Remarks on Psychology and Politics of Religion

Michael Starks

Reality Press   Las Vegas

Copyright © 2019 by Michael Starks

All rights reserved. No part of this publication may be reproduced, distributed, or transmitted without the express consent of the author.

Printed and bound in the United States of America.

First Edition 2019

ISBN 9781691873128

God is dead and man is free   Nietzsche

Heaven and Earth are inhumane--they view the myriad creatures as straw dogs   TaoTe Ching

This very body the Buddha, this very earth the lotus paradise   Osho

I can well imagine a religion in which there are no doctrines, so that nothing is spoken. Clearly, then, the essence of religion can have nothing to do with what is sayable   Wittgenstein

What we are supplying are really remarks on the natural history of man, not curiosities; however, but rather observations on facts which no one has doubted and which have only gone unremarked because they are always before our eyes. Wittgenstein RFM I p142

Philosophers constantly see the method of science before their eyes and are irresistibly tempted to ask and answer questions in the way science does. This tendency is the real source of metaphysics and leads the philosopher into complete darkness.   Wittgenstein BBB p18

I don't know why we are here, but I'm pretty sure that it is not in order to enjoy ourselves.   Wittgenstein

Death is not an event in life: we do not live to experience death. If we take eternity to mean not infinite temporal duration but timelessness, then eternal life belongs to those who live in the present.   Wittgenstein

He who understands baboon would do more towards metaphysics than Locke Charles Darwin 1838 Notebook M

TABLE OF CONTENTS

PREFACE I

1. The Logical Structure of Consciousness (behavior, personality, rationality, higher order thought, intentionality)..................................... 2

2. A Master Wittgensteinian Surveys Human Nature -A Review of Human Nature-the Categorial Framework by PMS Hacker (2010) (review revised 2019) 10

3. Review of "Are We Hardwired? by Clark & Grunstein Oxford (2000)<u>41</u>

4. Is JK Rowling More Evil Than Me? (revised 2019).................................. 44

5. Review of The New Science of the Mind by Marc Rowlands (2013)…49

6. Review of Religion Explained-- The Evolutionary Origins of Religious Thought by Pascal Boyer (2002) 65

7. Review of Sex, Ecology, Spirituality by Ken Wilber 2nd ed 851p (2001)-...79

9. The most profound spiritual autobiography of all time? - a review of "The Knee of Listening" by Adi Da (Franklin Jones) (1995).................. 96

10. Do our automated unconscious behaviors reveal our real selves and hidden truths about the universe? -- A review of David Hawkins 'Power vs Force--the hidden determinants of human behavior –author's official authoritative edition' 412p(2012)(original edition 1995)............................ 100

11. The Transient Suppression of the Worst Devils of our Nature—a review of Steven Pinker's 'The Better Angels of Our Nature: Why Violence Has Declined'(2012) 105

12. The Dead Hands of Group Selection and Phenomenology -- A Review of Individuality and Entanglement by Herbert Gintis 357p (2017)...............111

13. Altruism, Jesus and the End of the World—how the Templeton Foundation bought a Harvard Professorship and attacked Evolution, Rationality and Civilization. A review of E.O. Wilson 'The Social Conquest of Earth' (2012) and Nowak and Highfield 'SuperCooperators'(2012).........124

14. A Review of The Murderer Next Door by David Buss (2005)--.........139

15. Suicide by Democracy-an Obituary for America and the World (2019)-..151

16. How the Seven Sociopaths Who Rule China are Winning World War Three and Three Ways to Stop Them 202

PREFACE

This collection of articles was written over the last 10 years and revised to bring them up to date (2019). All the articles are about human behavior (as are all articles by anyone about anything), and so about the limitations of having a recent monkey ancestry (8 million years or much less depending on viewpoint) and manifest words and deeds within the framework of our innate psychology as presented in the table of intentionality. As famous evolutionist Richard Leakey says, it is critical to keep in mind not that we evolved from apes, but that in every important way, we are apes. If everyone was given a real understanding of this (i.e., of human ecology and psychology to actually give them some control over themselves), maybe civilization would have a chance. As things are however the leaders of society have no more grasp of things than their constituents and so collapse into anarchy is inevitable is spite of the near universal views that religion, politics or technology can save us. See my Suicidal Utopian Delusions in the 21st Century 5th ed (2019), for a detailed exposition of this view.

It is critical to understand why we behave as we do and so I start with a brief review of the logical structure of rationality, which provides some heuristics for the description of language (mind, rationality, personality) and gives some suggestions as to how this relates to the evolution of social behavior. This centers around the two writers I have found the most important in this regard, Ludwig Wittgenstein and John Searle, whose ideas I combine and extend within the dual system (two systems of thought) framework that has proven so useful in recent thinking and reasoning research. As I note, there is in my view essentially complete overlap between philosophy, in the strict sense of the enduring questions that concern the academic discipline, and the descriptive psychology of higher order thought (behavior). Once one has grasped Wittgenstein's insight that there is only the issue of how the language game is to be played, one determines the Conditions of Satisfaction (what makes a statement true or satisfied etc.) and that is the end of the discussion. No neurophysiology, no metaphysics, no postmodernism, no theology.

Many will find it strange that I spend little time discussing the topics common to most discussions of religion, but in my view it is essential to first understand the generalities of behavior and this necessitates a good understanding of biology and psychology which are mostly noticeable by their absence in works on religion, politics, history, morals and ethics, etc. In my view most such efforts have no grasp at all of the operation of System 2, the slow cortical functions of the brain which can be equated to linguistic behavior or the mind, and which I call the Descriptive Psychology of Higher Order Thought and which I regard as the province of philosophy in the narrow sense.

The key to everything about us is biology, and it is obliviousness to it that leads millions of smart educated people like Obama, Chomsky, Clinton, the Democratic Party and the Pope to espouse suicidal utopian ideals that inexorably lead straight to Hell on Earth. As W noted, it is what is always before our eyes that is the hardest to see. We live in the world of conscious deliberative linguistic System 2, but it is unconscious, automatic reflexive System 1 that rules. This is the source of the universal blindness described by Searle's The Phenomenological Illusion (TPI), Pinker's Blank Slate and Tooby and Cosmides' Standard Social Science Model.

The astute may wonder why we cannot see System 1 at work, but it is clearly counterproductive for an animal to be thinking about or second guessing every action, and in any case, there is no time for the slow, massively integrated System 2 to be involved in the constant stream of split second 'decisions' we must make. As W noted, our 'thoughts' (T1 or the 'thoughts' of System 1) must lead directly to actions.

It is my contention that the table of intentionality (rationality, mind, thought, language, personality etc.) that features prominently here describes more or less accurately, or at least serves as an heuristic for, how we think and behave, and so it encompasses not merely philosophy and psychology, but everything else (history, literature, mathematics, politics etc.). Note especially that intentionality and rationality as I (along with Searle, Wittgenstein and others) view it, includes both conscious deliberative System 2 and unconscious automated System 1 actions or reflexes.

Thus, all the articles, like all writing and all behavior, are intimately connected if one knows how to look at them. As I note, The Phenomenological Illusion (oblivion to our automated System 1) is universal and extends not merely throughout philosophy but throughout life. I am sure that Chomsky, Obama, Zuckerberg and the Pope would be incredulous if told that they suffer from the same problem as Hegel, Husserl and Heidegger, (or that that they differ only in degree from drug and sex addicts in being motivated by stimulation of their frontal cortices etc. by the delivery of dopamine (and over 100 other chemicals) via the ventral tegmentum and the nucleus accumbens), but it's clearly true. While the phenomenologists only wasted a lot of people's time, they are wasting the earth and their descendant's futures.

Several articles touch on The One Big Happy Family Delusion, i.e., that we are genetically selected for cooperation with everyone, and that the euphonious ideals of Democracy, Diversity, Equality and Religion will lead us into utopia, if we just manage things correctly (the possibility of politics). Again, the No Free Lunch Principle ought to warn us it cannot be true, and we see throughout history and all over the contemporary world, that without strict controls, selfishness and stupidity gain the upper hand and soon destroy any nation that embraces these delusions. In addition, the monkey mind steeply discounts the future, and so we cooperate in selling our descendant's heritage for temporary comforts, greatly exacerbating the problems.

I describe versions of this delusion (i.e., that we are basically 'friendly' if just given a chance) as it appears in some recent books on sociology/biology/economics. Even Sapolsky's otherwise excellent "Behave" (2017) embraces leftist politics and group selection and gives space to a discussion of whether humans are innately violent. I end with two essays on the great tragedy playing out in America and the world, which can be seen as a direct result of our evolved psychology manifested as the inexorable machinations of System 1. Our psychology, eminently adaptive and eugenic on the plains of Africa from ca. 6 million years ago, when we split from chimpanzees, to ca. 50,000 years ago, when many of our ancestors left Africa (i.e., in the EEA or Environment of Evolutionary Adaptation), is now maladaptive and dysgenic and the source of our Suicidal Utopian Delusions. So, like all discussions of behavior (theology, philosophy, psychology, sociology, biology, anthropology, politics, law, literature, history, economics, soccer strategies, business meetings, etc.), this book is about evolutionary strategies, selfish genes and inclusive fitness (kin selection, natural selection), though of course few grasp this, regardless of whether they are academics or peasants.

In several articles I refer to the pernicious stupidity of "group selection", roughly equitable to "true altruism". One thing rarely mentioned by the group selectionists is the fact that, even were 'group selection' possible, selfishness is at least as likely (probably far more likely in most contexts) to be group selected for as altruism. Just try to find examples of true altruism in nature –the fact that we can't (which we know is not possible if we understand evolution) tells us that its apparent presence in humans is an artefact of modern life, concealing the facts, and that it can no more be selected for than the tendency to suicide (which in fact it is). One might take this to imply that a just, democratic and enduring society for any kind of entity on any planet in any universe is only a dream, and that no being or power could make it otherwise. It is not only 'the laws' of physics that are universal and inescapable, or perhaps we should say that inclusive fitness is a law of physics.

The great mystic Osho, whose photo is on the cover, said that the separation of God and Heaven from Earth and Humankind was the most evil idea that ever entered the Human mind. In the 20th century an even more evil notion arose, or at least became popular with leftists—that humans are born with rights, rather than having to earn privileges. The idea of human rights is an evil fantasy created by leftists to draw attention away from the merciless destruction of the earth by unrestrained 3rd world motherhood. Thus, every day the population increases by 200,000, who must be provided with resources to grow and space to live, and who soon produce another 200,000 etc. And one almost never hears it noted that what they receive must be taken from those already alive, and their descendants. Their lives diminish those already here in both major obvious and countless subtle ways. Every new baby destroys the earth from the moment of conception. In a horrifically overcrowded world with vanishing resources, there cannot be human rights without destroying the earth and our descendents futures. It could not be more obvious, but it is rarely mentioned in a clear and direct way, and one will never see the streets full of protesters against motherhood.

The most basic facts, almost never mentioned, are that there are not enough resources in America or the world to lift a significant percentage of the poor out of poverty and keep them there. The attempt to do this is already bankrupting America and destroying the world. The earth's capacity to produce food decreases daily, as does our genetic quality. And now, as always, by far the greatest enemy of the poor is other poor and not the rich.

America and the world are in the process of collapse from excessive population growth, most of it for the last century, and now all of it, due to 3rd world people. Consumption of resources and the addition of 4 billion more ca. 2100 will collapse industrial civilization and bring about starvation, disease, violence and war on a staggering scale. The earth loses at least 1% of its topsoil every year, so as it nears 2100, most of its food growing capacity will be gone. Billions will die and nuclear war is all but certain. In America, this is being hugely accelerated by massive immigration and immigrant reproduction, combined with abuses made possible by democracy. Depraved human nature inexorably turns the dream of democracy and diversity into a nightmare of crime and poverty. China will continue to overwhelm America and the world, as long as it maintains the dictatorship which limits selfishness and permits long term planning. The root cause of collapse is the inability of our innate psychology to adapt to the modern world, which leads people to treat unrelated persons as though they had common interests (which I suggest may be regarded as an unrecognized -- but the commonest and most serious-- psychological problem -- Inclusive Fitness Disorder). This, plus ignorance of basic biology and psychology, leads to the social engineering delusions of the partially educated who control democratic societies. Few understand that if you help one person you harm someone else—there is no free lunch and every single item anyone consumes destroys the earth beyond repair. Consequently, social policies everywhere are unsustainable and one by one all societies without stringent controls on selfishness will collapse into anarchy or dictatorship. Without dramatic and immediate changes, there is no hope for preventing the collapse of America, or any country that follows a democratic system, especially now that the Neomarxist Third World Supremacists are taking control of the USA and other Western Democracies, and helping the Seven Sociopaths who run China to succeed in their plan to eliminate peace and freedom and religion worldwide. Hence my concluding essays. Of course, it is an easily defensible point of view that Artificial Intelligence (aka Artificial Stupidity or Artificial Sociopathy) researchers are even more evil than the Democrats and the CCP, and I make brief comments on this as well.

Finally, as with my other writings 3DTV and 3D Movie Technology-Selected Articles 1996-2017 2nd Edition (2018), Psychoactive Drugs-- Four Classic Texts (1976-1982) (2016), Talking Monkeys 3rd ed (2019), The Logical Structure of Philosophy, Psychology, Mind and Language in Ludwig Wittgenstein and John Searle 2nd ed (2019), Suicide by Democracy 4th ed (2019), The Logical Structure of Human Behavior (2019), The Logical Structure of Consciousness (2019, Understanding the Connections between Science, Philosophy, Psychology, Religion, Politics, and Economics (2019), and Suicidal Utopian Delusions in the 21st Century 5th ed (2019), and in all my letters and email and conversations for over 50 years, I have always used 'they' or 'them' instead of 'his/her', 'she/he', or the idiotic reverse sexism of 'she' or 'her', being perhaps the only one in this part of the galaxy to do so. The slavish use of these universally applied egregious vocables is of course intimately connected with the defects in our psychology which generate academic philosophy, the modern form of democracy, and the collapse of industrial civilization, and I leave the further description of these connections as an exercise for the reader.

I am aware of many imperfections and limitations of my work and continually revise it, but I took up these topics 13 years ago at 65, so it is miraculous, and an eloquent testimonial to the power of System 1 automatisms, that I have been able to do anything at all. It was thirteen years (or 78 years) of incessant struggle and I hope readers find it of some use.

vyupzz@gmail.com

Remarks on the Biology, Psychology and Politics of Religion

The Logical Structure of Consciousness (behavior, personality, rationality, higher order thought, intentionality)

Michael Starks

ABSTRACT

After half a century in oblivion, the nature of consciousness is now the hottest topic in the behavioral sciences and philosophy. Beginning with the pioneering work of Ludwig Wittgenstein in the 1930's (the Blue and Brown Books) and from the 50's to the present by his logical successor John Searle, I have created the following table as a heuristic for furthering this study. The rows show various aspects or ways of studying and the columns show the involuntary processes and voluntary behaviors comprising the two systems (dual processes) of the Logical Structure of Consciousness (LSC), which can also be regarded as the Logical Structure of Rationality (LSR-Searle), of behavior (LSB), of personality (LSP), of reality (LSOR), of Intentionality (LSI) -the classical philosophical term, the Descriptive Psychology of Consciousness (DPC), the Descriptive Psychology of Thought (DPT) –or better, the Language of the Descriptive Psychology of Thought (LDPT), terms introduced here and in my other very recent writings.

Those wishing a comprehensive up to date framework for human behavior from the modern two systems view may consult my books Talking Monkeys 3rd ed (2019), The Logical Structure of Philosophy, Psychology, Mind and Language in Ludwig Wittgenstein and John Searle 2nd ed (2019), Suicide by Democracy 4th ed (2019), The Logical Structure of Human Behavior (2019), The Logical Structure of Consciousness (2019, Understanding the Connections between Science, Philosophy, Psychology, Religion, Politics, and Economics (2019), and Suicidal Utopian Delusions in the 21st Century 5th ed (2019).

About a million years ago primates evolved the ability to use their throat muscles to make complex series of noises (i.e., speech) that by about 100,000 years ago had evolved to describe present events (perceptions, memory, reflexive actions with basic utterances that can be described as Primary Language Games (PLG's) describing System 1—i.e., the fast unconscious automated System One, true-only mental states with a precise time and location). We gradually developed the further ability to encompass displacements in space and time to describe memories, attitudes and potential events (the past and future and often counterfactual, conditional or fictional preferences, inclinations or dispositions) with the Secondary Language Games (SLG's) of System Two- slow conscious true or false propositional attitudinal thinking, which has no precise time and are abilities and not mental states). Preferences are Intuitions, Tendencies, Automatic Ontological Rules, Behaviors, Abilities, Cognitive Modules, Personality Traits, Templates, Inference Engines, Inclinations, Emotions, Propositional Attitudes, Appraisals, capacities, hypotheses. Emotions are Type 2 Preferences (W RPP2 p148). "I believe", "he loves", "they think" are descriptions of possible public acts typically displaced in spacetime. My first-person statements about myself are true-only (excluding lying) while third person statements about others are true or false (see my review of Johnston 'Wittgenstein: Rethinking the Inner').

"Preferences" as a class of intentional states --opposed to perceptions, reflexive acts and memories-- were first clearly described by Wittgenstein (W) in the 1930's and termed "inclinations" or "dispositions". They have commonly been termed "propositional attitudes" since Russell but this is a misleading phrase since believing, intending, knowing, remembering etc., are often not propositions nor attitudes, as has been shown e.g., by W and by Searle (e.g., Consciousness and Language p118). They are intrinsic, observer independent mental representations (as opposed to presentations or representations of System 1 to System 2 – Searle-C+L p53). They are potential acts displaced in time or space while the evolutionarily more primitive System One mental states of perceptions memories and reflexive actions are always here and now. This is one way to characterize System 2 and System 3--the second and third major advances in vertebrate psychology after System 1—the ability to represent events and to think of them as occurring in another place or time (Searle's third faculty of counterfactual imagination supplementing cognition and volition). S1 are potential or unconscious mental states (Searle-- Phil Issues 1:45-66(1991).

Perceptions, memories and reflexive (automatic) actions can be described as S1 or primary LG's (PLG's --e.g., I see the dog) and there are, in the normal case, no tests possible, so they can be true-only. Dispositions can be described as secondary LG's (SLG's –e.g. I believe I see the dog) and must also be acted out, even for me in my own case (i.e., how do I know what I believe, think, feel until I act). Dispositions also become Actions when spoken or written as well as being acted out in other ways, and these ideas are all due to Wittgenstein (mid 1930's) and are not Behaviorism (Hintikka & Hintikka 1981, Searle, Hutto, Read, Hacker etc.,). Wittgenstein can be regarded as the founder of evolutionary psychology, contextualism, enactivism, and the two systems framework, and his work a unique investigation of the functioning of our axiomatic System 1 psychology and its interaction with System 2. Though few have understood it well (and arguably nobody fully to this day) it was further developed by a few -- above all by John Searle, who made a simpler version of the table below in his classic book Rationality in Action (2001). It expands on W's survey of the axiomatic structure of evolutionary psychology developed from his very first comments in 1911 and so beautifully laid out in his last work On Certainty (OC) (written in 1950-51). OC is the foundation stone of behavior or epistemology and ontology (arguably the same), cognitive linguistics or the logical structure of Higher Order Thought (HOT), and in my view the single most important work in philosophy (descriptive psychology), and thus in the study of behavior. See my article The Logical Structure of Philosophy, Psychology, Mind and Language as Revealed in Wittgenstein and Searle (2016) and the recent work of Daniele Moyal-Sharrock.

Perception, Memory, Reflexive actions and Emotion are primitive partly Subcortical Involuntary Mental States, described in PLG's, in which the mind automatically fits the world (is Causally Self Referential --Searle) --the unquestionable, true-only, axiomatic basis of rationality over which no control is possible). Emotions evolved to make a bridge between desires or intentions and actions. Preferences, Desires, and Intentions are descriptions of slow thinking conscious Voluntary Abilities--described in SLG's-- in which the mind tries to fit the world.

Behaviorism and all the other confusions of our default descriptive psychology (philosophy) arise because we cannot see S1 working and describe all actions as SLG's (The Phenomenological Illusion or TPI of Searle). W understood this and described it with unequalled clarity with hundreds of examples of language (the mind) in action throughout his works. Reason has access to working memory and so we use consciously apparent but typically incorrect reasons to explain behavior (the Two Selves of current research). Beliefs and other Dispositions are thoughts which try to match the facts of the world (mind to world direction of fit), while Volitions are intentions to act (Prior Intentions — PI, or Intentions In Action-IAA- Searle) plus acts which try to match the world to the thoughts — world to mind direction of fit — cf. Searle e.g., C+L p145, p190).

Now that we have a reasonable start on the Logical Structure of Rationality (the Descriptive Psychology of Higher Order Thought) laid out we can look at the table of Intentionality that results from this work, which I have constructed over the last few years. It is based on a much simpler one from Searle, which in turn owes much to Wittgenstein. I have also incorporated in modified form tables being used by current researchers in the psychology of thinking processes which are evidenced in the last 9 rows. It should prove interesting to compare it with those in Peter Hacker's 3 recent volumes on Human Nature. I offer this table as an heuristic for describing behavior that I find more complete and useful than any other framework I have seen and not as a final or complete analysis, which would have to be three dimensional with hundreds (at least) of arrows going in many directions with many (perhaps all) pathways between S1 and S2 being bidirectional. Also, the very distinction between S1 and S2, cognition and willing, perception and memory, between feeling, knowing, believing and expecting etc. are arbitrary--that is, as W demonstrated, all words are contextuallysensitive and most have several utterly different uses (meanings or COS).

In accord with W's work and Searle's terminology, I categorize the representations of S2 as public Conditions of Satisfaction (COS) and in this sense S1 such as perceptions do not have COS. In other writings S says they do but as noted in my other reviews I think it is then essential to refer to COS1 (private presentations) and COS2 (public representations). To repeat this critical distinction, public Conditions of Satisfaction of S2 are often referred to by Searle and others as COS, Representations, truth makers or meanings (or COS2 by myself), while the automatic results of S1 are designated as presentations by others (or COS1 by myself).

Likewise, I have changed his 'Direction of Fit' to 'Cause Originates From' and his 'Direction of Causation' to 'Causes Changes In'. System 1 is involuntary, reflexive or automated "Rules" R1 while Thinking (Cognition) has no gaps and is voluntary or deliberative "Rules" R2 and Willing (Volition) has 3 gaps (see Searle).

Many complex charts have been published by scientists but I find them of minimal utility when thinking about behavior (as opposed to thinking about brain function). Each level of description may be useful in certain contexts but I find that being coarser or finer limits usefulness.

INTENTIONALITY can be viewed as personality or as the Construction of Social Reality (the title of Searle's well known book) and from many other viewpoints as well.

Beginning with the pioneering work of Ludwig Wittgenstein in the 1930's (the Blue and Brown Books) and from the 50's to the present by his successors Searle, Moyal-Sharrock, Read, Baker, Hacker, Stern, Horwich, Winch, Finkelstein etc., I have created the following table as an heuristic for furthering this study. The rows show various aspects or ways of studying and the columns show the involuntary processes and voluntary behaviors comprising the two systems (dual processes) of the Logical Structure of

Consciousness (LSC), which can also be regarded as the Logical Structure of Rationality (LSR), of behavior (LSB), of personality (LSP), of Mind (LSM), of language (LSL), of reality (LSOR), of Intentionality (LSI) -the classical philosophical term, the Descriptive Psychology of Consciousness (DPC), the Descriptive Psychology of Thought (DPT) –or better, the Language of the Descriptive Psychology of Thought (LDPT), terms introduced here and in my other very recent writings.

FROM THE ANALYSIS OF LANGUAGE GAMES

	Disposition*	Emotion	Memory	Perception	Desire	PI**	IA***	Action/Word
Cause Originates From****	World	World	World	World	Mind	Mind	Mind	Mind
Causes Changes In*****	None	Mind	Mind	Mind	None	World	World	World
Causally Self Reflexive******	No	Yes	Yes	Yes	No	Yes	Yes	Yes
True or False (Testable)	Yes	T only	T only	T only	Yes	Yes	Yes	Yes
Public Conditions of Satisfaction	Yes	Yes/No	Yes/No	No	Yes/No	Yes	No	Yes
Describe a Mental State	No	Yes	Yes	Yes	No	No	Yes/No	Yes
Evolutionary Priority	5	4	2,3	1	5	3	2	2
Voluntary Content	Yes	No	No	No	No	Yes	Yes	Yes
Voluntary Initiation	Yes/No	No	Yes	No	Yes/No	Yes	Yes	Yes
Cognitive System*******	2	1	2/1	1	2/1	2	1	2
Change Intensity	No	Yes	Yes	Yes	Yes	No	No	No
Precise Duration	No	Yes	Yes	Yes	No	No	Yes	Yes
Time, Place(H+N,T+T)********	TT	HN	HN	HN	TT	TT	HN	HN
Special Quality	No	Yes	No	Yes	No	No	No	No
Localized in Body	No	No	No	Yes	No	No	No	Yes
Bodily Expressions	Yes	Yes	No	No	Yes	Yes	Yes	Yes
Self Contradictions	No	Yes	No	No	Yes	No	No	No
Needs a Self	Yes	Yes/No	No	No	Yes	No	No	No
Needs Language	Yes	No	No	No	No	No	No	Yes/No

FROM DECISION RESEARCH

	Disposition*	Emotion	Memory	Perception	Desire	PI***	IA****	Action/Word
Subliminal Effects	No	Yes/No	Yes	Yes	No	No	No	Yes/No
Associative/Rule Based	RB	A/RB	A	A	A/RB	RB	RB	RB
Context Dependent/Abstract	A	CD/A	CD	CD	CD/A	A	CD/A	CD/A
Serial/Parallel	S	S/P	P	P	S/P	S	S	S
Heuristic/Analytic	A	H/A	H	H	H/A	A	A	A
Needs Working Memory	Yes	No	No	No	No	Yes	Yes	Yes
General Intelligence Dependent	Yes	No	No	No	Yes/No	Yes	Yes	Yes
Cognitive Loading Inhibits	Yes	Yes/No	No	No	Yes	Yes	Yes	Yes
Arousal Facilitates or Inhibits	I	F/I	F	F	I	I	I	I

*   Aka Inclinations, Capabilities, Preferences, Representations, possible actions etc.
**   Searle's Prior Intentions
***   Searle's Intention In Action
****   Searle's Direction of Fit
*****   Searle's Direction of Causation
****** (Mental State instantiates--Causes or Fulfills Itself). Searle formerly called this   causally self- referential.
******* Tversky/Kahneman/Frederick/Evans/Stanovich defined cognitive systems.
******** Here and Now or There and Then

I give detailed explanations of this table in my other writings.

I suggest we can describe behavior more clearly by changing Searle's "impose conditions of satisfaction on conditions of satisfaction" to "relate mental states to the world by moving muscles"—i.e., talking, writing and doing, and his "mind to world direction of fit" and "world to mind direction of fit" by "cause originates in the mind" and "cause originates in the world" S1 is only upwardly causal (world to mind) and contentless (lacking representations or information) while S2 has content and is downwardly causal (mind to world). I have adopted my terminology in this table.

One should always keep in mind Wittgenstein's discovery that after we have described the possible uses (meanings, truthmakers, Conditions of Satisfaction) of language in a particular context, we have exhausted its interest, and attempts at explanation (i.e., philosophy) only get us further away from the truth. It is critical to note that this table is only a highly simplified context-free heuristic and each use of a word must be examined in its context. The best examination of context variation is in Peter Hacker's recent 3 volumes on Human Nature, which provide numerous tables and charts that should be compared with this one.

A Master Wittgensteinian Surveys Human Nature -A Review of Human Nature-the Categorial Framework by PMS Hacker (2010) (review revised 2019)

Michael Starks

Abstract

Materialism, reductionism, behaviorism, functionalism, dynamic systems theory and computationalism are popular views, but they were shown by Wittgenstein and more recently by Searle to be incoherent. The study of behavior encompasses all of human life but behavior is largely automatic and unconscious and even the conscious part, mostly expressed in language (which Wittgenstein equates with the mind), is not perspicuous, so it is critical to have a framework which Searle calls the Logical Structure of Rationality (LSR) and I call the Descriptive Psychology of Higher Order Thought (DPHOT). After summarizing the framework worked out by Wittgenstein and Searle, as extended by myself and by modern reasoning research, I comment on this first book in a trilogy on Human Nature by P.M.S. Hacker, the leading authority on Wittgenstein and one of the best modern philosophers.

Those wishing a comprehensive up to date framework for human behavior from the modern two systems view may consult my books Talking Monkeys 3rd ed (2019), The Logical Structure of Philosophy, Psychology, Mind and Language in Ludwig Wittgenstein and John Searle 2nd ed (2019), Suicide by Democracy 4th ed (2019), The Logical Structure of Human Behavior (2019), The Logical Structure of Consciousness (2019, Understanding the Connections between Science, Philosophy, Psychology, Religion, Politics, and Economics (2019), and Suicidal Utopian Delusions in the 21st Century 5th ed (2019).

Before remarking on "Human Nature", I will first offer some comments on philosophy and its relationship to contemporary psychological research as exemplified in the works of Searle (S), Wittgenstein (W), Hacker (H) et al. It will help to see my reviews of PNC (Philosophy in a New Century), TLP, PI, OC by W, Making the Social World (MSW) and other books by and about these geniuses, who provide a clear description of higher order behavior, not found in psychology books, that I will refer to as the WS framework. I begin with some penetrating quotes from W and S.

"The confusion and barrenness of psychology is not to be explained by calling it a "young science"; its state is not comparable with that of physics, for instance, in its beginnings. (Rather with that of certain branches of mathematics. Set theory.) For in psychology there are experimental methods and conceptual confusion. (As in the other case, conceptual confusion and methods of proof). The existence of the experimental method makes us think we have the means of solving the problems that trouble us; though problem and method pass one another by." Wittgenstein (PI p.232)

"Philosophers constantly see the method of science before their eyes and are irresistibly tempted to ask and answer questions in the way science does. This tendency is the real source of metaphysics and leads the philosopher into complete darkness."(BBB p18).

"But I did not get my picture of the world by satisfying myself of its correctness: nor do I have it because I am satisfied of its correctness. No: it is the inherited background against which I distinguish between true and false." Wittgenstein OC 94

"The aim of philosophy is to erect a wall at the point where language stops anyway." Wittgenstein Philosophical Occasions p187

"The limit of language is shown by its being impossible to describe a fact which corresponds to (is the translation of) a sentence without simply repeating the sentence ..." Wittgenstein CV p10

"Many words then in this sense then don't have a strict meaning. But this is not a defect. To think it is would be like saying that the light of my reading lamp is no real light at all because it has no sharp boundary." BBB p27

"Every sign is capable of interpretation but the meaning mustn't be capable of interpretation. It is the last interpretation" BBB p34

"There is a kind of general disease of thinking which always looks for (and finds) what would be called a mental state from which all our acts spring, as from a reservoir." BBB p143

"And the mistake which we here and in a thousand similar cases are inclined to make is labeled by the word "to make" as we have used it in the sentence "It is no act of insight which makes us use the rule as we do", because there is an idea that "something must make us" do what we do. And this again joins onto the confusion between cause and reason. We need have no reason to follow the rule as we do. The chain of reasons has an end." BBB p143

"If we keep in mind the possibility of a picture which, though correct, has no similarity with its object, the interpolation of a shadow between the sentence and reality loses all point. For now the sentence itself can serve as such a shadow. The sentence is just such a picture, which hasn't the slightest similarity with what it represents."
BBB p37

"Thus, we may say of some philosophizing mathematicians that they are obviously not aware of the many different usages of the word "proof"; and that they are not clear about the differences between the uses of the word "kind", when they talk of kinds of numbers, kinds of proof, as though the word "kind" here meant the same thing as in the context "kinds of apples." Or, we may say, they are not aware of the different meanings of the word "discovery" when in one case we talk of the discovery of the construction of the pentagon and in the other case of the discovery of the South Pole." BBB p29

"Some of the most important logical features of intentionality are beyond the reach of phenomenology because they have no immediate phenomenological reality... Because the creation of meaningfulness out of meaninglessness is not consciously experienced...it does not exist...This is... the phenomenological illusion." Searle PNC p115-117

"...the basic intentional relation between the mind and the world has to do with conditions of satisfaction. And a proposition is anything at all that can stand in an intentional relation to the world, and since those intentional relations always determine conditions of satisfaction, and a proposition is defined as anything sufficient to determine conditions of satisfaction, it turns out that all intentionality is a matter of propositions." Searle PNC p193

"The intentional state represents its conditions of satisfaction...people erroneously suppose that every mental representation must be consciously thought...but the notion of a representation as I am using it is a functional and not an ontological notion. Anything that has conditions of satisfaction, that can succeed or fail in a way that is characteristic of intentionality, is by definition a representation of its conditions of satisfaction...we can analyze the structure of the intentionality of social phenomena by analyzing their conditions of satisfaction." Searle MSW p28- 32

"Superstition is nothing but belief in the causal nexus." TLP 5.1361

"Now if it is not the causal connections which we are concerned with, then the activities of the mind lie open before us." BBB p6

"We feel that even when all possible scientific questions have been answered, the problems of life remain completely untouched. Of course, there are then no questions left, and this itself is the answer." TLP 6.52

"Nonsense, Nonsense, because you are making assumptions instead of simply describing. If your head is haunted by explanations here, you are neglecting to remind yourself of the most important facts." Z 220

"Philosophy simply puts everything before us and neither explains nor deduces anything...One might give the name 'philosophy' to what is possible before all new discoveries and inventions." PI 126

"The more narrowly we examine actual language, the sharper becomes the conflict between it and our requirement. (For the crystalline purity of logic was, of course, not a result of investigation: it was a requirement.)"PI 107

"The wrong conception which I want to object to in this connexion is the following, that we can discover something wholly new. That is a mistake. The truth of the matter is that we have already got everything, and that we have got it actually present; we need not wait for anything. We make our moves in the realm of the grammar of our ordinary language, and this grammar is already there. Thus, we have already got everything and need not wait for the future." (said in 1930) Waismann "Ludwig Wittgenstein and the Vienna Circle (1979) p183

"Here we come up against a remarkable and characteristic phenomenon in philosophical investigation: the difficulty---I might say---is not that of finding the solution but rather that of recognizing as the solution something that looks as if it were only a preliminary to it. We have already said everything. ---Not anything that follows from this, no this itself is the solution!   This is connected, I believe, with our wrongly expecting an explanation, whereas the solution of the difficulty is a description, if we give it the right place in our considerations. If we dwell upon it, and do not try to get beyond it." Zettel p312-314

"Our method is purely descriptive, the descriptions we give are not hints of explanations." BBB p125

Incidentally, these quotes from W show that in spite of Searle's frequent disparaging of W for his famous rejection of 'theory', W makes far more and far broader and more profound generalizations than Searle.

These quotes are not chosen at random but (along with the others in my reviews) are an outline of behavior (human nature) from our two greatest descriptive psychologists. In considering these matters we must keep in mind that philosophy is the descriptive psychology of higher order thought (DPHOT), which is another of the obvious facts that are totally overlooked - i.e., I have never seen it clearly stated anywhere. In addition to failing to make it clear that what they are doing is descriptive psychology, philosophers rarely specify exactly what it is that they expect to contribute to this topic that other students of behavior (i.e., scientists) do not, so after noting W's above remark on science envy, I will quote again from Hacker who gives a good start on it.

"Traditional epistemologists want to know whether knowledge is true belief and a further condition ..., or whether knowledge does not even imply belief ... We want to know when knowledge does and when it does not require justification. We need to be clear what is ascribed to a person when it is said that he knows something. Is it a distinctive mental state, an achievement, a performance, a disposition or an ability? Could knowing or believing that p be identical with a state of the brain? Why can one say `he believes that p, but it is not the case that p', whereas one cannot say `I believe that p, but it is not the case that p'? Why are there ways, methods and means of achieving, attaining or receiving knowledge, but not belief (as opposed to faith)? Why can one know, but not believe who, what, which, when, whether and how? Why can one believe, but not know, wholeheartedly, passionately, hesitantly, foolishly, thoughtlessly, fanatically, dogmatically or reasonably? Why can one know, but not believe, something perfectly well, thoroughly or in detail? And so on - through many hundreds of similar questions pertaining not only to knowledge and belief, but also to doubt, certainty, remembering, forgetting, observing, noticing, recognising, attending, being aware of, being conscious of, not to mention the numerous verbs of perception and their cognates. What needs to be clarified if these questions are to be answered is the web of our epistemic concepts, the ways in which the various concepts hang together, the various forms of their compatibilities and incompatibilities, their point and purpose, their presuppositions and different forms of context dependency. To this venerable exercise in connective analysis, scientific knowledge, psychology, neuroscience and self-styled cognitive science can contribute nothing whatsoever." (Passing by the naturalistic turn: on Quine's cul- de-sac- p15-2005).

And also, Horwich gives one of the most beautiful summaries of where an understanding of Wittgenstein leaves us that I have ever seen.

"There must be no attempt to *explain* our linguistic/conceptual activity (PI 126) as in Frege's reduction of arithmetic to logic; no attempt to give it *epistemological foundations* (PI 124) as in meaning based accounts of *a priori* knowledge; no attempt to characterize *idealized* forms of it (PI 130) as in sense logics; no attempt to *reform* it (PI 124, 132) as in Mackie's error theory or Dummett's intuitionism; no attempt to *streamline* it (PI 133) as in Quine's account of existence; no attempt to make it more *consistent* (PI 132) as in Tarski's response to the liar paradoxes; and no attempt to make it more *complete* (PI 133) as in the settling of questions of personal identity for bizarre hypothetical 'teleportation' scenarios."

A major theme in all discussion of human behavior is the need to separate the genetically programmed automatisms from the effects of culture. All study of higher order behavior is an effort to tease apart not only fast S1 and slow S2 thinking (e.g., perceptions and other automatisms vs. dispositions), but the logical extensions of S2 into culture (S3).

Searle's (S) work as a whole provides a stunning description of higher order S2/S3 social behavior which is due to the recent evolution of genes for dispositional psychology, while the later Wittgenstein (W) shows how it is based on true-only unconscious axioms of S1 which evolved into conscious dispositional propositional thinking of S2.

S1 is the simple automated functions of our involuntary, System 1, fast thinking, mirror neuron, true-only, non- propositional, mental states- our perceptions and memories and reflexive acts including System 1 Truths and UA1 --Understanding of Agency 1-- and Emotions1- such as joy, love, anger) which can be described causally, while the evolutionarily later linguistic functions are expressions or descriptions of voluntary, System 2, slow thinking, mentalizing neurons, testable true or false, propositional, Truth2 and UA2 and Emotions2- joyfulness, loving, hating-- the dispositional (and often counterfactual) imagining, supposing, intending, thinking, knowing, believing, etc. which can only be described in terms of reasons (i.e., it's just a fact that attempts to describe System 2 in terms of neurochemistry, atomic physics, mathematics, make no sense--see W for many examples and Searle and Hacker (Human Nature)for disquisitions).

One should take seriously W's comment that even if God could look into our mind he could not see what we are thinking--this should be the motto of Cognitive Psychology. Yes, a cognitive psychologist of the future *may* be able to see what we are perceiving and remembering and our reflexive thinking and acting, since these S1 functions are always causal mental states (CMS) but S2 dispositions are only potentially CMS and so not realized or visible. This is not a theory but description of our language, mind, life, grammar (W). S, Carruthers (C) and others muddy the waters here because they sometimes refer to dispositions as mental states as well, but as W did long ago, S, Hacker and others show that the language of causality just does not apply to the higher order emergent S2 descriptions--again not a theory but a description of how our dispositional states (language, thinking) work.

S1 is composed of unconscious, fast, physical, causal, automatic, non-propositional, true only mental states, while slow S2 can only coherently be described in terms of reasons for actions that are more or less conscious dispositions to behavior (potential actions) that are or can become propositional (T or F). It seems quite obvious to me (as it was to W) that the mechanical view of mind exists for the same reason as nearly all behavior--it is the default operation of our evolved psychology (EP) which seeks explanations in terms of what we can deliberately think through slowly (S2), rather than in the automated S1, of which we mostly remain oblivious--called by S in PNC `The Phenomenological Illusion' (TPI). TPI is not a harmless philosophical error but a universal obliviousness to our biology which produces the illusion that we control our life and among the consequences are the inexorable collapse of what passes for civilization.

Our slow or reflective, more or less "conscious" (beware another network of language games!) second-self brain activity corresponds to what W characterized as "dispositions" or "inclinations", which refer to abilities or possible actions, are not mental states (or not in the same sense as S1 states), and do not have any definite time of occurrence and/or duration. But disposition words like "knowing", "understanding", "thinking", "believing", which W discussed extensively, have at least two basic uses. One is a peculiar philosophical use (but graduating into everyday uses) which refers to the true-only sentences resulting from direct perceptions and memory, i.e., our innate axiomatic S1 psychology (`I know these are my hands')--i.e., they are Causally Self Reflexive (CSR, termed Causally Self Referential by Searle in his earlier work)—i.e., to see a cat makes it true and in the normal case no test is possible, and the S2 use, which is their normal use as dispositions, which can be acted out, and which can become true or false (`I know my way home')--i.e., they have external, public, testable Conditions of Satisfaction (COS) and are not CSR.

The investigation of involuntary fast thinking of System 1 has revolutionized psychology, economics and other disciplines under names like "cognitive illusions", "priming", "framing", "heuristics" and "biases". Of course these too are language games so there will be more and less useful ways to use these words, and studies and discussions will vary from "pure" System 1 to combinations of 1 and 2 (the norm as W made clear), but presumably not ever of slow System 2 dispositional thinking only, since any System 2 thought or intentional action cannot occur without involving much of the intricate network of "cognitive modules", "inference engines", "intracerebral reflexes", "automatisms", "cognitive axioms", "background" or "bedrock" --as W and later Searle call our Evolutionary Psychology (EP).

One way of regarding this is that the unconscious automatic System 1 activates the higher cortical conscious personality of System 2, bringing about throat muscle contractions which inform others that it sees the world in certain ways, which commit it to potential actions. A huge advance over prelinguistic or protolinguistic interactions in which only gross muscle movements were able to convey very limited information about intentions.

The deontic structures or `social glue' are the automatic fast actions of S1 producing the slow dispositions of S2 which are inexorably expanded during personal development into a wide array of automatic universal cultural deontic relationships (S3). I expect this fairly well describes the basic structure of behavior.

These descriptions of cognition and volition are summarized in Table 2.1 of MSW, which Searle has used for many years and is the basis for an extended one I have created. In my view, it helps enormously to relate this to modern psychological research by using my S1, S2, S3 terminology and W's true-only vs propositional (dispositional) description. Thus, CSR references S1 true-only perception, memory and prior intention, while S2 refers to dispositions such as belief and desire.

So, recognizing that S1 is only upwardly causal (world to mind) and contentless (lacking representations or information) while S2 has content and is downwardly causal (mind to world) (e.g., see my review of Hutto and Myin's `Radical Enactivism'), I would change the paragraphs from MSW p39 beginning "In sum" and ending on pg 40 with "conditions of satisfaction" as follows.

In sum, perception, memory and reflexive prior intentions and actions (`will') are caused by the automatic functioning of our S1 true-only axiomatic EP. Via prior intentions and intentions-in-action, we try to match how we desire things to be with how we think they are. We should see that belief, desire (and imagination--desires time shifted and decoupled from intention) and other S2 propositional dispositions of our slow thinking later evolved second self, are totally dependent upon (have their COS originating in) the CSR rapid automatic primitive true- only reflexive S1. In language and neurophysiology there are intermediate or blended cases such as intending (prior intentions) or remembering, where the causal connection with COS (i.e., with S1) is time shifted, as they represent the past or the future, unlike S1 which is always in the present. S1 and S2 feed into each other and are often orchestrated seamlessly by the learned deontic cultural relations of S3, so that our normal experience is that we consciously control everything that we do. This vast arena of cognitive illusions that dominate our life S has described as 'The Phenomenological Illusion.'

It follows in a very straightforward and inexorable fashion, both from W's 3rd period work and from the observations of contemporary psychology, that 'will', 'self' and 'consciousness' are axiomatic true-only elements of System 1 just like seeing, hearing, etc., and there is no possibility (intelligibility) of demonstrating (of giving sense to) their falsehood. As W made so wonderfully clear numerous times, they are the basis for judgment and so cannot be judged. The true-only axioms of our psychology are not evidential.

Like Carruthers and others, S sometimes states (e.g., p66-67 MSW) that S1 (i.e., memories, perceptions, reflex acts) has a propositional (i.e., true-false) structure. As I have noted above, and many times in other reviews, it seems crystal clear that W is correct, and it is basic to understanding behavior, that only S2 is propositional and S1 is axiomatic and true-only. They both have COS and Directions of Fit (DOF) because the genetic, axiomatic intentionality of S1 generates that of S2 but if S1 were propositional in the same sense it would mean that skepticism is intelligible, the chaos that was philosophy before W would return, and in fact if true, life would not be possible. As W showed countless times and biology demonstrates, life must be based on certainty--automated unconscious rapid reactions. Organisms that always have a doubt and pause to reflect will die-no evolution, no people, no philosophy.

Language and writing are special because the short wavelength of vibrations of vocal muscles enable much higher bandwidth information transfer than contractions of other muscles and this is on average several orders of magnitude higher for visual information.

Thinking is propositional and so deals with true or false statements, which means that it is a typical S2 disposition which can be tested, as opposed to the true-only automatic cognitive functions of S1. Or you can say that spontaneous utterances and actions are the primitive reflexes or Primary Language Games (PLG) of S1, while conscious representations are the dispositional Secondary Language Games (SLG's) of S2. It sounds trivial and indeed it is, but this is the most basic statement of how behavior works and hardly anyone has ever understood it.

I would translate S's summary of practical reason on p127 of MSW as follows: "We yield to our desires (need to alter brain chemistry), which typically include Desire -Independent Reasons for Action (DIRA--i.e., desires displaced in space and time, most often for reciprocal altruism), which produce dispositions to behavior that commonly result sooner or later in muscle movements that serve our inclusive fitness (increased survival for genes in ourselves and those closely related)." And I would restate his description on p129 of how we carry out DIRA2/3 as "The resolution of the paradox is that the unconscious DIRA1 serving long term inclusive fitness generate the conscious DIRA2 which often override the short term personal immediate desires." Agents do indeed consciously create the proximate reasons of DIRA2/3, but these are very restricted extensions of unconscious DIRA1 (the ultimate cause).

Evolution by inclusive fitness has programmed the unconscious rapid reflexive causal actions of S1 which often give rise to the conscious slow thinking of S2 (often modified into the cultural extensions of S3), which produces reasons for action that often result in activation of body and/or speech muscles by S1 causing actions. The general mechanism is via both neurotransmission and by changes in neuromodulators in targeted areas of the brain. The overall cognitive illusion (called by S `The Phenomenological Illusion', by Pinker `The Blank Slate' and by Tooby and Cosmides `The Standard Social Science Model') is that S2/S3 has generated the action consciously for reasons of which we are fully aware and in control of, but anyone familiar with modern biology and psychology can see that this view is not credible.

Though W is correct that there is no mental state that constitutes meaning, S notes (as quoted above) that there is a general way to characterize the act of meaning-- "Speaker meaning... is the imposition of conditions of satisfaction on conditions of satisfaction" which is an act and not a mental state. This can be seen as another statement of W's argument against private language (personal interpretations vs publicly testable ones). Likewise, with rule following and interpretation --they can only be publicly checkable acts--no private rules or private interpretations either. And one must note that many (most famously Kripke) miss the boat here, being misled by W's frequent referrals to community practice into thinking it's just arbitrary public practice that underlies language and social conventions. W makes clear many times that such conventions are only possible given an innate shared psychology which he often calls the background, and it this which underlies all behavior and which is schematized in the table.

As I have noted in my other reviews, few if any have fully understood the later W and, lacking the S1, S2 framework it is not surprising. Thus, one can understand why one cannot imagine an object while seeing it as the domination of S2 by S1. There is no test for my inner experiences, so whatever comes to mind when I imagine Jack's face is the image of Jack. Similarly, with reading and calculation which can refer to S1, S2 or a combination and there is the constant temptation to apply S2 terms to S1 processes where the lack of any test makes them inapplicable. Two of W's famous examples used for combatting this temptation are playing tennis without a ball (`S1 tennis'), and a tribe that had only S2 calculation so `calculating in the head (`S1 calculating') was not possible.

`Playing' and `calculating' describe actual or potential acts--i.e., they are disposition words but with plausible reflexive S1 uses so as I have said before one really ought to keep them straight by writing `playing1' and `playing2' etc. But we are not taught to do this and so we want to either dismiss `calculating1' as a fantasy, or we think we can leave its nature undecided until later. Hence another of W's famous comments--"The decisive movement in the conjuring trick has been made, and it was the very one we thought quite innocent." That is, the first few sentences or often the title commit one to a way of looking at things (a language game) which prevents clear use of language in the present context.

A sentence expresses a thought (has a meaning), when it has clear COS, and this means has public truth conditions. Hence the comment from W: " When I think in language, there aren't 'meanings' going through my mind in addition to the verbal expressions: the language is itself the vehicle of thought." And, if I think with or without words, the thought is whatever I (honestly) say it is as there is no other possible criterion (COS). Thus, W's lovely aphorisms (p132 Budd) "It is in language that wish and fulfillment meet" and "Like everything metaphysical, the harmony between thought and reality is to be found in the grammar of the language." And one might note here that 'grammar' in W can usually be interpreted as the logical structure of language, and that in spite of his frequent warnings against theorizing and generalizing, this is about as broad a characterization of philosophy and higher order descriptive psychology as one canfind.

Likewise, with the question "What makes it true that my image of Jack is an image of him?" Imagining is another disposition and the COS is that the image I have in my head is Jack and that's why I will say 'YES' if shown his picture and 'NO' if shown one of someone else. The test here is *not* that the photo matches the vague image I had but that I intended it (had the COS that) to be an image of him. Hence the famous quote from W: "If God had looked into our minds he would not have been able to see there whom we were speaking of (PI p217)" and his comments that the whole problem of representation is contained in "that's Him" and "...what gives the image its interpretation is the path on which it lies," or as S says its COS. Hence W's summation (p140 Budd) that "What it always comes to in the end is that without any further meaning, he calls what happened the wish that that should happen"..." the question whether I know what I wish before my wish is fulfilled cannot arise at all. And the fact that some event stops my wishing does not mean that it fulfills it. Perhaps I should not have been satisfied if my

23

wish had been satisfied"...Suppose it were asked `Do I know what I long for before I get it? If I have learned to talk, then I do know." Disposition words refer to Potential Events (PE's) which I accept as fulfilling the COS and my mental states, emotions, change of interest etc. have no bearing on the way dispositions function. I am hoping, wishing, expecting, thinking, intending, desiring etc. depending on the state I take myself to be in-- on the COS that I express. Thinking and intending are S2 dispositions which can only be expressed by reflexive S1 muscle contractions, especially those of speech.

Now that we have a reasonable start on the Logical Structure of Rationality (the Descriptive Psychology of Higher Order Thought) laid out we can look at the table of Intentionality that results from this work, which I have constructed over the last few years. It is based on a much simpler one from Searle, which in turn owes much to Wittgenstein. I have also incorporated in modified form tables being used by current researchers in the psychology of thinking processes which are evidenced in the last 9 rows. It should prove interesting to compare it with those in Peter Hacker's 3 recent volumes on Human Nature. I offer this table as an heuristic for describing behavior that I find more complete and useful than any other framework I have seen and not as a final or complete analysis, which would have to be three dimensional with hundreds (at least) of arrows going in many directions with many (perhaps all) pathways between S1 and S2 being bidirectional. Also, the very distinction between S1 and S2, cognition and willing, perception and memory, between feeling, knowing, believing and expecting etc. are arbitrary--that is, as W demonstrated, all words are contextually sensitive and most have several utterly different uses (meanings or COS). Many complex charts have been published by scientists but I find them of minimal utility when thinking about behavior (as opposed to thinking about brain function). Each level of description may be useful in certain contexts but I find that being coarser or finer limits usefulness.

The Logical Structure of Rationality (LSR), or the Logical Structure of Mind (LSM), the Logical Structure of Behavior (LSB), the Logical Structure of Thought (LST), the Logical Structure of Consciousness (LSC), the Logical Structure of Personality (LSP), the Descriptive Psychology of Consciousness

(DSC), the Descriptive Psychology of Higher Order Thought (DPHOT), Intentionality-the classical philosophical term.

System 1 is involuntary, reflexive or automated "Rules" R1 while Thinking (Cognition) has no gaps and is voluntary or deliberative "Rules" R2 and Willing (Volition) has 3 gaps (see Searle)

I suggest we can describe behavior more clearly by changing Searle's "impose conditions of satisfaction on conditions of satisfaction" to "relate mental states to the world by moving muscles" —i.e., talking, writing and doing, and his "mind to world direction of fit" and "world to mind direction of fit" by "cause originates in the mind" and "cause originates in the world" S1 is only upwardly causal (world to mind) and contentless (lacking representations or information) while S2 has content and is downwardly causal (mind to world). I have adopted my terminology in this table.

FROM THE ANALYSIS OF LANGUAGE GAMES

	Disposition*	Emotion	Memory	Perception	Desire	PI**	IA***	Action/Word
Cause Originates From****	World	World	World	World	Mind	Mind	Mind	Mind
Causes Changes In*****	None	Mind	Mind	Mind	None	World	World	World
Causally Self Reflexive******	No	Yes	Yes	Yes	No	Yes	Yes	Yes
True or False (Testable)	Yes	T only	T only	T only	Yes	Yes	Yes	Yes
Public Conditions of Satisfaction	Yes	Yes/No	Yes/No	No	Yes/No	Yes	No	Yes
Describe A Mental State	No	Yes	Yes	Yes	No	No	Yes/No	Yes
Evolutionary Priority	5	4	2,3	1	5	3	2	2
Voluntary Content	Yes	No	No	No	No	Yes	Yes	Yes
Voluntary Initiation	Yes/No	No	Yes	No	Yes/No	Yes	Yes	Yes
Cognitive System *******	2	1	2/1	1	2/1	2	1	2
Change Intensity	No	Yes	Yes	Yes	Yes	No	No	No
Precise Duration	No	Yes	Yes	Yes	No	No	Yes	Yes
Time, Place (H+N, T+T) ********	TT	HN	HN	HN	TT	TT	HN	HN
Special Quality	No	Yes	No	Yes	No	No	No	No
Localized in Body	No	No	No	Yes	No	No	No	Yes
Bodily Expressions	Yes	Yes	No	No	Yes	Yes	Yes	Yes
Self Contradictions	No	Yes	No	No	Yes	No	No	No
Needs a Self	Yes	Yes/No	No	No	Yes	No	No	No
Needs Language	Yes	No	No	No	No	No	No	Yes/No

FROM DECISION RESEARCH

	Disposition*	Emotion	Memory	Perception	Desire	PI**	IA***	Action/Word
Subliminal Effects	No	Yes/No	Yes	Yes	No	No	No	Yes/No
Associative/Rule Based	RB	A/RB	A	A	A/RB	RB	RB	RB
Context Dependent/Abstract	A	CD/A	CD	CD	CD/A	A	CD/A	CD/A
Serial/Parallel	S	S/P	P	P	S/P	S	S	S
Heuristic/Analytic	A	H/A	H	H	H/A	A	A	A
Needs Working Memory	Yes	No	No	No	No	Yes	Yes	Yes
General Intelligence Dependent	Yes	No	No	No	Yes/No	Yes	Yes	Yes
Cognitive Loading Inhibits	Yes	Yes/No	No	No	Yes	Yes	Yes	Yes
Arousal Facilitates or Inhibits	I	F/I	F	F	I	I	I	I

Public Conditions of Satisfaction of S2 are often referred to by Searle and others as COS, Representations, truthmakers or meanings (or COS2 by myself), while the automatic results of S1 are designated as presentations by others (or COS1 by myself).

*   Aka Inclinations, Capabilities, Preferences, Representations, possible actions etc.
**   Searle's Prior Intentions
***   Searle's Intention In Action
****   Searle's Direction of Fit
*****   Searle's Direction of Causation
****** (Mental State instantiates--Causes or Fulfills Itself). Searle formerly calls this causally self- referential.
******* Tversky/Kahneman/Frederick/Evans/Stanovich defined cognitive systems.
******** Here and Now or There and Then

It is of interest to compare this with the various tables and charts in Peter

Hacker's recent 3 volumes on Human Nature. One should always keep in mind Wittgenstein's discovery that after we have described the possible uses (meanings, truthmakers, Conditions of Satisfaction) of language in a particular context, we have exhausted its interest, and attempts at explanation (i.e., philosophy) only get us further away from the truth. He showed us that there is only one philosophical problem — the use of sentences (language games) in an inappropriate context, and hence only one solution — showing the correct context.

EXPLANATION OF THE TABLE System 1 (i.e., emotions, memory, perceptions, reflexes) which parts of the brain present to consciousness, are automated and generally happen in less than 500msec, while System 2 is abilities to perform slow deliberative actions that are represented in conscious deliberation (S2D-my terminology) requiring over 500msec, but frequently repeated S2 actions can also become automated (S2A-my terminology). There is a gradation of consciousness from coma through the stages of sleep to full awareness. Memory includes short term memory (working memory) of system 2 and long term memory of System 1. For volitions one would usually say they are successful or not, rather than true or false. S1 is causally self-reflexive since the description of our perceptual experience-the presentation of our senses to consciousness, can only be described in the same words (as the same COS - Searle) as we describe the world, which I prefer to call the percept or COS1 to distinguish it from the representation or public COS2 of S2.

Of course, the various rows and columns are logically and psychologically connected. E.g., Emotion, Memory and Perception in the True or False row will be True-Only, will describe a mental state, belong to cognitive system 1, will not generally be initiated voluntarily, are causally self-reflexive, cause originates in the world and causes changes in the mind, have a precise duration, change in intensity, occur here and now, commonly have a special quality, do not need language, are independent of general intelligence and working memory, are not inhibited by cognitive loading, will not have voluntary content, and will not have public conditions of satisfaction etc.

There will always be ambiguities because the words (concepts, language games) cannot precisely match the actual complex functions of the brain (behavior), that is, there is a combinatorial explosion of contexts in sentences and in the brain states), and this is why it's not possible to reduce higher order behavior to a system of laws, which would have to state all the possible contexts –hence Wittgenstein's warnings against theories. This is a special case of the irreducibility of higher level descriptions to lower level ones that has been explained many times by Searle, Daniele Moyal-Sharrock (DMS), P.M.S. Hacker, Wittgenstein and others.

About a million years ago primates evolved the ability to use their throat muscles to make complex series of noises (i.e., primitive speech) to describe present events (perceptions, memory, reflexive actions) with some Primary or Primitive Language Games (PLG's). System 1 is comprised of fast, automated, subcortical, nonrepresentational, causally self-reflexive, intransitive, informationless, true-only mental states with a precise time and location, and over time there evolved in higher cortical centers S2 with the further ability to describe displacements in space and time of events (the past and future and often hypothetical, counterfactual, conditional or fictional preferences, inclinations or dispositions-the Secondary or Sophisticated Language Games (SLG's) of System 2 that are slow, cortical, conscious, information containing, transitive (having public Conditions of Satisfaction-Searle's term for truthmakers or meaning which I divide into COS1 and COS2 for private S1 and public S2), representational (which I again divide into R1 for S1 representations and R2 for S2), true or false propositional thinking, with all S2 functions having no precise time and being abilities and not mental states. Preferences are Intuitions, Tendencies, Automatic Ontological Rules, Behaviors, Abilities, Cognitive Modules, Personality Traits, Templates, Inference Engines, Inclinations, Emotions (described by Searle as agitated desires), Propositional Attitudes (correct only if used to refer to events in the world and not to propositions), Appraisals, Capacities, Hypotheses. Some Emotions are slowly developing and changing results of S2 dispositions (W- 'Remarks on the Philosophy of Psychology' V2 p148) while others are typical S1 — automatic and fast to appear and disappear. "I believe", "he loves", "they think" are descriptions of possible public acts typically displaced in space-time. My first-person statements about myself are true-only (excluding lying) –i.e. S1, while third person statements about others are true or false –i.e., S2 (see my reviews of Johnston 'Wittgenstein: Rethinking the Inner' and of Budd 'Wittgenstein's Philosophy of Psychology').

"Preferences" as a class of intentional states --opposed to perceptions, reflexive acts and memories-- were first clearly described by Wittgenstein (W) in the 1930's and termed "inclinations" or "dispositions". They have commonly been termed "propositional attitudes" since Russell but it has often been noted that this is an incorrect or misleading phrase since believing, intending, knowing, remembering etc., are often not propositional nor attitudes, as has been shown e.g., by W and by Searle (e.g., cf Consciousness and Language p118).

Preferences are intrinsic, observer independent public representations (as opposed to presentations or representations of System 1 to System 2 – Searle-Consciousness and Language p53). They are potential acts displaced in time or space, while the evolutionarily more primitive S1 perceptions memories and reflexive actions are always here and now. This is one way to characterize System 2 -the second major advance in vertebrate psychology after System 1 — the ability to represent (state public COS for) events and to think of them as occurring in another place or time (Searle's third faculty of counterfactual imagination supplementing cognition and volition). S1 'thoughts' (my T1-i.e., the use of "thinking" to refer to automatic brain processes of System One) are potential or unconscious mental states of S1 --Searle-- Phil Issues 1:45-66(1991).

Perceptions, memories and reflexive (automatic) actions can be described by primary LG's (PLG's -- e.g., I see the dog) and there are, in the normal case, NO TESTS possible so they can be True-Only- i.e., axiomatic as I prefer or animal reflexes as W and DMS describe. Dispositions can be described as secondary LG's (SLG's –e.g. I believe I see the dog) and must also be acted out, even for me in my own case (i.e., how do I KNOW what I believe, think, feel until I act or some event occurs—see my reviews of the well-known books on W by Johnston and Budd. Note that Dispositions become Actions when spoken or written as well as being acted out in other ways, and these ideas are all due to Wittgenstein (mid 1930's) and are NOT Behaviorism (Hintikka & Hintikka 1981, Searle, Hacker, Hutto etc.,). Wittgenstein can be regarded as the founder of evolutionary psychology and his work a unique investigation of the functioning of our axiomatic System 1 psychology and its interaction with System 2. After Wittgenstein laid the groundwork for the Descriptive Psychology of Higher Order Thought in the Blue and Brown Books in the early 30's, it was extended by John Searle, who made a simpler version of this table in his classic book Rationality in Action (2001). It expands on W's survey of the axiomatic structure of evolutionary psychology developed from his very first comments in 1911 and so beautifully laid out in his last work 'On Certainty' (OC) (written in 1950-51). OC is the foundation stone of behavior or epistemology and ontology (arguably the same as are semantics and pragmatics), cognitive linguistics or Higher Order Thought, and in my view (shared e.g., by DMS) the single most important work in philosophy (descriptive psychology) and thus in the study of behavior. Perception, Memory, Reflexive actions and Emotion are primitive partly Subcortical Involuntary Mental States, that can be described in PLG's, in which the mind automatically fits (presents) the world (is Causally Self Reflexive--Searle) --the unquestionable, true-only, axiomatic basis of rationality over which no control is possible).

Preferences, Desires, and Intentions are descriptions of slow thinking conscious Voluntary Abilities— that can be described in SLG's-- in which the mind tries to fit (represent) the world. Behaviorism and all the other confusions of our default descriptive psychology (philosophy) arise because we cannot see S1 working and describe all actions as the conscious deliberate actions of S2 (The Phenomenological Illusion—TPI—Searle). W understood this and described it with unequalled clarity with hundreds of examples of language (the mind) in action throughout his works. Reason has access to memory and so we use consciously apparent but often incorrect reasons to explain behavior (the Two Selves or Systems or Processes of current research). Beliefs and other Dispositions can be described as thoughts which try to match the facts of the world (mind to world direction of fit), while Volitions are intentions to act (Prior Intentions—PI, or Intentions In Action-IA-Searle) plus acts which try to match the world to the thoughts—world to mind direction of fit—cf. Searle e.g., Consciousness and Language p145, 190).

Sometimes there are gaps in reasoning to arrive at belief and other dispositions. Disposition words can be used as nouns which seem to describe mental states ('my thought is…') or as verbs or adjectives to describe abilities (agents as they act or might act -'I think that…) and are often incorrectly called "Propositional Attitudes".

Perceptions become Memories and our innate programs (cognitive modules, templates, inference engines of S1) use these to produce Dispositions — (believing, knowing, understanding, thinking, etc., -actual or potential public acts such as language (thought, mind) also called Inclinations, Preferences, Capabilities, Representations of S2) and Volition -and there is no language (concept, thought) of private mental states for thinking or willing (i.e., no private language, thought or mind). Higher animals can think and will acts and to that extent they have a public psychology. Perceptions: (X is True): Hear, See, Smell, Pain, Touch, Temperature Memories, Remembering: (X was true)

PREFERENCES, INCLINATIONS, DISPOSITIONS: (X might become True)

CLASS 1: PROPOSITIONAL (True or False) PUBLIC ACTS of Believing, Judging, Thinking, Representing, Understanding, Choosing, Deciding, Preferring, Interpreting, Knowing (including skills and abilities), Attending (Learning), Experiencing, Meaning, Remembering, Intending, Considering, Desiring, Expecting, Wishing, Wanting, Hoping (a special class), Seeing As (Aspects),

CLASS 2: DECOUPLED MODE-(as if, conditional, hypothetical, fictional) - Dreaming, Imagining, Lying, Predicting, Doubting

CLASS 3: EMOTIONS: Loving, Hating, Fearing, Sorrow, Joy, Jealousy, Depression. Their function is to modulate Preferences to increase inclusive fitness (expected maximum utility) by facilitating information processing of perceptions and memories for rapid action. There is some separation between S1 emotions such as rage and fear and S2 such as love, hate, disgust and anger. We can think of them as strongly felt or acted out desires.

DESIRES: (I want X to be True—I want to change the world to fit my thoughts): Longing, Hoping, Expecting, Awaiting, Needing, Requiring, obliged to do

INTENTIONS: (I will make X True) Intending

ACTIONS (I am making X True) : Acting, Speaking , Reading, Writing, Calculating, Persuading, Showing, Demonstrating, Convincing, Doing Trying, Attempting, Laughing, Playing, Eating, Drinking, Crying, Asserting (Describing, Teaching, Predicting, Reporting), Promising , Making or Using Maps, Books, Drawings, Computer Programs–these are Public and Voluntary and transfer Information to others so they dominate over the Unconscious, Involuntary and Informationless S1 reflexes in explanations of behavior (The Phenomenological Illusion, The Blank Slate or the Standard Social Science Model--SSSM).

Words express actions having various functions in our life and are not the names of objects nor of a single type of event. The social interactions of humans are governed by cognitive modules—roughly equivalent to the scripts or schemata of social psychology (groups of neurons organized into inference engines), which, with perceptions and memories, lead to the formation of preferences which lead to intentions and then to actions. Intentionality or intentional psychology can be taken to be all these processes or only preferences leading to actions and in the broader sense is the subject of cognitive psychology or cognitive neurosciences when including neurophysiology, neurochemistry and neurogenetics. Evolutionary psychology can be regarded as the study of all the preceding functions or of the operation of the modules which produce behavior, and is then coextensive in evolution, development and individual action with preferences, intentions and actions. Since the axioms (algorithms or cognitive modules) of our psychology are in our genes, we can enlarge our understanding and increase our power by giving clear descriptions of how they work and can extend them (culture) via biology, psychology, philosophy (descriptive psychology), math, logic, physics, and computer programs, thus making them faster and more efficient. Hajek (2003) gives an analysis of dispositions as conditional probabilities which are algorithmatized by Rott (1999), Spohn etc.

Intentionality (cognitive or evolutionary psychology) consists of various aspects of behavior which are innately programmed into cognitive modules which create and require consciousness, will and self, and in normal human adults nearly all except perceptions and some memories are purposive, require public acts (e.g., language), and commit us to relationships in order to increase our inclusive fitness (maximum expected utility or Bayesian utility maximization). However, Bayesianism is highly questionable due to severe underdetermination-i.e., it can 'explain' anything and hence nothing. This occurs via dominance and reciprocal altruism, often resulting in Desire Independent Reasons for Action (Searle)- which I divide into DIRA1 and DIRA2 for S1 and S2) and imposes Conditions of Satisfaction on Conditions of Satisfaction (Searle)-(i.e., relates thoughts to the world via public acts (muscle movements), producing math, language, art, music, sex, sports etc. The basics of this were figured out by our greatest natural psychologist Ludwig Wittgenstein from the 1930's to 1951 but with clear foreshadowings back to 1911, and with refinements by many, but above all by John Searle beginning in the 1960's. "The general tree of psychological phenomena. I strive not for exactness but for a view of the whole." RPP Vol 1 p895 cf Z p464. Much of intentionality (e.g., our language games) admits of degrees. As W noted, inclinations are sometimes conscious and deliberative. All our templates (functions, concepts, language games) have fuzzy edges in some contexts as they must to be useful.

There are at least two types of 'thinking' (i.e., two language games or ways of using the dispositional verb "thinking")—nonrational without awareness and rational with partial awareness(W), now described as the fast and slow thinking of S1 and S2. It is useful to regard these as language games and not as mere phenomena (W RPP Vol2 p129). Mental phenomena (our subjective or internal "experiences") are epiphenomenal, lack criteria, hence lack info even for oneself and thus can play no role in communication, thinking or mind. Thinking like all dispositions lacks any test, is not a mental state (unlike perceptions of S1), and contains no information until it becomes a public act or event such as in speech, writing or other muscular contractions. Our perceptions and memories can have information (meaning-i.e., a public COS) only when they are manifested in public actions, for only then do thinking, feeling etc. have any meaning (consequences) even for ourselves.

Memory and perception are integrated by modules into dispositions which become psychologically effective when they are acted upon—i.e., S1 generates S2. Developing language means manifesting the innate ability of advanced humans to substitute words (fine contractions of oral or manual muscles) for acts (gross contractions of arm and leg muscles). TOM (Theory of Mind) is much better called UA-Understanding of Agency (my term) and UA1 and UA2 for such functions in S1 and S2 —and can also be called Evolutionary Psychology or Intentionality--the innate genetically programmed production of consciousness, self, and thought which leads to intentions and then to actions by contracting muscles—i.e., Understanding is a Disposition like Thinking and Knowing. Thus, "propositional attitude" is an incorrect term for normal intuitive deliberative S2D (i.e., the slow deliberative functioning of System 2) or automated S2A (i.e., the conversion of frequently practiced System 2 functions of speech and action into automatic fast functions). We see that the efforts of cognitive science to understand thinking, emotions etc. by studying neurophysiology is not going to tell us anything more about how the mind (thought, language) works (as opposed to how the brain works) than we already know, because "mind" (thought, language) is already in full public view (W). Any 'phenomena' that are hidden in neurophysiology, biochemistry, genetics, quantum mechanics, or string theory, are as irrelevant to our social life as the fact that a table is composed of atoms which "obey" (can be described by) the laws of physics and chemistry is to having lunch on it. As W so famously said "Nothing is hidden". Everything of interest about the mind (thought, language) is open to view if we only examine carefully the workings of language. Language (mind, public speech connected to potential actions) was evolved to facilitate social interaction and thus the gathering of resources, survival and reproduction. Its grammar (i.e., evolutionary psychology, intentionality) functions automatically and is extremely confusing when we try to analyze it. This has been explained frequently by Hacker, DMS and many others.

As W noted with countless carefully stated examples, words and sentences have multiple uses depending on context. I believe and I eat have profoundly different roles as do I believe and I believed or I believe and he believes. The present tense first person use of inclinational verbs such as "I believe" normally describe my ability to predict my probable acts based on knowledge (i.e., S2) but can also seem (in philosophical contexts) to be descriptive of my mental state and so not based on knowledge or information (W and see my review of the book by Hutto and Myin). In the former S1 sense, it does not describe a truth but makes itself true in the act of saying it --i.e., "I believe it's raining" makes itself true. That is, disposition verbs used in first person present tense can be causally self-reflexive--they instantiate themselves but then they are not testable (i.e., not T or F, not S2). However past or future tense or third person use--"I believed" or "he believes" or "he will believe' contain or can be resolved by information that is true or false, as they describe public acts that are or can become verifiable. Likewise, "I believe it's raining" has no information apart from subsequent actions, even for me, but "I believe it will rain" or "he will think it's raining" are potentially verifiable public acts displaced in spacetime that intend to convey information (or misinformation).

Nonreflective or Nonrational (automatic) words spoken without Prior Intent (which I call S2A—i.e., S2D automated by practice) have been called Words as Deeds by W & then by Daniel Moyal-Sharrock in her paper in Philosophical Psychology in 2000). Many so-called Inclinations/Dispositions/Preferences/Tendencies/Capacities/Abilities are Non-Propositional (NonReflective) Attitudes (far more useful to call them functions or abilities) of System 1 (Tversky and Kahnemann). Prior Intentions are stated by Searle to be Mental States and hence S1, but again I think one must separate PI1 and PI2 since in our normal language our prior intentions are the conscious deliberations of S2. Perceptions, Memories, type 2 Dispositions (e.g., some emotions) and many Type 1 Dispositions are better called Reflexes of S1 and are automatic, nonreflective, NON-Propositional and NON-Attitudinal functioning of the hinges (axioms, algorithms) of our Evolutionary Psychology (Moyal-Sharrock after Wittgenstein).

Now for some comments on "Human Nature: The Categorical Framework" (HN).

Hacker is the world's leading authority on W and much of his work has been dedicated to explaining him so there is inevitably a Wittgensteinian feel to much of this book. This is the first of 3 volumes on Human Nature (the second The Intellectual Powers: A Study of Human Nature has now appeared and the third on ethics should follow soon) and its aim is to lay out the classes or categories of the psychology of intentionality. The quote from H above gives the best brief overview of what needs to be described as I have seen. And this description is, as both H and W insist, a conceptual and not scientific one for reasons that should be obvious from their work. This is totally at odds with the views of many others (most notoriously e.g. Dennett, Carruthers and the Churchlands) who think that not only must philosophy explain behavior but that it must fundamentally change as science progresses.

A capsule summary of what H is getting at here can be gained by looking at the various charts and I again suggest comparing them with my table above. Sadly, there is no bibliography-a major failing, but this is trivial compared to the lack of any serious discussion of the work of John Searle (S)--in my view, next to W, the major philosopher of recent times. Since I have referenced S many times above and in my other reviews I will not repeat the reasons for this view here. Recently there have been some exchanges between the two recorded in "Neuroscience and Philosophy" which appeared as a result of H's views expressed e.g. in Philosophical Foundations of Neuroscience which I will review soon. Both authors score some points and miss critical ideas in the others work. I have noted S's failure to appreciate W before. Hacker is representing W's views or at least Wittgensteinian views most of the time so we get as close as we ever will to a confrontation between the two geniuses of descriptive psychology --W and S.

Though H gives the best characterization of the task of philosophy I have seen (see above) nevertheless his comment on p10 makes me note again that it is just the descriptive psychology of higher order thought.

Anyone interested in a concise demolition of Quine (another great mind who totally missed W and thus the whole enterprise of philosophy) should see Hacker's paper 'PASSING BY THE NATURALISTIC TURN: ON QUINE'S CUL-DE-SAC' (though of course Q's deconstruction has been done by many including S).

The discussion of the logical (psychological) difference between the S1 causes and the S2 reasons in Chapter 7, esp. on p226-32 is critical for any student of behavior. It is a nearly universal delusion that "cause" is a precise logically exact term while "reason" is not but W exposed this many times and so have others, but this discussion is the best and most concise I can recall and it is basic to any understanding of behavior. Of course, the same issue arises with all scientific and mathematical concepts. The discussion of mental states vs. dispositions is excellent and reminds me that S's continued reference to dispositions as mental states and his reference to mental states as representations (actually `presentations" in his latest work) with COS, is (in my view) counterproductive. Though I accept most of S's ontology and epistemology I don't see the advantage of regarding our seeing an apple as the COS of a perception rather than that they are the true only results of the unconscious actions of S1.

The table on p147 and the whole chapter on agency reminds me again of how greatly this work would have benefited from the S, S2 notions and S's concepts such as Prior Intention, Intention in Action, intentional gaps, DOF, COS, CSR etc. And of course, one must keep constantly in mind that `action', `condition', `satisfaction',`intention', and even `and', `or', `prior', `true' etc. are all complex language games able to trip us up as W so beautifully described in BBB in the early 30's.

The footnote on p235-6 reminds us that it was Descartes mistake that played a major role in laying the dead hand of private language and introspection on philosophy.

I see as another failing H's obliviousness (which as noted he shares with S and almost all philosophers) to the modern two systems framework and to the full implications of W's "radical" epistemology as stated most dramatically in his last work `On Certainty', as I have noted in many reviews (and as DMS noted in her superb book on OC). This is sad, as I have described how it was W who did the first and best job of describing the two systems (though nobody else has noticed) and that OC represents a major event in intellectual history. One of the

39

numerous places this comes out is p245 in the discussion of doubt where he could have noted that `grammar' is another word for the axiomatic true only EP of S1. Likewise, with his table on p19 where one kind of `proposition' is listed as conceptual truths--i.e., what W called true-only sentences or ideas, the axiomatic EP or `grammar' that is the basis for judging.

In spite of what I see as its limitations, this is a unique work of great interest to philosophers, psychologists, linguists, AI researchers and many others. One hopes that Hacker is able to complete a second edition.

Those wishing a comprehensive up to date account of Wittgenstein, Searle and their analysis of behavior from the modern two systems view may consult my book 'The Logical Structure of Philosophy, Psychology, Mind and Language as Revealed in Ludwig Wittgenstein and John Searle' 2nd ed. (2019).

Review of "Are We Hardwired? by Clark & Grunstein Oxford (2000)

Michael Starks

ABSTRACT

This is an excellent review of gene/environment interactions on behavior and, in spite of being a bit dated, is an easy and worthwhile read. They start with twin studies which show the overwhelming impact of genetics on behavior. They note the increasingly well-known studies of Judith Harris which extend and summarize the facts that shared home environment has almost no effect on behavior and that adopted children grow up to be as different from their stepbrothers and sisters as people chosen at random. One basic point that they (and nearly all who discuss behavioral genetics) fail to note is that the hundreds (thousands depending on your viewpoint) of human behavioral universals, including all the basics of our personalities, are 100% determined by our genes, with no variation in normals. Everyone sees a tree as a tree and not a stone, seeks and eats food, gets angry and jealous etc. So, what they are mostly talking about here is how much environment (culture) can affect the degree to which various traits are shown, rather than their appearance.

Finally, they discuss eugenics in the usual politically correct fashion, failing to note that we and all organisms are the products of nature's eugenics and that attempts to defeat natural selection with medicine, agriculture, and civilization as a whole, are disastrous for any society that persists in doing this. As much as 50% of all conceptions, or some 100 million/year, end in early spontaneous abortion, nearly all without the mother being aware. This natural culling of defective genes drives evolution, keeps us relatively genetically sound and makes society possible. Dysgenics is sufficient to destroy civilization but overpopulation will do it first.

Those wishing a comprehensive up to date framework for human behavior from the modern two systems view may consult my book 'The Logical Structure of Philosophy, Psychology, Mind and Language in Ludwig Wittgenstein and John Searle' 2nd ed (2019). Those interested in more of my writings may see 'Talking Monkeys--Philosophy, Psychology, Science, Religion and Politics on a Doomed Planet--Articles and Reviews 2006-2017' 3rd ed (2019).

This is an excellent review of gene/environment interactions on behavior and, in spite of being a bit dated, is an easy and worthwhile read.

They start with twin studies, which show the overwhelming impact of genetics on behavior. They note the increasingly well-known studies of Judith Harris which extend and summarize the facts that shared home environment has almost no effect on behavior and that adopted children grow up to be as different from their stepbrothers and sisters as people chosen at random. There is lots of impact on personality (ca 50% of variation) from early environment, presumably peer interaction, TV etc., but we really don't know.

They summarize the genetics of behavior in the earliest true animals, the protozoa, and note that many of the genes and mechanisms underlying our behavior are already present. There is strong selective advantage to identifying the genes of one's potential mates and even protozoa have such mechanisms. There is data showing that people tend to pick out mates with different HLA types but the mechanism is obscure. They present various lines of evidence that we communicate unconsciously with pheromones via the vomeronasal organs and this is not mediated by smell neurons.

One chapter reviews the biology of the nematode C. elegans, noting the fact that it shares many mechanisms and genes with protozoa and with us due to the extreme conservativism of evolution. Some human genes have been inserted into it with apparent preservation of their function in us.

Moreover, they show what seem to be mechanisms of long term and short term memory controlled by genes in a fashion similar to that in higher organisms.

They note the general similarity of the nonvisual cryptochome mediated regulation of circadian rhythms in yeasts and fruitflies to those in higher animals and even to those in plants. It has been shown that both cry-1 and cry-2 cryptochrome genes are present in fruit flies, mice and humans and that the photoreceptor system is active in many body cells other than the retina, and researchers have even been able to trigger circadian rhythms from light shined on our leg!

After a brief survey of work on the famous slug Aplysia and the cAMP and Calmodulin systems, they review the data on human neurotransmitters. The chapter on aggression notes the impulsive aggression of low serotonin mice and the effects on aggressive behavior of mutations/drugs that affect the chemistry of nitric oxide— recently, to the amazement of all, identified as a major neurotransmitter or neuromodulator.

In a chapter on consumption, they recount the now well known story of leptin and its role in regulation of food intake. Then a summary of the genetics of sexual behavior.

One basic point that they (and nearly all who discuss behavioral genetics) fail to note is that the hundreds (thousands depending on your viewpoint) of human behavioral universals, including all the basics of our personalities, are 100% determined by our genes, with no variation in normals. Everyone sees a tree as a tree and not a stone, seeks and eats food, gets angry and jealous etc. So, what they are mostly talking about here is how much environment (culture) can affect the degree to which various traits are shown, rather than their appearance.

There are also highly active fields studying human behavior which they barely mention— evolutionary psychology, cognitive psychology, parts of sociology, anthropology and behavioral economics—which are casting brilliant lights on behavior and showing that it is to a large extent automatic and unconscious with little voluntary awareness or control. The authors bias towards biology is a huge defect.

Finally, they discuss eugenics in the usual politically correct fashion, failing to note that we and all organisms are the products of nature's eugenics and that attempts to defeat natural selection with medicine, agriculture, and civilization as a whole, are disastrous for any society that persists in it. As much as 50% of all conceptions, or some 100 million/year, end in early spontaneous abortion, nearly all without the mother being aware. This natural culling of defective genes drives evolution, keeps us relatively genetically sound and makes society possible. However, it is now clear that overpopulation will destroy the world before dysgenics has a chance.

Is JK Rowling More Evil Than Me? (revised 2019)

Michael Starks

ABSTRACT

How about a different take on the rich and famous? First the obvious—the Harry Potter novels are primitive superstition that encourages children to believe in fantasy rather than take responsibility for the world-- the norm of course. JKR is just as clueless about herself and the world as most people, but about 200 times as destructive as the average American and about 800 times more than the average Chinese. She has been responsible for the destruction of maybe 30,000 hectares of forest to produce these trash novels and all the erosion ensuing (not trivial as it's at least 6 and maybe 12 tons/year soil into the ocean for everyone on earth or maybe 100 tons per American, and so about 5000 tons/year for Rowling's books and movies and her 3 children). The earth loses at least 1% of its topsoil every year, so as it nears 2100, most of its food growing capacity will be gone. Then there is the huge amount of fuel burned and waste made to make and distribute the books and films, plastic dolls etc. She shows her lack of social responsibility by producing children rather than using her millions to encourage family planning or buy up the rain forest, and by promoting the conventional liberal stupidity of 3rd world supremacy that is destroying Britain, America, the world and her descendant's future. Of course, she's not that different from the other 7.8 billion clueless - just noisier and more destructive.

It is the no free lunch problem writ large. The mob just can't see that there is no such thing as helping one person without harming others. Rights or privileges given to new entrants into an overcrowded world can only diminish those of others. In spite of the massive ecological disasters happening in front of them everywhere everyday, they can't pin them to the unrestrained motherhood of "the diverse", which accounts for most of the population increase of the last century and all of that in this one. They lack some combination of intelligence, education, experience and sanity required to extrapolate the daily assaults on the resources and functioning of society to the eventual collapse of industrial civilization. Each meal, each trip by car or bus, each pair of shoes is another nail in the earth's coffin. It has likely never crossed her mind that one seat on a plane from London to San Francisco produces about one ton of carbon which melts about 3 square meters of sea ice and as one of the overprivileged she has probably flown hundreds of such flights.

Not only the rich and famous, but nearly any public figure at all, including virtually all teachers, are pressured to be politically correct, which in the Western Democracies, now means social democratic (Neomarxist—i.e., diluted communist) third world supremacists working for the destruction of their own societies and their own descendants. So, those whose lack of education, experience, intelligence (and basic common sense), which should prohibit them from making any public statements at all, totally dominate all the media, creating the impression that the intelligent and civilized must favor democracy, diversity and equality, while the truth is that these are the problems and not the solutions, and that they themselves are the prime enemies of civilization. See e.g., my Suicide by Democracy 4th ed (2019).

How about a different take on the rich and famous? First the obvious—the Harry Potter novels are primitive superstition that encourages children to believe in fantasy rather than take responsibility for the world-- the norm of course. JKR is just as clueless about herself and the world as all the other monkeys, but about 200 times as destructive as the average American and about 800 times more than the average Chinese. She has been responsible for the destruction of maybe 30,000 hectares of forest to produce these trash novels and all the erosion ensuing (not trivial as it's 6 to 12 tons/year soil into the ocean for everyone on earth or maybe 100 tons per American, and so about 5000 tons/year for Rowling's books and movies and her 3 children). The earth loses at least 1% of its topsoil every year, so as it nears 2100, most of its food growing capacity will be gone. Then there is the huge amount of fuel burned and waste made to make and distribute the books and films, plastic dolls etc. She shows her lack of social responsibility by producing children rather than using her millions to encourage family planning or buy up the rain forest, and by promoting the conventional liberal stupidity of 3rd world supremacy that is destroying Britain, America, the world and her descendant's future. Of course, she's not that different from the other 7.8 billion clueless - just noisier and more destructive.

Like all the rich, she is able to multiply her destruction by causing others to destroy on her behalf. Each child she produced results in about 50 tons of topsoil into the ocean, 300 lbs of toxic chemicals produced, 1 acre of forest/wetland/ gone forever, every year. Like all people, her family steals from all people on the earth and from their own descendants (no human rights without human wrongs), and, like the vast majority, she is poorly educated, egomaniacal, and lacking self-awareness, so these issues never cross her mind. In addition to the material destruction to make and distribute her books and movies, there is the vast amount of time wasted in reading and viewing them.

In addition, the extreme immaturity shown by the characters in them and their preoccupation with infantile superstitious fantasies can only do harm to impressionable minds. The world would be a better place if she had never been born, but one can say it of nearly everyone.

It has long been the understanding of spiritually aware people that all but a tiny number of us spend their whole lives asleep, and this view is powerfully supported by modern psychological research, which shows that nearly all our actions are done mechanically, for reasons of which we are not aware and over which we have no control. Our personality is an illusion produced by evolution to ensure reproduction. We are only a package for selfish genes carrying out their blind programs and, like all organisms, we live to replicate our genes and to accumulate and consume resources to that end. In our case that means we live to destroy the earth and our own descendants. It is essential to this game that we remain unaware of it, for, to the extent we become aware and live our lives as conscious beings, we diminish our reproduction and the genes which produce this behavior are selected against.

Rowling is a typical example of a seemingly intelligent aware person who will walk through their whole life sound asleep—just like nearly all of the other 11 billion (I extrapolate to 2100) —and like them, lives only to destroy the earth and to leave her toxic offspring behind to continue the destruction. Like so many, she, with Obama and the Pope, share the common delusion that the poor are more noble and deserving, but the rich differ only in having the chance to be more destructive. The poor are the rich in waiting. So, 800 Chinese or Indians do about as much damage as JKR and her family. Rich or poor they do the only things monkeys can do - consume resources and replicate their genes until the collapse of industrial civilization about the middle of the next century. In the blink of an eye, centuries and millennia will pass and, in the hellish world of starvation, disease, war and violence that their ancestors created, nobody will know or care that any of them existed. She is no more inherently evil than others, but also no better and, due to the accidents of history, she is high on the list of Enemies of Life on Earth.

It is the no free lunch problem writ large. The mob just can't see that there is no such thing as helping one person without harming others. Rights or privileges given to new entrants into an overcrowded world can only diminish those of others. In spite of the massive ecological disasters happening in front of them everywhere everyday, they can't pin them to the unrestrained motherhood of "the diverse", which accounts for most of the population increase of the last century and all of that in this one. They lack some combination of intelligence, education, experience and sanity required to extrapolate the daily assaults on the resources and functioning of society now to the eventual collapse of industrial civilization, as well as the courage to say so even if they do realize it. Each meal, each trip by car or bus, each pair of shoes is another nail in the earth's coffin. It has likely never crossed her mind that one seat on a plane from London to San Francisco produces about one ton of carbon which melts about 3 square meters of sea ice and as one of the overprivileged she has probably flown hundreds of such flights.

It never crosses most people's minds that the average American lower class family of 4 take out in goods, services, and infrastructure costs perhaps $50,000 more every year than they contribute, and in 100 years (when it will have expanded to perhaps 10 people) will have cost the country about $15 million, and immeasurably more in long term ecological and social costs (what is the value for the collapse of civilization?).

Not only the rich and famous, but nearly any public figure at all, including virtually all teachers, are pressured to be politically correct, which in the Western Democracies, now means social democratic (diluted communist) third world supremacists working for the destruction of their own societies and their own descendants. So, those whose lack of free speech (and basic common sense), which should prohibit them from making any public statements at all, totally dominate all the media, creating the impression that the intelligent and civilized must favor democracy, diversity and equality, while the truth is that these are the problems and not the solutions, and that they themselves are the prime enemies of civilization.

America and the world are in the process of collapse from excessive population growth, most of it for the last century and now all of it due to 3rd world people. Consumption of resources and the addition of 4 billion more ca. 2100 will collapse industrial civilization and bring about starvation, disease, violence and war on a staggering scale. Billions will die and nuclear war is all but certain. In America, this is being hugely accelerated by massive immigration and immigrant reproduction, combined with abuses made possible by democracy. Depraved human nature inexorably turns the dream of democracy and diversity into a nightmare of crime and poverty. China will continue to overwhelm America and the world, as long as it maintains the dictatorship which limits selfishness. The root cause of collapse is the inability of our innate psychology to adapt to the modern world, which leads people to treat unrelated persons as though they had common interests. I have termed this the Inclusive Fitness Delusion. This, plus ignorance of basic biology and psychology, leads to the social engineering delusions of the partially educated who control democratic societies. Few understand that if you help one person you harm someone else—there is no free lunch and every single item anyone consumes destroys the earth beyond repair. Consequently, social policies everywhere are unsustainable and one by one all societies without stringent controls on selfishness will collapse into anarchy or dictatorship. Without dramatic and immediate changes, there is no hope for preventing the collapse of America, or any country that follows a democratic system.

Those wishing a comprehensive up to date framework for human behavior from the modern two systems view may consult my books Talking Monkeys 3rd ed (2019), The Logical Structure of Philosophy, Psychology, Mind and Language in Ludwig Wittgenstein and John Searle 2nd ed (2019), Suicide by Democracy 4th ed (2019), The Logical Structure of Human Behavior (2019), The Logical Structure of Consciousness (2019, Understanding the Connections between Science, Philosophy, Psychology, Religion, Politics, and Economics (2019), and Suicidal Utopian Delusions in the 21st Century 5th ed (2019).

Review of The New Science of the Mind by Marc Rowlands (2013)

Michael Starks

ABSTRACT

Before remarking on "The New Science of the Mind", I first offer some comments on philosophy and its relationship to contemporary psychological research as exemplified in the works of Searle (S), Wittgenstein (W), Hacker (H) et al. It will help to see my reviews of PNC (Philosophy in a New Century), TLP, PI, OC, Making the Social World (MSW) and other books by and about these geniuses, who provide a clear description of higher order behavior, not found in psychology nor philosophy, that I will refer to as the WS framework.

As with so many philosophy books, we might stop with the title. As the quotes and comments above and in my other reviews and the books they cover indicate, there are compelling reasons for regarding the problems we face in describing the psychology of higher order thought as conceptual and not scientific. This ought to be crystal clear to all, but science envy and almost complete oblivion to WSH etc. is a la mode! But as H notes above, the issues discussed here are all about language games and have nothing to do with science. In fact, as usual, if one translates into plain English there is very little of interest here, and certainly nothing not said before and better by WS etc.
countless times since the 30's (see e.g., The Blue and Brown Books from 1933-35). It is not surprising that he makes no significant references to any of the above books or persons (the only reference to S is an article from 1958!), though in my view they are at the top of the list of the major figures in descriptive psychology.

On p119 he tells us that the key to all this is to figure out how "...a personal level cognitive process can belong to a representational subject. This is the task of the second half of the book." But W did this 80 years ago and since we have the beautifully clear explanations of WSH, H&M etc., there is no point to torturing oneself with the rather aimless and opaque prose that veers off at the end into Sartre, Heidegger, Husserl, and Frege, with a dash of postmodernist word salad for good measure. A valiant effort on an interesting topic, but ultimately exhausting and fruitless

Those wishing a comprehensive up to date framework for human behavior from the modern two systems view may consult my books Talking Monkeys 3rd ed (2019), The Logical Structure of Philosophy, Psychology, Mind and Language in Ludwig Wittgenstein and John Searle 2nd ed (2019), Suicide by Democracy 4th ed (2019), The Logical Structure of Human Behavior (2019), The Logical Structure of Consciousness (2019, Understanding the Connections between Science, Philosophy, Psychology, Religion, Politics, and Economics (2019), and Suicidal Utopian Delusions in the 21st Century 5th ed (2019).

"The confusion and barrenness of psychology is not to be explained by calling it a "young science"; its state is not comparable with that of physics, for instance, in its beginnings. (Rather with that of certain branches of mathematics. Set theory.) For in psychology there are experimental methods and conceptual confusion. (As in the other case, conceptual confusion and methods of proof). The existence of the experimental method makes us think we have the means of solving the problems that trouble us; though problem and method pass one another by." Wittgenstein (PI p.232)

"Philosophers constantly see the method of science before their eyes and are irresistibly tempted to ask and answer questions in the way science does. This tendency is the real source of metaphysics and leads the philosopher into complete darkness." (Blue Book p18, 1933).

"But I did not get my picture of the world by satisfying myself of its correctness: nor do I have it because I am satisfied of its correctness. No: it is the inherited background against which I distinguish between true and false." Wittgenstein OC 94

"Now if it is not the causal connections which we are concerned with, then the activities of the mind lie open before us." Wittgenstein "The Blue Book" p6 (1933)

"The aim of philosophy is to erect a wall at the point where language stops anyway." Wittgenstein Philosophical Occasions p187

"The limit of language is shown by its being impossible to describe a fact which corresponds to (is the translation of) a sentence without simply repeating the sentence ..." Wittgenstein CV p10 (1931)

"Some of the most important logical features of intentionality are beyond the reach of phenomenology because they have no immediate phenomenological reality... Because the creation of meaningfulness out of meaninglessness is not consciously experienced...it does not exist...This is... the phenomenological illusion." Searle PNC p115-117

"...the basic intentional relation between the mind and the world has to do with conditions of satisfaction. And a proposition is anything at all that can stand in an intentional relation to the world, and since those intentional relations always determine conditions of satisfaction, and a proposition is defined as anything sufficient to determine conditions of satisfaction, it turns out that all intentionality is a matter of propositions." Searle PNC p193

"But you cannot explain a physical system such as a typewriter or a brain by identifying a pattern which it shares with its computational simulation, because the existence of the pattern does not explain how the system actually works as a physical system. In sum, the fact that the attribution of syntax identifies no further causal powers is fatal to the claim that programs provide causal explanations of cognition   There is just a physical mechanism, the brain, with its various real physical and physical/mental causal levels of description." Searle Philosophy in a New Century (PNC) p101-103

"In short, the sense of `information processing' that is used in cognitive science is at much too high a level of abstraction to capture the concrete biological reality of intrinsic intentionality We are blinded to this difference by the fact that the same sentence `I see a car coming toward me,' can be used to record both the visual intentionality and the output of the computational model of vision...in the sense of `information' used in cognitive science, it is simply false to say that the brain is an information processing device." Searle PNC p104-105

"The intentional state represents its conditions of satisfaction...people erroneously suppose that every mental representation must be consciously thought...but the notion of a representation as I am using it is a functional and not an ontological notion. Anything that has conditions of satisfaction, that can succeed or fail in a way that is characteristic of intentionality, is by definition a representation of its conditions of satisfaction...we can analyze the structure of the intentionality of social phenomena by analyzing their conditions of satisfaction." Searle MSW p28- 32

"Here we come up against a remarkable and characteristic phenomenon in philosophical investigation: the difficulty---I might say--- is not that of finding the solution but rather that of recognizing as the solution something that looks as if it were only a preliminary to it. We have already said everything. --- Not anything that follows from this, no this itself is the solution! This is connected, I believe, with our wrongly expecting an explanation, whereas the solution of the difficulty is a description, if we give it the right place in our considerations. If we dwell upon it, and do not try to get beyond it." Zettel p312-314

These quotes are not chosen at random but (along with the others in my reviews) are an outline of behavior (human nature) from our two greatest descriptive psychologists. In considering these matters we must keep in mind that philosophy is descriptive psychology.

Before remarking on "The New Science of the Mind", I will first offer some comments on philosophy and its relationship to contemporary psychological research as exemplified in the works of Searle (S), Wittgenstein (W), Hacker (H) et al. It will help to see my reviews of PNC (Philosophy in a New Century), TLP, PI, OC, Making the Social World (MSW) and other books by and about these geniuses, who provide a clear description of higher order behavior, not found in psychology books, that I will refer to as the WS framework. To serve as an heuristic framework I have generated a table which is very useful but no room here (see other reviews such as that of Shoemaker's Physical Realization).

Here is how the leading Wittgenstein scholar summarized his work: "Wittgenstein resolved many of the deep problems that have dogged our subject for centuries, sometimes indeed for more than two millennia, problems about the nature of linguistic representation, about the relationship between thought and language, about solipsism and idealism, self-knowledge and knowledge of other minds, and about the nature of necessary truth and of mathematical propositions. He ploughed up the soil of European philosophy of logic and language. He gave us a novel and immensely fruitful array of insights into philosophy of psychology. He attempted to overturn centuries of reflection on the nature of mathematics and mathematical truth. He undermined foundationalist epistemology. And he bequeathed us a vision of philosophy as a contribution not to human knowledge, but to human understanding – understanding of the forms of our thought and of the conceptual confusions into which we are liable to fall." —Peter Hacker--'Gordon Baker's late interpretation of Wittgenstein'

To this I would add that W was the first to clearly and extensively describe the two systems of thought--fast automatic prelinguistic S1 and the slow reflective linguistic dispositional S2. He explained how behavior only is possible with a vast inherited background that is the axiomatic basis for judging and cannot be doubted or judged, so will (choice), consciousness self, time and space are innate true-only axioms. He noted in thousands of pages and hundreds of examples how our inner mental experiences are not directly describable in language, this being possible only with terms that substitute for public behavior (the impossibility of private language). He invented truth tables and predicted the utility of paraconsistent logic. He patented helicopter designs which anticipated by three decades the use of blade-tip jets to drive the rotors and which had the seeds of the centrifugal-flow gas turbine engine, designed a heart-beat monitor, designed and supervised the building of a modernist house, and sketched a proof of Euler's Theorem, subsequently completed by others. He can be viewed as the first evolutionary psychologist since he constantly explained the necessity of the innate background and demonstrated how it generates behavior. He described the psychology behind the Wason test--a fundamental measure used in EP decades later. He noted the indeterminate nature of language and the game-like nature of social interaction. He described and refuted the notions of the mind as machine and the computational theory of mind, long before practical computers. He decisively laid to rest skepticism and metaphysics. He showed that, far from being inscrutable, the activities of the mind lie open before us, a lesson few have learned since.

In addition to failing to make it clear that what they are doing is descriptive psychology, philosophers rarely specify exactly what it is that they expect to contribute to this topic that other students of behavior (i.e., *scientists*) do not, so after noting W's above remark on science envy, I will quote again from Hacker who gives a good start on it.

"Traditional epistemologists want to know whether knowledge is true belief and a further condition ..., or whether knowledge does not even imply belief ... We want to know when knowledge does and when it does not require justification. We need to be clear what is ascribed to a person when it is said that he knows something. Is it a distinctive mental state, an achievement, a performance, a disposition or an ability? Could knowing or believing that p be identical with a state of the brain? Why can one say 'he believes that p, but it is not the case that p', whereas one cannot say 'I believe that p, but it is not the case that p'? Why are there ways, methods and means of achieving, attaining or receiving knowledge, but not belief (as opposed to faith)? Why can one know, but not believe who, what, which, when, whether and how? Why can one believe, but not know, wholeheartedly, passionately, hesitantly, foolishly, thoughtlessly, fanatically, dogmatically or reasonably? Why can one know, but not believe, something perfectly well, thoroughly or in detail? And so on – through many hundreds of similar questions pertaining not only to knowledge and belief, but also to doubt, certainty, remembering, forgetting, observing, noticing, recognising, attending, being aware of, being conscious of, not to mention the numerous verbs of perception and their cognates. What needs to be clarified if these questions are to be answered is *the web of our epistemic concepts,* the ways in which the various concepts hang together, the various forms of their compatibilities and incompatibilities, their point and purpose, their presuppositions and different forms of context dependency. To this venerable exercise in connective analysis, scientific knowledge, psychology, neuroscience and self-styled cognitive science can contribute nothing whatsoever." (Passing by the naturalistic turn: on Quine's *cul- de-sac-* p15-2005)

A major theme in all discussion of human behavior is the need to separate the genetically programmed automatisms from the effects of culture. All study of higher order behavior is an effort to tease apart not only fast S1 and slow S2 thinking (e.g., perceptions and other automatisms vs. dispositions or abilities to act), but the logical extensions of S2 into culture (S3).

Searle's work as a whole provides a stunning description of higher order S2/S3 social behavior due to the recent evolution of genes for dispositional psychology, while the later W shows how it is based on true-only unconscious axioms of S1 which evolved into conscious dispositional propositional thinking of S2.

S1 is the simple automated functions of our involuntary, System 1, fast thinking, mirror neuron, true-only, non- propositional, prelinguistic mental states- our perceptions and memories and reflexive acts including System 1 Truths and UA1 --Understanding of Agency 1-- and Emotions1- such as joy, love, anger) which can be described causally, while the evolutionarily later linguistic functions are expressions or descriptions of voluntary, System 2, slow thinking, mentalizing neurons. That is, of testable true or false, propositional, Truth2 and UA2 and Emotions2 (joyfulness, loving, hating) -- the dispositional (and often counterfactual) imagining, supposing, intending, thinking, knowing, believing, etc. which can only be described in terms of reasons (i.e., it's just a fact that attempts to describe System 2 in terms of neurochemistry, atomic physics, mathematics, make no sense--see W, S, Hacker etc.).

Disposition words have at least two basic uses. One is a peculiar philosophical use (but graduating into everyday uses) which refers to the true-only sentences resulting from direct perceptions and memory, i.e., our innate axiomatic S1 psychology (`I know these are my hands')--i.e., they are Causally Self Referential (CSR), and the S2 use, which is their normal use as dispositions, which can be acted out, and which can become true or false (`I know my way home')--i.e., they have Conditions of Satisfaction (COS) and are not CSR.

The investigation of System 1 has revolutionized psychology, economics and other disciplines under names like "cognitive illusions", "priming", "framing", "heuristics" and "biases". Of course, these too are language games so there will be more and less useful ways to use these words, and studies and discussions will vary from "pure" System 1 to combinations of 1 and 2 (the norm as W made clear), but not of S2 only, since it cannot occur without involving much of the intricate S1 network of "cognitive modules", "inference engines", "intracerebral reflexes", "automatisms", "cognitive axioms", "background" or "bedrock" --as W and later S call our Evolutionary Psychology (EP).

The deontic structures or `social glue' are the automatic fast actions of S1 producing the slow dispositions of S2 which are inexorably expanded during personal development into a wide array of automatic universal cultural deontic relationships (S3). I expect this fairly well describes the basic structure of behavior.

So, recognizing that S1 is only upwardly causal (world to mind) and contentless (lacking representations or information) while S2 has content and is downwardly causal (mind to world) (e.g., see my review of Hutto and Myin's 'Radical Enactivism'), I would change the paragraphs from S's MSW p39 beginning "In sum" and ending on pg 40 with "conditions of satisfaction" as follows.

In sum, perception, memory and reflexive prior intentions and actions ('will') are caused by the automatic functioning of our S1 true-only axiomatic EP as modified by S2 ('free will'). We try to match how we desire things to be with how we think they are. We should see that belief, desire (and imagination--desires time shifted and decoupled from intention) and other S2 propositional dispositions of our slow thinking later evolved second self, are totally dependent upon (have their COS originating in) the CSR rapid automatic primitive true- only reflexive S1. In language and neurophysiology there are intermediate or blended cases such as intending (prior intentions) or remembering, where the causal connection of the COS with S1 is time shifted, as they represent the past or the future, unlike S1 which is always in the present. S1 and S2 feed into each other and are often orchestrated seamlessly by the learned deontic cultural relations of S3, so that our normal experience is that we consciously control everything that we do. This vast arena of cognitive illusions that dominate our life Searle has described as 'The Phenomenological Illusion' (TPI).

It follows both from W's 3rd period work contemporary psychology, that 'will', 'self' and 'consciousness' are axiomatic true-only elements of S1 composed of perceptions and reflexes., and there is no possibility (intelligibility) of demonstrating (of giving sense to) their falsehood. As W made so wonderfully clear numerous times, they are the basis for judgment and so cannot be judged. The true-only axioms of our psychology are not evidential.

Like Carruthers and others, S sometimes states (e.g., p66-67 MSW) that S1 (i.e., memories, perceptions, reflex acts) has a propositional (i.e., true-false) structure. As I have noted above, and many times in other reviews, it seems crystal clear that W is correct, and it is basic to understanding behavior, that only S2 is propositional and S1 is axiomatic and true-only. They both have COS and Directions of Fit (DOF) because the genetic, axiomatic intentionality of S1 generates that of S2 but if S1 were propositional in the same sense it would mean that skepticism is intelligible, the chaos that was philosophy before W would return, and in fact if true, life would not be possible. As W showed countless times and biology demonstrates, life must be based on certainty-- automated unconscious rapid reactions. Organisms that always have a doubt and pause to reflect will die-no evolution, no people, no philosophy.

I would translate S's summary of practical reason on p127 of MSW as follows: "We yield to our desires (need to alter brain chemistry), which typically include Desire - Independent Reasons for Action (DIRA--i.e., desires displaced in space and time), which produce dispositions to behavior that commonly result sooner or later in muscle movements that serve our inclusive fitness (increased survival for genes in ourselves and those closely related)." And I would restate his description on p129 of how we carry out DIRA2/3 as "The resolution of the paradox is that the unconscious DIRA1 serving long term inclusive fitness generate the conscious DIRA2 which often override the short term personal immediate desires." Agents do indeed consciously create the proximate reasons of DIRA2/3, but these are very restricted extensions of unconscious DIRA1 (the ultimate cause). Obama and the Pope wish to help the poor because it is right but the ultimate cause is a change in their brain chemistry that increased the inclusive fitness of their distant ancestors.

Evolution by inclusive fitness has programmed the unconscious rapid reflexive causal actions of S1 which often give rise to the conscious slow thinking of S2 (often modified into the cultural extensions of S3), which produces reasons for action that often result in activation of body and/or speech muscles by S1 causing actions. The general mechanism is via both neurotransmission and by changes in neuromodulators in targeted areas of the brain. The overall cognitive illusion (called by S 'The Phenomenological Illusion', by Pinker 'The Blank Slate' and by Tooby and Cosmides 'The Standard Social Science Model') is that S2/S3 has generated the action consciously for reasons of which we are fully aware and in control of, but anyone familiar with modern biology and psychology can see that this view is not credible.

A sentence expresses a thought (has a meaning), when it has clear COS, i.e., public truth conditions. Hence the comment from W: " When I think in language, there aren't 'meanings' going through my mind in addition to the verbal expressions: the language is itself the vehicle of thought." And, if I think with or without words, the thought is whatever I (honestly) say it is as there is no other possible criterion (COS). Thus, W's lovely aphorisms (p132 Budd) "It is in language that wish and fulfillment meet" and "Like everything metaphysical, the harmony between thought and reality is to be found in the grammar of the language." And one might note here that `grammar' in W can usually be translated as `EP' and that in spite of his frequent warnings against theorizing and generalizing, this is about as broad a characterization of higher order descriptive psychology as one can find.

Though W is correct that there is no mental state that constitutes meaning, S notes that there is a general way to characterize the act of meaning-- "Speaker meaning... is the imposition of conditions of satisfaction on conditions of satisfaction" which means to speak or write a well-formed sentence in a context that can be true or false and this is an act and not a mental state. Hence the famous quote from W: "If God had looked into our minds he would not have been able to see there whom we were speaking of (PI p217)" and his comments that the whole problem of representation is contained in "that's Him" and "...what gives the image its interpretation is the path on which it lies," or as S says its COS. Hence W's summation (p140 Budd) that "What it always comes to in the end is that without any further meaning, he calls what happened the wish that that should happen"..." the question whether I know what I wish before my wish is fulfilled cannot arise at all. And the fact that some, event stops my wishing does not mean that it fulfills it. Perhaps I should not have been satisfied if my wish had been satisfied"...Suppose it were asked `Do I know what I long for before I get it? If I have learned to talk, then I do know."

Disposition words refer to Potential Events which I accept as fulfilling the COS and my mental states, emotions, change of interest etc. have no bearing on the way dispositions function. I am hoping, wishing, expecting, thinking, intending, desiring etc. depending on the state I take myself to be in-- on the COS that I express and which can only be expressed by reflexive S1 muscle contractions, especially those of speech.

This is another statement of W's argument against private language. Likewise, with rule following and interpretation --they can only be publicly checkable acts. And one must note that many (most famously Kripke) miss the boat here, being misled by W's frequent referrals to community practice into thinking it's just arbitrary public practice that underlies language and social conventions. W makes clear many times that such conventions are only possible given an innate shared axiomatic psychology which he often calls the background.

W's definitive arguments against introspection and private language are as clear as day—we must have a test to differentiate between A and B and tests can only be public. He famously illustrated this with the 'Beetle in the Box'. I have explained the functioning of dispositional language ('propositional attitudes') and W's dismantling of the notion of introspection above and in my reviews of Budd, Johnston and several of S's books. Basically, he showed that the causal relation and word and object model that works for S1 does not apply to S2.

W famously rejected behaviorism and much of his work is devoted to describing why it cannot serve as a description of behavior. "Are you not really a behaviourist in disguise? Aren't you at bottom really saying that everything except human behavior is a fiction? If I do speak of a fiction, then it is of a *grammatical* fiction." (PI p307) But *real* behaviorism is rampant in its modern 'functionalist', 'computationalist','dynamic systems' forms. See my review of Carruthers' 'The Opacity of Mind' for a recent egregious example.

Behaviorism etc. have no practical impact. Unlike other cartoon views of life, they are too cerebral and esoteric to be grasped by more than a tiny fringe and it is so unrealistic that even its adherents totally ignore it in their everyday life. Unfortunately, not so with other cartoon theories like SSSM, BS and TPI, widely shared by religions, governments, sociology, anthropology, pop psychology, history, literature, and mom and dad, in spite of well-known facts, such as that personalities of adults adopted as children are as different from those of their adoptive siblings and parents as people chosen randomly off the street. Religions big and small, political movements, and economics often generate or embrace already existing cartoons that ignore physics and biology (human nature), posit forces terrestrial or cosmic that reinforce our superstitions, wishful thinking and selfishness and help to accelerate the destruction of the earth (the real purpose of nearly every social practice). The point is to realize that these fantasies are on a continuum and have the same source. All of us are born with a cartoon view of life and few ever grow out of it. But the world is not a cartoon, so a great tragedy is being played out as the cartoons collide with reality.

In spite of the fact that most of the above has been known to many for decades (and even ¾ of a century in the case of some of W's teachings), I have never seen anything approaching an adequate discussion in behavioral science texts and commonly there is barely a mention.

Now for some comments on "The New Science of the Mind" (NSM).
As with so many philosophy books, we might stop with the title. As the quotes and comments above and in my other reviews and the books they cover indicate, there are compelling reasons for regarding the problems we face in describing the psychology of higher order thought as conceptual and not scientific. This ought to be crystal clear to all, but science envy and almost complete oblivion to WSH etc. is a la mode! But as H notes above, the issues discussed here are all about language games and have nothing to do with science. In fact, as usual, if one translates into plain English there is very little of interest here, and certainly nothing not said before and better by WS etc.
countless times since the 30's (see e.g., The Blue and Brown Books from 1933-35—if you don't see the connection with all this try harder). It is not surprising that he makes no significant references to any of the above books or persons (the only reference to S is an article from 1958!), though in my view they are at the top of the list of the major figures in descriptive psychology.

Rowland wants to discern the precise roles of the 4 E 'aspects' of mind (Enactive, Embodied, Embedded, Extended see p3) with the aim to show that he can combine the Extended and Embodied into the Amalgamated to yield a clear theory of mind. Recall that W insisted that the activities of the mind lie open before us and theories or theses must be replaced by descriptions.

Some sections of the book are reasonably successful at describing the nonsense 61that passes as philosophy of mind but there is much aimless wandering and many mistakes and confusions, all couched in infelicitous jargon. This will hopefully be obvious to those who read the above and my other reviews as I cannot record more than a few of the comments I made in my two readings of this book. Major flaws, common to most writing in the behavioral sciences, are the lack of awareness of the S1/S2 two selves mode of describing personality that W pioneered (though nobody has noticed), the partial (or perhaps complete) embracing of the mechanical view of mind, and a failure to be clear about nature/nuture issues which the 4 E's seem eager to fuse. The fast, automatic perceptions, 'rules' and behaviors of S1 are mushed together with the slow conscious dispositional thinking, believing and rule following of S2 and neither are clearly or consistently distinguished from the arbitrary cultural behaviors of S3.

Thus, he is severely limited by failing to note clearly the difference between the automatic unconscious 'rules' of S1 perception and reflexive actions and the deliberate conscious 'rules' of S2 thinking and understanding, both innate, and the arbitrary learned S3 rules that constitute the cultural veneer on behavior. S2 rule following is just dispositional behavior of understanding propositions with COS. He says things somewhat like this (e.g., see p116, but not in clear and consistent terms and I doubt many will be able to wade thru it with any good results.

It fails anywhere to make it clear that thinking, believing etc. are dispositions, hence propositional and true or false S2 functions and, like all dispositions, have clear meaning due to their *public outer* Conditions of Satisfaction and not to any *private internal* phenomena. This is another demonstration of the impossibility of private language and introspection and contrary to its supposed complexity, it is a simple fact that there can be no such thing as a private test to determine the truth of any statement. This is the major topic of the fine books by Budd and Johnston—the Inner phenomena that we experience vs the Outer behavior that constitutes language and social interaction. That is why this can be seen as a poor man's version of W's Inner and Outer watered down and smothered in jargon. If one thinks that where there's smoke, there's fire, then please see Hutto and Myin's book for a razor-sharp account of the 4 E's by someone who understands the critical need to differentiate the various LG's of 'information', 'representation', 'content' etc. and why none of these can be part of S1. Yes, the brain can only express itself via the muscles of mouth, arms and legs and yes, it is thus unavoidable that S2 dispositions can only be manifested in public acts like speech and movement—that is, in the WS framework they have Conditions of Satisfaction (COS). "I am driving to Ohio" has to be said and heard and yes it needs a car, a road and the cognitive act of driving and if you like you can call these these external embodiments, enactive, embedded or extended aspects of mind, but exactly what is achieved? It is the most trivial of truisms that our mind needs a brain and the brain a body and the body a world but what is useful about including the car, the gas, the engine, the road and Ohio as part of cognition? Yes, in some sense they are all signs or creations of intentionality since created by us, but how about the trees, birds and clouds? Only theists could be happy with that. We inherit our genes, biochemistry, physiology, anatomy and abilities (e.g., dispositions such as thinking) but not the car in any useful sense and certainly not the clouds, and isn't this the crucial thing? The 4 E's and Rowlands' Amalgamated Mind seem to want to fuse dispositions with intentions and actions and results and the world (see p127-129) and look a lot like back door attempts to merge nature and nurture, a return to blank slateism and TPI. Not a happy ending.

W destroyed the mechanical or reductionist, computationalist, behaviorist, functionalist, Strong AI view of mind (yes, they seem to be different, but the mistakes are pretty much the same) and for those who didn't get it, S, H and many others carried on. Nevertheless, these incoherencies continue to dominate cognitive science and philosophy. Rowlands says he will mostly avoid functionalism, yet if he realized its bankruptcy why bring it up again and again, and he tells us p103 that the extended mind (one of the two pillars of his theory) is "predicated on a liberal conception of functionalism" and in detail on p100 and 104 how they go hand in hand.

Rowlands' discussion of cognitive bloat (p128 etc.) makes reference to S's "underived" content but his only ref to S's work is over 50 years old. Since then S has called this "intrinsic intentionality" that includes all of S1 and S2 (i.e., all cognition) and which contrasts with "derived" or "ascribed" which is ascribed by us to machines and other artifacts and events and is of course NOT intentionality (cognition or psychology). In this sense animals have only intrinsic and not ascribed intentionality. But he seems to get this sense of derived mixed up with his sense in which it refers to the personal level S2, as opposed to the nonderived or subpersonal level S1 (see p117-19). If you want to be *really* serious about your laptop being asleep and awake, and the car and the road being part of the mind, then cognition will extend into the universe, at least when doing philosophy, but it will not in this sense (except maybe in bizarre, rare, amusing or quite scary cases) enter into nor have any impact at all on *real life*. So, for me the 4 E's as presented here are just more cartoon views of life.

In contrast, the almost mathematically precise Radical Enactivism of Hutto and Myin only insists on the fact that S1 blends into the world as our perceptions, memories and reflex actions are automatic, unconscious, prelinguistic, contentless, informationless and without representation. Only the slow, conscious S2 dispositions fed by S1 have information, content and representation (COS). If you insist to apply these terms to S1 as well then please differentiate I1, C1, R1, COS1 etc from I2, C2, R2, COS2 etc. for reasons I have mentioned above and in many other reviews.

On p119 he tells us that the key to all this is to figure out how "…a personal level cognitive process can belong to a representational subject. This is the task of the second half of the book." But W did this 80 years ago and since we have the beautifully clear explanations of WSH, H&M etc., there is no point to torturing oneself with the rather aimless and opaque prose that veers off at the end into Sartre, Heidegger, Husserl, and Frege, with a dash of postmodernist word salad for good measure. A valiant effort on an interesting topic, but ultimately exhausting and fruitless.

Review of Religion Explained-- The Evolutionary Origins of Religious Thought by Pascal Boyer (2002) (review revised 2019)

Michael Starks

ABSTRACT

You can get a quick summary of this book on p 135 or 326. If you are not up to speed on evolutionary psychology, you should first read one of the numerous recent texts with this term in the title. One of the best is "The Handbook of Evolutionary Psychology" 2nd ed by Buss. Until about 15 years ago,
'explanations' of behavior have not really been explanations of mental processes at all, but rather vague and largely useless descriptions of what people did and what they said, with no insight into why. We might say that people gather to commemorate an event, praise god, receive his (or her or their) blessings, etc., but none of this describes the relevant mental processes, so we might say they are explanations in much the same way that it explains why an apple drops to the ground if we say its because we released it, and it's heavy- there is no mechanism and no explanatory or predictive power. This book continues the elucidation of the genetic basis of human behavior which has been almost universally ignored and denied by academia, religion, politics and the public (see Pinker's excellent book ``The Blank Slatè`). His statement (p3) that it is meaningless to ask if religion is genetic is mistaken as the percentage of variation of any behavior due to genes and environment can be studied, just as they are for all other behaviors (see e.g., Pinker). The title should be "Preliminary Attempts to Explain Some Aspects of Primitive Religion", since he does not treat higher consciousness at all (e.g., satori, enlightenment etc.) which are by far the most interesting phenomena and the only part of religion of personal interest to intelligent, educated people in the 21st century. Reading this entire book, you would never guess such things exist. Likewise, for the immense field of drugs and religion. It lacks a framework for rationality and does not mention the dual systems of thought view which is now so productive. For this I suggest my own recent papers. Nevertheless, the book has much of interest, and in spite of being dated is still worth reading.

Those wishing a comprehensive up to date framework for human behavior from the modern two systems view may consult my books Talking Monkeys 3rd ed (2019), The Logical Structure of Philosophy, Psychology, Mind and

Language in Ludwig Wittgenstein and John Searle 2nd ed (2019), Suicide by Democracy 4th ed (2019), The Logical Structure of Human Behavior (2019), The Logical Structure of Consciousness (2019, Understanding the Connections between Science, Philosophy, Psychology, Religion, Politics, and Economics (2019), and Suicidal Utopian Delusions in the 21st Century 5th ed (2019).

"God is dead and man is free" Nietzsche

"This very body the Buddha, this very earth the lotus paradise" Osho

''I can well imagine a religion in which there are no doctrines, so that nothing is spoken. Clearly, then, the essence of religion can have nothing to do with what is sayable'' Wittgenstein

When this book appeared, it was a pioneering effort, but now there are endless discussions of this topic and so I will give a sufficiently detailed and accurate summary that only specialists will need to read it. You can get a quick summary of this book on p 135 or 326. If you are not up to speed on evolutionary psychology you should first read one of the numerous recent texts with this term in the title. The best are "The Handbook of Evolutionary Psychology" 2nd ed (2015) and The 5th ed. of Evolutionary Psychology by Buss, readily available free on the net.

Until about 15 years ago, 'explanations'' of behavior have not really been explanations of mental processes at all, but rather vague and largely useless descriptions of what people did and what they said, with no insight into why. We might say that people gather to commemorate an event, praise god, receive their blessings, etc., but none of this describes the relevant mental processes, so we might say they are explanations in much the same way that it explains why an apple drops to the ground if we say it's because we released it and it's heavy--there is no mechanism and no explanatory or predictive power.

This book continues the elucidation of the genetic basis of human behavior which has been almost univerally ignored and denied by academia, religion, politics and the public (see Pinker's excellent book ``The Blank Slate``). His statement (p3) that it is meaningless to ask if religion is genetic is mistaken as the percentage of variation in any behavior due to genes and environment can be studied, just as they are for all other behaviors (see e.g., Pinker).

The title should be "Preliminary Attempts to Explain Some Aspects of Primitive Religion" since he does not treat higher consciousness at all (e.g., satori, enlightenment etc.) which are by far the most interesting phenomena and the only part of religion of personal interest to intelligent, educated people in the 21st century. Reading this entire book, you would never guess such things exist. Likewise, for the immense field of drugs and religion. How and why do entheogens trigger the inference engines and what role have they played in religion and life for the last million years? There is a huge mine of info on drugs and behavioral templates, but you won't find even a clue here. You can start with the recent books "Entheogens and the Future of Religion" and "Buddhism and Psychedelics" or you can read my friend Alexander Shulgin's amazing probing of the 'cognitive templates in PHIKAL and TIKAL, available, as almost everything now, free on the net. One of the most unusual of the drug probes is ketamine, described by many, most notably in "Journeys into the Bright World" by Altounian and Moore, Jansen in "Ketamine" and in probably the most detailed account of a single entheogenic drug by a single user in the last two chapters of John Lilly's "The Scientist". Lilly, almost single handedly the founder of dolphin research, was a generation or more ahead of nearly everyone on many topics and he also probed his own mind with LSD and isolation tanks. See his `Simulations of God` (1975 and my review of it) for his speculations on Mind, God and Brain and more aspects of the spiritual and mental not touched upon by Boyer. Also for recent heroic self therapy with entheogens see 'Xenolinguistics' by Slattery and 'DMT & My Occult Mind' by Khan.

There is also virtually nothing here about the relation between physical and mental states. The practice of the many forms of yoga was highly advanced thousands of years ago. Its primary aim was to trigger spiritual states with body energy and the reverse. There is an immense literature and hundreds of millions have practiced it. The best personal account I know of by a mystic detailing the interaction of the mental and physical via yoga is found in `The Knee of Listening` by Adi Da (see my review). Interwoven with the spellbinding account of his spiritual progress are the details of his work with the shakti energy of yoga (e.g., p95-9, 214-21, 249,281-3, 439-40 of the 1995 edition-- preferable to the later ones). These few pages are worth more than a whole shelf of yoga books if you want to get to the heart of the mind/body relation in spirituality.

Zen and other practices probe the brain's templates with meditation and tricks. Boyer does not understand that the major religions (and countless minor ones) were started by persons who broke the mold—i.e., somehow blocked or evaded some templates to destroy much of the ego and to discover aspects of their mind normally hidden. It is not hard to see why full blown enlightenment is rare, as those who have it stop behaving like monkeys (i.e., fighting, deceiving, reproducing, accumulating) and this would be heavily selected against. One might say those who achieved it are the only ones who became fully human (i.e., Jesus, Adi Da, Mohammed, Buddha, Mahavira, Rumi, Osho and 1000 or so others we know of). It seems Boyer has no personal experience with meditation, entheogens and higher consciousness (e.g., see pages 317, 320-324) so he clearly does not treat all of religion. This is again evident (p32) when he says religion has no origin or clear explanation which is curious as he provides exactly this. Of course, this is true in a sense of the primitive religions he discusses, but Buddhism, Christianity, Islam, etc., have very clear origins and explanations in the enlightenment of Jesus, Buddha, Mohammed etc. He is mistaken (p308) in his belief that Eastern religion is mostly about ritual, rather than personal experience and inner states and that it got such ideas from Western philosophy (3000 years ago!).

Amazingly, he rejects William James's notion that religion is a result of the experiences of exceptional individuals that are subsequently degraded by the masses (p310). James is clearly right and Boyer is again, only thinking of primitive religion. Perhaps the best personal account of the various states of samadhi, enlightenment, etc. is Adi Da's book--'The Knee of Listening` but by far the best source for personal accounts by an enlightened master are the numerous books, audios and videos by Osho, all free on the net.

Witnessing one's thoughts is one of the commonest techniques of beginning meditators in many different traditions. Further progress fuses the perceiver and perceived (all is one). One wonders how this relates to the templates—do they enter consciousness, does spiritual change open new neural connections or close some? Cognitive psychology has barely started on this, but is would be interesting to see PET or fMRI on an enlightened person or one in a samadhi state with good controls and has been done. Though he is right that many experiences are of some agent, advanced states have been described in a vast literature which shows they typically have no thoughts, no mind, no person, no god. This would seem to be the ultimate in decoupling System 2 templates in a functional person.

For supernatural types of religious concepts to evolve and survive, they should belong to one of the basic ontological categories or templates (plant, tool, natural object, animal, person etc.) which the brain uses to organize perception and thought. These are commonly given counterintuitive properties such as prescience, telepathy, immortality, abilility to hear one's words or read one's thoughts, ability to heal or confer great power etc. Good supernatural concepts usually allow all inferences not specifically barred by the violation of intuition—i.e., a god will have all human properties but does not age or die. The huge number of religious concepts is contained in this short list of templates. It is the counterintuitive nature of the concepts that makes them easy to remember and to transmit to others and this seems to by one reason why supernatural concepts are a central part of nearly all religions. Supernatural concepts interact with other types of templates such as intuitive psychology, intuitive physics, structure function and goal detection. If it activates physics, goal detection, intuitive psychology and intentional use, then it will be a human-like being with superhuman properties. This is standard cognitive psychology and counterintuitive parts are added on for religious use. There is abundant evidence that brain areas that are activated when we do something are also activated when we see someone else doing a similar thing (mirror neurons). It is feasible that this is correlated with the need to join in and the satisfaction from participating in the rituals integral to society (sports, politics, music etc.) and religion.

There is also evidence that seeing other people's emotions activates the same areas as our own. Our theory of mind (i.e., of other people's mental life--intuitive psychology which I prefer to call Understandingof Agency -UA) seems not to be one inference engine, but the sum of many and, as more research is done, more modules will be discovered. Another critical feature of inference engines is that they often run in decoupled (counterfactual or imaginary) mode while we consider the past or the future. This starts quite early as shown by the common presence of imaginary playmates in children, their ability to grasp stories and TV, and he notes that research seems to show that children who create playmates seem to be better at grasping other people's mental states and emotions. The point in this context is that it seems quite natural to ascribe humanlike characteristics to spirits, ghosts, gods, etc. when there is no evidence at all for their actual presence.

The innate inference engines are automatic as they have to be fast and not distract us (i.e., they are System 1 but sadly he fails to use the two systems framework here—see my papers for this). The mind was not evolved as an explanation machine and before the recent rise of science, nobody ever tried to explain why our foot moves when we walk, an apple falls to the ground, we get hungry or angry or why we experience or do anything. Only bizarre or cosmic occurrences like lightning or sunrise needed a cause. Our intuitive psychology and agency templates also prompted us to ascribe good and bad luck to some agent. Much of this may sound speculative but now that EP (evolutionary psychology) is a major paradigm, the evidence of such innate S1 functions in early childhood and infancy is mounting rapidly.

Supernatural agents (including deceased ancestors) are treated by intuitive psychology as intentional agents, by the social exchange system (a part of or variant on the cost/benefit systems) by the moral system as witnesses to moral actions, and by the person-file system as individuals. Since all these systems can operate in decoupled mode, there is no need to consider whether these agents really exist. They are driven by relevance, by the richness of inferences that result and by the ease with which they can be remembered and communicated. The templates are highly tuned to gather info, get cooperation and calculate benefits in a very rapid, subconscious and normally error-free way, while conscious reason is slow and fallible. In modern times, the ego has time to waste on debate, explanation, and interpretation in endless attempts to deceive and manipulate others for personal gain. With large, mobile populations and fast communication the results of our social exchange, evaluation of trust, cheater detection and other templates are often useless and self-destructive. Strategic info (that which passes the relevance filters) activates the engines related to social interaction and our knowledge of what info others have is a critical part of the social mind. The supernatural agents typically have perfect knowledge. Though he does not seem to mention it, powerful people often come to have some of the characteristics of supernatural agents and so people will start to respond to them as to gods. Aliens, UFO's, new age mysticism, astrology, fantasy and sci-fi draw great attention due to activation, and often possess agents with strategic info. However, hundreds of millions have followed charismatic leaders with false strategic info (i.e., quasi-supernatural agents) to their deaths (The Branch Davidians of Waco, Communism, Nazism, Vietnam, Jonestown, George Bush, Comet Kahoutek etc.).

Social interactions require a social mind—i.e., mental systems that organize them. Like most behavior, it is only recently that it was generally realized that we needed built-in mechanisms to do this. Strategic information is whatever activates the social mind. Our theory of mind (UA) tells us to what agents this info is also available. It is common to attribute to supernatural agents the ability to fully access info that would normally be partly or totally unavailable to others.

All the engines must have some kind of relevance filter so that they are not constantly activated by trivia. We have taxonomies that tell us how to group things in ways relevant to their behavior or properties in the world now called System 1 (S1), and we then use our more recently evolved slow deliberate linguistic System 2 (S2) when there is time. We expect large catlike things with big teeth and claws to be predators and not herbivores. Spirits fit human taxonomy and automatically have needs and desires, likes and dislikes and will thus give rewards and punishments and all any culture has to do is specify what these are. Those concepts giving the richest inferences with the least effort have been selected into S1.

A common viewpoint is given by relevance theory, which tries to determine how and why some 'concepts' (i.e., the language games of System 2) are more easily transmitted. Presumably, concepts which trigger engines (S1 'concepts') more intensely or frequently, or more different engines, will be superior. So, we may have many language games that are easier to remember and apply, rather than because they make sense or are more useful in some way than others. This may help to explain the existence of many concepts or practices that seem arbitrary or stupid, or which make life more difficult and applies to all of culture, not just to religion.

Nearly all religions have full access agents—i.e., they know all or nearly all about us and Boyer distinguishes 3 classes--divine brutes with little or no access but which nevertheless have power, Aquinas agents which know everything and full strategic agents which have access to all the strategic or important info. He says that this may account for our interest in knowing other person's religious ideas or in converting them to ours. Only in this way can we understand how they may behave and interact.

Agents that are aware of and able to affect our social interaction are richer in inferences, and so are easier to mentally represent and remember and thus enjoy a great advantage in cultural transmission. Thus, we can now say that religion does not create or even support morality, but that our built in moral intuitions (i.e., the fast automatic prelinguistic mental reflexes of S1) make religion plausible and useful. Likewise, our mechanisms to explain good and bad luck makes their connection with supernatural agents simple. And since we share our moral system and our information with them, it is natural to expect they will enforce our attitudes.

Recipcrocal altruism and cheating are central parts of human behavior. To show passionate feelings and honesty that are genuine (difficult to fake) is of great social (and genetic) value. This can be reinforced by religion as one would choose to cooperate with such persons rather than with rational calculators who may change their mind or cheat anytime their inference engines calculate that it is in their best interests. This system also requires that cheaters be punished, even when the cheating has minimal social cost. One common group of religious concepts are those that make cheating immoral. The mechanism is feelings (e.g., the rapid S1 reflexes of anger, jealousy, resentment, confusion) rather than the slow rational cogitation of S2. This may sound strange but it has been shown not only in monkeys but in lower animals. Yes there are endless elaborations of cheating in modern society but like all our behavior it is built on genetics and S1..We feel that it is wrong for someone to steal another's money rather than needing to sit down and think--well if he takes that money, then maybe he will take mine or he will have some future advantage over me etc. Perhaps here is one place that guilt enters in order to make the socially (genetically) destructive practice of cheating less appealing. This takes us into the huge literature on cheaters and cooperators, hawks and doves and pretenders and into reciprocal altruism and game theory. Keep in mind that 'true altruism' or group selection is clearly a fantasy as I have detailed in my review of Wilson's 'The Social Conquest of Earth'. So, like all behavior, religion evolved because it had survival value for individuals.

Many types of commitment gadgets have evolved which tend to ensure cooperation--keeping track of reputation, legal or quasi-legal binds (contracts), strong passions, compulsive honesty, resentment and need to punish cheaters. Cooperation gadgets are built in also--moral intuitions, guilt, pride, gratefulness, hostility. In contrast to the nearly universal idea that moral realism (that behavior itself has a specific moral value that does not depend on one's viewpoint) is only developed by adults or is given by religion, it is now clear that this appears in 3 and 4 year olds and changes little with age. Methods have now been developed to study infants and in late 2007 a study appeared in Nature which showed that they can distinguish helper from non- helper objects and there has been lots of work on humans and other animals since. Of course, intuitive morality will often give the wrong results for adults in the modern world, as may all of our S1 reflexes in many contexts.

Most of the basics of what has formerly been regarded as culture, is now known or suspected to be inherited. Pinker lists hundreds of different aspects of human societies that are universal and thus good candidates. One can compile a very long list of religious concepts that we don't need to be taught---spirits understand human thoughts, emotions and intentions and differentiate between wishes or images and reality etc.

It seems that the only feature of humans that is always projected onto gods, spirits, ghosts, etc, is a mind much like our own. Intuitive psychology applies to intentional agents in general (i.e., persons, animals and anything that appears to move in pursuit of its own goals). Intuitive physics is probably also composed of many subsegments and must be connected with the intentionality module –e.g., when a lion is chasing an antelope, we know that if it changes course, the lion will probably do so. One would expect that detecting such agents was a very ancient evolutionary priority and even 500 million years ago a trilobite that lacked such genes would soon be lunch. As more behavioral genes are mapped we are finding the same or similar ones in fruitflies, just as we have for other genes such as the ones controlling body segmentation and immunity, and great strides in this direction have been made since this book appeared. Just search Drosophila behavior.

Like our other concepts, religious ones are often vague and their use idiosyncratic due to the fact that they result from the unconscious functioning of inference engines (S1) as elaborated upon by the vagaries of culture. We cannot say precisely even what simple words mean, but we know how to use them. Just as Chomsky discovered depth grammar, one might say that Wittgenstein discovered depth semantics.

Wittgenstein was the first (and still one of the few) who understood that what philosophy—which I term the descriptive psychology of higher order thought-(and all attempts to understand behavior) was struggling with was first and foremost these built-in S1 functions that are inaccessible to conscious thought. Though I have never seen it stated, it seems reasonable to regard him as a pioneer in cognitive and evolutionary psychology.

Boyer takes a new view of death also. Corpses have properties that make supernatural concepts relevant apart from our need for comfort and this part of religion may be less about death than about dead bodies. They produce a dissociation between the animacy, intuitive psychology and person 'file systems'. We see such dissociation in autism and odd neurological states such as Capgras syndrome.

He sees this as another way that culture makes use of salient gadgets (events, objects etc.) which are highly relevant and grab the attention of the inference engines. And since this book appeared, evidence continues to accumulate that genes create culture to a much greater extent than most people (including scholars) ever imagined. It has its own field—implicit cognition.

Nobody ever thinks to inquire as to the motives if a rock that falls and hits us, but we always do if it comes from the hand of a person. Even a very young child knows this, due to its intuitive psychology, agency, animism and other engines. These engines (genes, reflexive behaviors) must, in their orginal forms, be hundreds of millions of years old. A carboniferous era dragonfly differentiated between animate and inanimate objects and calculated the trajectory of its prey.

Religion originally worked in an atmosphere of perpetual fear. Inference engines evolved to find mates and food and shelter and avoid death, hence the approach to the gods as a powerless supplicant and the use of appeasement rituals and offerings (as we would to a person). Our danger avoidance is highly imperfect in the modern world due to guns, drugs and fast transport (cars, skis). Everywhere in the world you can see people walking or riding bicycles in the streets just a step away from speeding vehicles, even though at least a million a year are run down.

He says (p40) that memes (Dawkins famous cultural analog of the gene) are not a very good concept for cultural transmission since ideas are changed by each person, while genes remain the same. However, what about media—i.e., film, TV, print, email? They can replicate more precisely than genes. These are now the prime means for transmitting and checking the validity of memes, not just what someone says. In any case, genes are not perfect either. Just as there is a phenotype corresponding to the genotype, there is a phene corresponding to the meme.

Why do we invoke supernatural agents for good and bad luck? They activate our social exchange systems and since we regard them as having strategic info they can control what happens.

It occurs to me that perhaps there is such great opposition to genetic explanations for behavior because people feel anyone who accepts this will automatically reject the social exchange and other templates and will always cheat. Or perhaps they fear the intuitive psychology will no longer work. And it calls their attention to The Phenomenological Illusion (the illusory feeling we have that our behavior is due to conscious decisions- see my other writings).

Social rituals are examples of what psychologists have termed precautionary rules and these commonly include concerns about pollution, purification rituals (activation of the contagion system), contact avoidance, special types of touching, special attention to boundaries and thresholds, rule violations, use of certain numbers of bright colors, symmetrical arrays and precise patterns, special sounds or music, special dance and other movements, etc. All these trigger certain groups of templates, create satisfying feelings, and are commonly coupled to religious concepts, and to politics, sports, hunting and agriculture, marriage, child rearing, music, art, folklore, literature etc.

The agency detecting systems (e.g., predator and prey detection) are biased for over-detection—i.e., they do not need to see a lion or a person to be activated, but only a footprint or a sound of the right kind. Based on very little info, these systems then produce feelings and expectations about the agents' nature and intentions. In the case of supernatural agencies our intuitive psychology templates are also activated and generally produce a person-like entity plus the counterintuitive features, but their precise characteristics are generally left vague.

The attaching of a counterintuitive tag (e.g., rising from the dead) to an agent (e.g., Jesus) or other ontological category makes it easy to remember and a good candidate for religion.

All these modules are inherited but of course a baby does not have them fully developed and only with time and a `normal` environment will they emerge.

I read this shortly before reading Ken Wilber's "Sex, Ecology and Spirituality" and could see on nearly every page how outdated and empty are most of the works which Wilber is discussing. A large part of Wilbur's book and of the hundreds he analyzes on religion, psychology and philosophy are now archaic. However, Wilbur has written many books of great interest on spirituality and it is sad that Boyer does not even reference him-- but neither does he reference drugs, Wittgenstein, meditation, yoga, satori or enlightenment in his index!

One might say that the Nobel peace prize is given to those who are best at encouraging us to extend coalitions to include other outgroups or even other countries or the whole world. Or, one might say they get the prize for efforts to turn off the `cheater detector` or social exchange templates which require that only those who reciprocate are included in one's group and given access to resources (which most of the world's poor clearly cannot do).

He gives a brief summary of some of the self-deceptive inferences which play a role in religion as in all of life--consensus, false consensus, generation effect, memory illusions, source monitoring defects, confirmation bias and cognitive dissonance. Like the other templates, these gave very good results 100,000 years ago, but with life in the fast lane, they can now prove fatal for individuals and for the world. Coalitional intuitions and essence concepts are delineated as critical parts of human behavior. Humans automatically form groups and show hostility to persons not in the group and wholly undeserved friendship to those in the group (coalitional intuitions), even when the group is composed of total strangers. This relates to operation engines such as cost/benefit and calculation of reliability mentioned before. Essences are the concepts we use to describe our feelings (intuitions) about coalitions and other social categories (e.g., hierarchies and dominance). Although these mechanisms evolved in small groups, nowadays these are commonly operating with people to whom we are not closely related, so they often give false results. Stereotyping, racism and its accompaniments (i.e., arbitrary (or not so arbitrary) set distinctions) are probably the results of the operation of coalitional intuitions built into our brains, rather than stereotyping being an S2 psychological function and the coalitions with their exclusion, dominance, and antipathy being the results. These engines may well explain the 'social magic' that forms and guides societies.

He suggests that one might explain fundamentalism as a natural reaction to the common violation of coalitional thinking in modern societies. Freedom to act as one chooses and in direct opposition to others in the same community creates strong and often violent feelings in those without the education or experience to deal with diversity and change. They often want public and spectacular punishment to assuage their feelings. Fundamentalism may best be explained as attempts to preserve hierarchies based on coalitions, when these are threatened by easy defection or inattention. These are functioning in all people all the time, but they come to the surface mainly when there is a situation that creates some special threat (i.e., modern life). Of course, as always, we need to keep in mind that the ultimate source and payoff for all behavior is in the genes.

Though he says little about it, the notions of ontological S1 categories and counterintuitive tags that 'stick' to them also go far to explain magic, the paranormal, folklore, mythology, folk medicine, astrology, theology, miracle workers, demonic and angelic possession, the arts, and formerly even much of science. Rituals act as snares for thought. Our contagion templates are powerful activators of behavior and it is natural to include many purification rituals in religion. They also make use of our planning systems, which we can see in extreme form in obsessive compulsive disorder. There is preoccupation with colors, spaces, boundaries, movements and contact. Salient gadgets are incorporated. We have a powerful need to imitate others.

Rituals activate our undetected hazard systems. Sacrificial offerings to the unseen agents make use of our social exchange systems. Our coalitional intuitions are satisfied by group rites and marriage. The 'naive sociology' of the common man extends into much philosophy, sociology, theology, anthropology, psychology, economics, politics and is the result of our attempts to make sense of our own behavior but this is the result of the automatic and unconscious functioning of our templates. Thus, much of culture seems magical-- hence the term 'social magic'. Inevitably, naive sociology is weak, so rituals and belief systems emphasize the benefits of cooperation and the costs of cheating or defection. The rituals and gadgets stimulate memory and satisfy the contagion system. Participation signals cooperation and the gods and spirits are optional. So, templates lead to religion which leads to doctrines and not the reverse.

I think he goes seriously astray when discussing science vs. religion (p320). He says it is wrong to talk about religion as a real object in the world (whatever that might be), but of course the external and internal (mental) phenomena can be studied as well as any other, and he shows in this book that religion is a branch of cognitive psychology. He says there is no science as such, and we know that he means it's complex, but then there is no religion, law, sports, auto racing or anything at all, as such. He objects to `pop theology` which says religion makes the world more beautiful or meaningful or that it addresses ultimate questions, but all religion addresses the ultimate questions and tries to make the world meaningful and less ugly. In addition, what I call `advanced religion` --i.e., the way it starts in the no-minds of Jesus, Buddha, Osho etc.-- has a quite different take on the world than the primitive religion he discusses in this book (e.g., see the 200 books and DVD's of Osho at Oshoworld.com or on p2p etc., or see Wilber, Adi Da etc.). Again, on p 327 he thinks there is no religious center in the brain and though this is probably true for primitive religion, it seems more likely that there are centers (networks of connections) for the experiences of satori and enlightenment and maybe for entheogens too. He also thinks (p321) that science is less natural and more difficult than religion, but in view of the huge number of scientists and the facts that nearly everyone is able to absorb science in grade school, and that there have probably been less than 1000 enlightened persons in all of human history, it seems clear that the situation is quite the reverse for advanced spirituality. It is vastly less difficult to become a botanist or a chemist than to dissolve one's ego! Natural selection will clearly eliminate higher consciousness genes, but the rational calculus of science is quite consistent with gathering resources and producing children. Of course, the problem is that he is again fixated on primitive religion.

He sums it up by saying (p 135) that religious activities activate inference systems that 'govern our most intense emotions, shape our interaction with other people, give us moral feelings and organize social groups`. Of course, these have nothing to do with satori or enlightenment! He notes that religious ideas are parasitic upon our intuitive ontology (i.e., they are relevant). They are transmitted successfully due to mental capacities that evolution has already created. As with other behaviors, religion is a result of aggregate relevance — i.e., the sum of the operation of all the inference engines. Thus, religious concepts and behavior are present not because they are necessary or even useful, but because they easily activate our templates, are easy to remember and transmit, and so they survive over time. He gives a final summary (p326) of ``The Full History of all Religion (ever)`` as follows (of course it leaves out `advanced religion (spirituality, mysticism)`). Among the millions of things people discussed were some which violated our intuitions and this made them easier to remember and transmit. Those that were about agents were especially salient as they activated rich domains of possible inferences such as those about predators and intuitive psychology. Agents with counterintuitive properties, especially ability to understand and affect human behavior or the world were strongly transmitted. They became connected with other strange and somewhat counterintuitive events such as death and feelings about the continued presence of the dead. Somehow rituals arise and become associated with the powerful supernatural agents. Some persons will be more skilled at conducting such rituals and guiding the interactions with the spirits. Inevitably they will create more abstract versions and start to acquire power and wealth. However, people will continue to have their own inferences about religion.

He notes that religion owes much to the probably recent (in hominoid evolution) appearance of the decoupling ability and it occurs to me that one might regard entheogenic drug experiences, satori and enlightenment as the ultimate in decoupling--no past, no future, and not even a present-- no here, no there, no me, no you and all is one thing and illusory. The other key transition in evolution is posited to be the ability to accept the violation of intuitive expectations at the level of ontological domains (i.e., the classes of things-- plants, people, moving things etc.). He regards these capacities as leading to the invention of religion (and of course much else) but it's clear that Buddha, Jesus and Osho went quite a bit further. He rejects the idea that religious thoughts made minds more flexible and open (rather they became susceptible to certain concepts that activated the inferences of agency, predation, morality, social exchange, death etc.), but something made us susceptible also to the entheogens, satori and enlightenment and this is as flexible and open as people can be and remain sane. So it is clear that much remains to be discovered about spirituality and religion and the progress in understanding behavior will bring this about.

Review of Sex, Ecology, Spirituality by Ken Wilber 2nd ed 851p (2001) (review revised 2019)

Michael Starks

ABSTRACT

It is both amazing and fitting that this huge, jargon-laden (this book really needs a glossary!), heavily academic work has become a best seller in the world of the educated. One has to be dedicated to learn the jargon and then plow through 551 pages of text and 238 pages of notes. Meanwhile, we are told time and again that this is just an outline of what is to come!

Though he severely criticizes the excesses of the three movements, this is a deconstructive and New Age Mystical and postmodern interpretation of religion, philosophy and the behavioral sciences from a very liberal, spiritual point of view—i.e., without the worst of decon, pm and NAM jargon, rabid egalitarianism and anti-scientific anti-intellectualism.

He analyzes in some detail the various world views of philosophy, psychology, sociology and religion, exposing their fatal reductionistic flaws with (mostly) care and brilliance, but most of the sources he analyzes are of almost no relevance today. They use terminology and concepts that were already outdated when he was researching and writing 20 years ago. One has to slog thru endless pages of jargon –laden discussion of Habermas, Kant, Emerson, Jung et.al. to get to the pearls.

You get a terrific sampling of bad writing, confused and outdated ideas and obsolete jargon.

If one has a good current education, it is doubly painful to read this book (and most writing on human behavior). Painful because it's so tortured and confusing, and then again when you realize how simple it is with modern psychology and philosophy. The terminology and ideas are horrifically confused and dated (but less so in Wilber's own analysis than in his sources).

This book and most of its sources are would-be psychology texts, though most of the authors did not realize it. It is about human behavior and reasoning-about why we think and act the way we do and how we might change in the future. But (like all such discussion until recently) none of the explanations are really explanations, and so they give no insight into human behavior. Nobody discusses the mental mechanisms involved. It is like describing how a car works by discussing the steering wheel and metal and paint without any knowledge of the engine, fuel or drive train. In fact, like most older 'explanations' of behavior, the texts quoted here and the comments by Wilber are often more interesting for what kinds of things they accept (and omit!) as explanations, and the kind of reasoning they use, than for the actual content.

If one is up on philosophy and cognitive and evolutionary psychology, most of this is archaic. Like nearly everyone (scholars and public alike—e.g., see my review of Dennett's Freedom Evolves and other books), he does not understand that the basics of religion and ethics-- in fact all human behavior, are programmed into our genes. A revolution in understanding ourselves was taking place while he was writing his many books and it passed him by.

Those wishing a comprehensive up to date framework for human behavior from the modern two systems view may consult my books Talking Monkeys 3rd ed (2019), The Logical Structure of Philosophy, Psychology, Mind and Language in Ludwig Wittgenstein and John Searle 2nd ed (2019), Suicide by Democracy 4th ed (2019), The Logical Structure of Human Behavior (2019), The Logical Structure of Consciousness (2019, Understanding the Connections between Science, Philosophy, Psychology, Religion, Politics, and Economics (2019), and Suicidal Utopian Delusions in the 21st Century 5th ed (2019).

'Anything that can be said can be said clearly' Ludwig Wittgenstein

'Heaven and Earth are inhumane--they view the myriad creatures as straw dogs' TaoTe Ching

It is both amazing and fitting that this huge, jargon-laden (this book really needs a glossary!), heavily academic work has become a best seller in the world of the educated. One has to be dedicated to learn the jargon and then plow through 551 pages of text and 238 pages of notes. Meanwhile, we are told time and again that this is just an outline of what is to come!

This book and most of its sources are would-be psychology texts, though most of the authors did not realize it. It is about human behavior and reasoning- about why we think and act the way we do and how we might change in the future. But (like all such discussion until recently) none of the explanations are really explanations and so they gave no insight into human behavior. Nobody discusses the mental mechanisms involved. It is like describing how a car works by discussing the steering wheel and metal and paint and the wheels without any knowledge of the engine or drive train. In fact, like most older 'explanations' of behavior, the texts quoted here and the comments by Wilber are often more interesting for what kinds of things they accept (and omit!) as explanations, and the kind of reasoning they use, than for the actual content.

As with all reasoning and explaining one now wants to know which of the brains inference engines are activated to produce the results and how fast thinking automated prelinguistic system 1 (S1) and slow thinking deliberative linguistic system 2 (S2) are involved and what is the Logical Structure of Rationality that explains (or rather describes as Wittgenstein insisted) behavior. It is the relevance filters (the reflexive processes) of S1 which determine what sorts of things that can be input as appropriate data for each engine and their automatic and unconscious operation and interaction that determines what our brain will pass on to S2 for higher order expression in language.

Cognitive and evolutionary psychology are still not evolved enough to provide full explanations (descriptions) but an interesting start has been made. Boyer's 'Religion Explained' is a good place to see what a modern scientific explanation of human behavior looks like as of 2002 (though it completely misses enlightenment!). Pinker's 'How the mind Works' is a good general survey and his 'The Blank Slate' (see my reviews) by far the best discussion of the heredity-environment issue in human behavior. They do not 'explain' all of intelligence or thinking but summarize what is known. See several of the recent texts (i.e., 2004 onwards) with evolutionary psychology in the title (above all "The Handbook of Evolutionary Psychology" 2nd ed by Buss) or the web for further info.

We now recognize that the bases for art, music, math, philosophy, psychology, sociology, language and religion are found in the automatic functioning of templates or inference engines of S1. This is why we can expect similarities and puzzles and inconsistencies or incompleteness and often, dead ends as without careful probing by experiments or philosophical (linguistic) analysis it is invisible to us ('The Phenomenological Illusion' of Searle). The brain has no general intelligence but numerous specialized modules, each of which works on certain aspects of some problem and the results are then added, resulting in the feelings which lead to behavior. Wilber, like everyone, can only generate or recognize explanations that are consistent with the operations of his own inference engines, which were evolved to deal with such things as resource accumulation, coalitions in small groups, social exchanges and the evaluation of the intentions of other persons. It is amazing they can produce philosophy and science, and not surprising that figuring out how they work together to produce consciousness or choice or spirituality is way beyond reach.

Wilber is a bookworm and he has spent decades analyzing classic and modern texts. He is extremely bright, has clearly had his own awakening, and also knows the minutiae of Eastern religion as well as anyone. I doubt there are more than a handful in the world who could write this book. However, this is a classic case of being too smart for your own good and his fascination with intellectual history and his ability to read, analyze and write about hundreds of difficult books has bogged him down in the dead past.

Though he severely criticizes the excesses of the three movements, this is a deconstructive and New Age Mystical and postmodern interpretation of religion, philosophy and the behavioral sciences from a very liberal, spiritual point of view—i.e., without the worst of decon, pm and NAM jargon, anti-scientific anti-intellectualism, and the oppressive rabid Neomarxist Third World Supremacist Egalitarianism that is destroying America and the world by handing power over to the low class rabble in the West and to the Jihadists and the Seven Sociopaths who run China.

Boyer points out (p20), when fear and poverty give way to security and wealth, the results of the inference engines change and you find religion changing from appeasement rituals for the powerful gods in a hostile universe to self empowerment and control in a benevolent one (i.e., New Age Mysticism etc.).

He analyzes in some detail the various world views of philosophy, psychology, sociology and religion, exposing their fatal reductionistic flaws with (mostly) care and brilliance, but most of the sources he analyzes are of questionable relevance today. They use terminology and concepts that were already outdated when he was researching and writing 20 years ago. One has to slog thru endless pages of jargon –laden discussion of Habermas, Kant, Emerson, Jung et.al. to get to the pearls. He immerses himself in Freud and the psychoanalytic interpretation of dreams (eg, p92), though most now regard these as merely quaint artifacts of intellectual history.

If one is up to date on philosophy and cognitive and evolutionary psychology, most of this is archaic. Like nearly everyone (scholars and public alike--eg, see my review of Dennett's Freedom Evolves and other books), he does not understand that the basics of religion and ethics-- in fact all human behavior, are programmed into our genes. A revolution in understanding ourselves was taking place while he was writing his many books and it largely passed him by, though I have not read his latest works.

If one has a good current education, it is doubly painful to read this book (and most writing on human behavior). Painful because it's so tortured and confusing and then again when you realized how simple it is with modern psychology and philosophy. The terminology and ideas are horrifically confused and dated (but less so in Wilber's own analysis than in his sources). We now think in terms of cognitive templates which evolved about 100,000 years ago (in most cases several hundreds of millions of years earlier in their original forms). They operate automatically, are not accessible to consciousness and there is abundant evidence that they severely limit the behaviorial options for individuals and for society. His new preface notes one such study, but the book needs a total rewriting.

There is an enormous resistance in us to accepting ourselves as part of nature, and in particular, any gene based explanations of behavior, in spite of the fact that all our behavior, like all of our physiology, is at its roots gene based. Like all our thinking, these feelings are due to the operation of the cognitive templates, so perhaps it is the conflict between biological explanations and our automatic intuitive psychology or social mind systems that is responsible (the obviousness of our linguistic conventions and culture and the opacity of our automatisms which Searle has called 'The Phenomenological Illusion'). These genetic systems have operated for hundreds of thousands or millions of years and the new data from science is telling us the results of their operations (our feelings about what to do) are often wrong in our complex modern world. There is a huge research program in social, economic and political behavior from this new viewpoint.

Some jargon you will need is on pg X of the new preface where you find that the constantly used vision-logic is postformal cognition or network-logic or integral-aperspectival (all points of view are equal and must be considered). He also states the postmodern manifesto here: all views equal, dependent on limitless contexts, and merely interpretations. As he notes in great detail, this puts one on the slippery slope leading to much irrational and incoherent rant and there are very basic flaws in it. Nevertheless, it virtually took over US and European universities for several decades and is far from dead, having transformed itself into Neomarxist Third World Supremacist Egalitarianism. You will also need his definition of eros from p528.

You get a terrific sampling of bad writing, confused and outdated ideas and obsolete jargon. On p52 there is a quote from Jakobson which can be replaced by 'the inference engines for psychology and language develop as we mature';

and paragraphs from Jantsch (p58) which say that evolution is evolution and cells are cells and (p71) the environment changes as organisms evolve. There is a quote from Foucault to open Book Two (p327) which, translated from deconstructese, says 'knowledge helps to understand the world'.

There is a long quote (p60-61) from Rupert Sheldrake which, when it is intelligible at all, says things that translate as 'proteins are proteins' and 'cells are cells'. There are numerous linguistic disasters from Habermas (e.g., if you have time to waste, try figuring out the quotes on p77 or 150), but some are actually translatable, such as those on p153-4, which say that people have morals, so society has laws and language evolved so society evolved. And lots of this from Wilber himself, as on p109 where he spends most of the page to say most mutations and recombinations fail and the surviviors are compatible with their evirons. In spite of his acquaintance with Searle's work, he is often confused about consciousness. He says (p117-8) that we can regard whatever we want as conscious, but clearly, once we leave the realm of animals that have eyes and a brain and walk around, it becomes a joke. Likewise, he is on very thin ice when discussing our interior and the need to interpret the minds of others. This is very far off the mark if one knows some Searle, Wittgenstein and cognitive psychology (see my other writings). Likwise with the 'explanations' of Wolf on p742 which are wrong for the same reasons that 'explanations' of consciousness are wrong. It must be true that mind and spirit are based in physics (at least there is no intelligible alternative) but we don't know how to conceptualize this or even how to recognize such a concept (i.e., the language games or Conditions of Satisfaction are unclear). Many suspect we will never understand this but rather its just a matter of accepting how things are and likewise with the fundamentals of the universe (eg, see my review of Kaku's 'Hyperspace' and Dennett).

His notes (p129) that cultural studies have made little headway but neither he nor his sources understand that they lacked any framework to do so and typically because they embraced the sterile idea of the blank slate. They want to be factual, even scientific, but they constantly veer off into fantasy. He delineates the integration of art, science and morality as the great task of postmodernism and he and others go to immense lengths to make connections and organize it all into a coherent plan for thinking and living. However, I cannot see any really useful sense in which this is possible. Life is not a game of chess. Even in the limited realm of art or morality it is not at all clear that there is anything other than that these are parts of human experience which draws them together, i.e., genes make brains and unconscious automatic System 1 rules. One can put paintings and sculpture and clothing and buildings and stick figures in an art book but is this really getting us anywhere? Please see my reviews for details on how to describe behavior using the modern two systems of thought and a logical structure for rationality. Boyer (see my review) shows in detail how religion is due to a complex of brain systems that serve many different functions which evolved long before there was anything like religion.

The brain has numerous templates that take in data, organize it and relate it realtime to other data, but they each serve a specific purpose and those purposes are not ART, MORALITY, RELIGION, and SCIENCE.

Cognitive psychology shows that we have many modules working simultaneously to produce any behavior and that we relate to people in many ways for many reasons. One basic function is coalitional intuition. This gives us feelings that guide our entrance into groups and our interactions with other groups. We automatically and immediately overestimate the qualities of those in our group even if it's composed of randomly chosen total strangers we met five minutes before. Likewise, we immediately underestimate the good qualities of those in other groups, and always we heavily favor those who closely genetically related (kin selection or inclusive fitness which are other names for natural selection).

This and many other automatisms guide and commonly rule individual behavior, groups, nations and the world, but hardly anyone had a real understanding of this until quite recently. So, it is not surprising that almost all of his sources from Plato to Kant to Habermas have been wandering around in the dark and that Wilber is frantically running from one to the other with a flashlight trying to help them find their way out of the woods.

He notes (p199) that the only serious global social movement to date was Marxism but thinks its fatal flaw was reductionism. It seems far more cogent to note that, like virtually all of modern society (and most of his sources and to a significant extent this book), it denied (or ignored or failed to understand) human nature and basic biology. Nobody seems to notice that most social institutions and ideals, (including equality and democracy) have this same flaw. Debate on human nature, the environment and the future is endless, but reality is an acid that will eat through all fantasy. To paraphrase Lincoln, you can fool some of the people all of the time and all of the people some of the time but you can't fool mother nature anytime. The mob is programmed to accumulate resources and replicate their genes, and this means the collapse of civilization. Neomarxism, Diversity, Democracy, Islam, Hinduism, Buddhism, Christianity, Social Justice, and Human Rights are the means to this end and nothing can resist.

He details intellectual history (philosophy, psychology, religion, ecology, feminism, sociology, etc) and shows where nearly everyone went too far in the direction of Ascent (to the spirit or religious life only) or Descent (to science, materialism, reductionism or Flatland). He tries to show how to heal the rifts by combining sense and soul (spiritual and material life, science and religion, internal and external, individual and social). Everything is related to everything else (holons in holarchies--ie, things in nested hierarchies—see p26,135 for his definition).

The Age of Enlightenment denied the the spirit, the individual and the interior life, but developed art, morals and science and led to democracy, feminism, equality and ecology. This reductionism compressed the intellect and the spirit into the Flatland of science, rationality and materialism. He sees the loss of the spiritual point of view with the Age of Enlightenment as the major factor responsible for the malaise of modern times, but `true spirituality` or `advanced religion`--my terms--(i.e., the quest for enlightenment), as opposed to `primitive religion` (everything else-see Boyer) was always rare. It is advanced religion he sees as the panacea, but it is primitive religion that the masses understand, and it too has only materialistic goals (money, power and all else serving to replicate genes).

He understands that Jesus was a mystic in the same sense as Buddha and many others, and that what was to become the Catholic church largely destroyed his mystical aspects and the personal search for enlightenment- e.g., Gnosticism, in favor of primitive religion, priests, tithes and a structure seemingly modeled on the Roman army (p363). But, for the early Christian church, as for most religion, the cognitive templates were servants of the genes and enlightenment was not on the menu. Jesus was not a Christian, he had no bible, and he did not believe in a god any more than did Buddha. We have Christianity without the real intelligence of Jesus and this, as he explains in detail, is one cause of the West's extended stay in Flatland. I am not a Christian nor even a theist but it is one of the saddest things in history that the enlightened master who was to serve as the model of spirituality for the West had his vision of personal enlightenment destroyed and distorted by his own followers (but of course they are not really HIS followers). See the Gnostics and the Nag Hammadi manuscripts and above all Osho's discourses on the Gospel of Thomasfrom these.

Like everyone until recently, the many authors he discusses lacked any real explanation for human behavior. It rarely occurred to them to ask why we have such ideas and behavior and the few who did had no coherent solution.

Though he has read some of John Searle's superb philosophy, and has passing references to research in cognitive psychology, it is amazing that he could do 20 years research in philosophy without studying Wittgenstein, religion without reading Osho and watching his videos, and psychology without Buss, Tooby, Cosmides et al. Much of cognitive and evolutionary psychology was only published in journals at the time he was writing and Wilber has almost no references to journals. But Wittgenstein is the most famous philosopher of modern times, and Osho the most famous spiritual teacher. It is remarkable that although he spends much time in his books discussing the intellectual aspects of therapy (Freud, Beck, Maslow etc) and clearly understands that the spiritual path is the ultimate therapy, he totally ignores Osho, who had the most advanced therapeutic community in history functioning worldwide for the last 30 years. Osho never wrote a thick book containing a theory of human behavior, though his 200 books and many videos, all free online, explain it as beautifully and clearly as has ever been done.

Though he tries hard to heal the world, Wilber spends too much time in the airy realms of intellectual debate. As a postmodernist, and holist new age mystic, he wants to unite art, morality and science, but science gets the short straw. As in some of his other books (e.g., A Brief History of Everything- see my review), by far the worst mistakes he makes (along with nearly all his sources and most of the planet) are ignoring and misunderstanding basic biology. This is apparent thoughout the book. He starts chapter 7 with a quote from Aurobindo, who had the same failing. They have no grasp of the fact that the eugenic effects of evolution are driven by natural selection and when society became firmly established, this ceased and it's been totally dysgenic ever since. Genetic engineers have been at work and they have released on a helpless world the most horrifically destructive mutant imaginable. Society is the engineer and we are that mutant. If one gets the big picture, preoccupation with the possible destructive effects of GMOs (genetically modified organisms) -- other than ourselves -- is simply stupid and is perhaps a result of the operation of the contagion templates discussed by Boyer. That is, the potential destructive effect of all the GMOs we will ever make is unlikely to approach what humans have already done themselves.

He says (p 508, p519) that Darwin does not explain evolution, supposedly well known before him, and accuses him of `massive obscurantism' (he should be saying this about most of his sources!). The truth is that nothing in human behaviour or the world or the universe makes sense except in the light of evolution and no person did more to make this clear than Darwin. The work before him was little more than idle speculation and did not even approach a serious scientific treatment. This is why it had NO EFFECT on science or society, as opposed to Darwin's complete transformation of them.

Of course, Darwin did not know genetics nor plate tectonics, and modern Neodarwinism adds many refinements, but it shows a total misunderstanding of science and history to say that this invalidates or diminishes his contributions. Wilber is clearly sliding sideways into the Creationist camp and one can only speculate as to which of his inference engines produce this. He shows in many places that he has a poor grasp of genetics and evolution. E.g., on p561--as Dawkins has so patiently explained, the unit of evolution is the gene, and none of the other things Wilber mentions work as a genetic unit. Though he lists 'The Selfish Gene' in his bibliography, it's clear he has not understood it, and it's over 40 years old. Dawkins has written half a dozen superb works since and there are hundreds of others.

Wilber seems to have an allergy to good biology books--most of those he quotes are very old and others are classics of confusion. He wastes a page (p51) on the idea (mostly due to the Noemarxist pseudoscientist Gould and his coauthor Eldredge) of punctuated evolution, which is of very little interest. Gould loved to make a big fuss about his 'discoveries' and his energy got him alot of airtime, but when all was said and done, he had nothing new to say and dragged millions into his own confusions (as Dawkins, Conway Morris and many others have noted). Yes, evolution is sometimes faster but so what? Sometimes it rains a little, sometimes a lot. If you zoom in, in time or space, you always see more detail, and if you zoom out it starts to look the same. Gould was also responsible for the 'spandrels of San Marcos' debacle and, with his Neomarxist colleagues Lewontin and Rose, for endless insipid attacks on 'determinist biology', including the scandalous verbal and physical assaults on E.O Wilson (who, unlike themselves, made numerous major contributions to biology, though he recently disgraced himself—see my review of his 'The Social Conquest of Earth'). Modern research (e.g., see Pinker and Boyer) makes it clear that Wilson was right on the money regarding evolution, except for his unfortunate recent embrace of 'group selection'.

It is quite careless to say (p775) that there is no single pregiven world. Perhaps he only means we ought to be multicultural, egalitarian etc., but if there really were none, then how can we live and communicate? This is the ugliness of postmodernism creeping in. A large dose of Wittgenstein and cognitive psychology is an appropriate cure. Neither Wilber nor Derrida nor Foucault (nor most people) understand that there MUST be a single point of view or life would be impossible. This single point of view, resident in our genes, is integral to how we think and behave and largely dictates the vagaries of philosophy, politics and religion. The cognitive templates of S1 that underlie language, thought and our perception of reality logically must be the same and the evidence for this is overwhelming. Even the smallest changes, even one gene gone wrong, and you have autism, imbecility or schizophrenia.

The brute fact that Wilber (and most of the world) largely ignores, is that there are 8 billion (11 billion or so by 2100) sets of selfish genes carrying out their programs to destroy the earth. They are an acid that will eat through any intellectual conclusions, egalitarian fanatasies and spiritual rebirths. Selfishness, dishonesty, tribalism and shortsightedness are not due to accidents of intellectual or spiritual history. He says that the lack of spirit is destroying the earth, and though there is this aspect to things, it is much more to the point to say that it is selfish genes that are responsible. Likewise, he says `Biology is no longer Destiny`, but it is an easily defensible point of view that the reverse is far more likely. The attempt to understand history in terms of ideas ignores biology and denies human nature. Selfish genes always live in Flatland and less than 1000 people in all of human history have escaped the tyranny of the monkey mind into enlightenment.

Most of chapter 6 on myth and magic is outdated, confused or just wrong. To give just a few examples, we now understand that most of a child's psychological and social development is built in and does not have to be learned (eg, pg 233-4). The child does not have to deconstruct anything--the inferences engines do it all (p260). Joseph Campbell is quoted extensively and he too was clueless about how we develop and how to explain the differences and similarities in cultures (p245-50). E.g., Campbell says mythology can only lay claim to childhood, but a look around the world shows how false this is and a reading of Boyer's 'Religion Explained' (see my review) tells why. His discussion of thinking about the nonfactual on pg 279 to 80 is now often referred to as running the inference engines in decoupled or counterfactual mode. To his contorted comments in the middle of pg 560 (and finally....) I want to say `explanation ends with the templates! P580-4 and 591-3 are so full of dubious and plain wrong statements I don't even want to begin but suggest that Wilber and the reader start with Searle's 'The Mystery of Consciousness` or better with almost any one of my reviews of Searle or Wittgenstein. Time and again, it is clear he shares the lack of a scientific viewpoint with most of his sources. What info or procedures can solve the questions of consciousness or of any social science and philosophical theories? How do you recognize an answer when you see it? He and they go on for pages and whole books without ever having any idea (e.g., see my review of Dennett's Freedom Evolves).

On p702- bottom- he talks about the fulcrum driving development, but if one understands templates, the logical structure of rationality and the two systems of thought (and I mean here and elsewhere the entire corpus of cognitive and evolutionary psychology) then one either needs to rewrite this or eliminate it. Ditto for most of pgs 770-77. The tortured prose on pg 771-2 is only saying that the templates (S1 reflexes) are probed by drugs or other input but not changed and that nobody knows (in a way they can clearly convey) what these are. The background or intersubjective worldspace is the templates and they develop very early in children and then stay fixed for life. The deliberate destruction of Jesus` mysticism has created a powerful bias against higher consciousness in the West. Though he does not understand or discuss enlightenment, Boyer gives the basis for understanding how and why this happened.

Wilber embraces a simple utilitarianism (greatest good for greatest number) — i.e., the greatest depth for he greatest span (p334). This basic principle of much philosophy, religion and economics has serious problems and is probably unworkable. Which people should we make happy and how happy and when (i.e., now or in the future)? On what basis do we distribute resources now and how much do we save for the future population, and who decides and how to enforce this? He calls upon our Basic Moral Intuition (ie, the operation of our templates, as we now know), but our BMI is not really to help others but to help ourselves and our close relatives (inclusive fitness), and the few thousand (or let's be very optimistic and say few million) who are spritually advanced do not run the world and never will. The BMI-- eg, social exchange, coalitional intuitions, intuitive psychology, etc, evolved to serve our own interests (not those of the group--if, like Wilber, you think this way please read some of Dawkin's books or my recent review of Wilson's 'The Social Conquest of Earth') and in any case is hopelessly at sea in the modern world with it's advanced education, instant communications, firearms, mood altering drugs, clothes and cosmetics, a huge and mobile population and vanishing resources.

Instead of the intellectual or spiritual approach Wilber takes to history, others take ecological, genetic or technogical approaches (eg, Diamond's 'Guns, Germs and Steel' or Pinkers 'The Blank Slate'). In the long run, it appears that only biology really matters and we see daily how overpopulation is overwhelming all attempts to civilize the masses. The democracy and equality which Wilber values so highly are means created by selfish genes to facilitate their destruction of the planet. In spite of the hope that a new age is dawning and we will see the biological and psychic evolution of a new human, the fact is that we are the most degenerate species there ever was and the planet is nearing collapse. The billions of years of eugenics (natural selection) that thrust life up out of the slime and gave us the amazing ability to write and read books like this is now over. There is no longer selection for the healthier and more intelligent and in fact they produce a smaller percentage of the children every year. Nature does not tolerate physical and mental aberrations but society encourages them. Our physical and mental peak was probably CroMagnon man or maybe even Neanderthals (who had larger brains (yes, I know they seem not to have contributed more than a few percent of our DNA) about 100,000 years ago. It seems plausible that only genetic engineering and an enlightened oligarchy can save us. See my essay Suicide by Democracy.

He thinks (eg, p12 etc.) that it is our fractured world view (i.e., denial of the spirit) that is responsible for our ecological catastrophes and preoccupation with material goods, but this is another example of the denial of human nature. Nobody views heart conditions or Alzheimer disease as due to a fractured world view, but few seem to have any problem thinking you can change the fundamentals of behavior just by education or psychological manipulation. Modern science refutes this view conclusively (see Pinker, Boyer etc). The intuitive psychology templates tell us that we can manipulate the behavior of others, but these templates were evolved hundreds of thousands to millions of years ago, and they often fail to give correct results in modern contexts. Nearly every parent thinks they can profoundly influence the adult character (patience, honesty, irritability, depression, persistence, compulsiveness etc.) of their children in spite of clear evidence to the contrary (e.g., Pinker).

He thinks that animal rights people are illogical and excessive when they value animals over humans and likewise with those who value the environment over people's needs. This may be logical in his system but of course humans are typically (and often reasonably) illogical. In any case, if we always put human needs first, then it is surely the end of peace, tranquility, beauty and sanity.

Wilber defends Piaget, but like him he shows many places that he does not understand that the child does not have to learn the important things--they are built in and it only has to grow up. There seems to be no evidence that any of our templates, i.e., S1 change with time one we mature. The things that we learn are mostly trivial in comparison (i.e., even a computer can learn them!).

His sources are mostly lost in confusion and jargon, but he is brilliant and if one bothers to read his explanations and translate Wilberspeak into English, it usually makes sense. On pg 545- 7 he explains holonic ecology. Here is a translation. All organisms have value in themselves and are related to all others in the ecosystem and we must wake up spiritually. There is a web of life (i.e., Gaia or ecosystem) and all have intrinsic value, but higher organisms have more value, which requires a spiritual point of view. Neither the spiritual nor scientific approach works alone (i.e., dualism is bad).

Translated, it loses most of it's appeal but it is not fair to deny the poetry and majesty of his vision. But, this does not excuse him from writing clearly. Opacity is a nearly universal characteristic of the books he treats here. However, when Katz wrote a book denigrating mysticism Wilber took the time to do a `Searleian` analysis to show how incoherence has passed for scholarship (p629-31). Unfortunately, he does not continue this throughout the book and uses the jargon-laden incoherence of Habermas and others to explain other vague or incoherent texts (e.g., using Habermas instead of Searle or Wittgenstein or cognitive psychology to explicate Emerson p633).

In the USA, some 120 million (about 250 million by 2100) third world refugees from unrestrained motherhood are now the most powerful single force for destruction, having easily displaced fundamentalist European Christians. But all lowclass people are united in being against (or at least unwilling/unable to practice) population control and for environmental devastation in order to maximize the number of and resource use by their genes (though lacking any insight into this of course). This was a rational survival strategy when it was fixed in the genes millions of years ago, but it is suicidal now. The spiritual rebirth he talks about is not that of the "diverse" or the lower classes anywhere.

His view is that it is the poor and ignorant who are the major environmental problem and that this is somehow due to our Flatland approach, so if we just wake up, get spritual and help them out this will solve it. However, the rich destroy as much as 20 times more than the poor per capita and the third world will pass the first in CO_2 production about 2025. But there is nothing noble about the poor—they are only the rich in waiting.

Everyone is part of the problem and if one does the math (vanishing resources divided by increasing population) it's clear that the worldwide collapse of industrial society and a drastic reduction in population will happen and its only a matter of how and when (2150 is a good guess). Like so many, he suggests living lightly on the earth, but to live (and above all, to reproduce), is to do harm and if reproduction remains a right then it's hard to see any hope for the future. As is politically correct, he emphasizes rights and says little about responsibilities. It is a reasonable view that if society is to accept anyone as human, they must take responsibility for the world and this must take precedence over their personal needs. It is unlikely that any government will implement this, and equally unlikely that the world will continue to be a place any civilized person will wish to live in (or be able to).

I present here a table of rationality which I have worked out over the last 10 years. The rows show various aspects or ways of studying and the columns show the involuntary processes and voluntary behaviors comprising the two systems (dual processes) of the Logical Structure of Consciousness (LSC), which can also be regarded as the Logical Structure of Rationality (LSR-Searle), of behavior (LSB), of personality (LSP), of Mind(LSM), of language (LSL), of reality (LSOR), of Intentionality (LSI) -the classical philosophical term, the Descriptive Psychology of Consciousness (DPC), the Descriptive Psychology of Thought (DPT) –or better, the Language of the Descriptive Psychology of Thought (LDPT), terms introduced here and in my other very recent writings.

The ideas for this table originated in the work by Wittgenstein, a much simpler table by Searle, and correlates with extensive tables and graphs in the three recent books on Human Nature by P.M.S Hacker. The last 9 rows come principally from decision research by Johnathan St. B.T. Evans and colleagues as revised by myself.

System 1 is involuntary, reflexive or automated "Rules" R1 while Thinking (Cognition) has no gaps and is voluntary or deliberative "Rules" R2 and Willing (Volition) has 3 gaps (see Searle).

I suggest we can describe behavior more clearly by changing Searle's "impose conditions of satisfaction on conditions of satisfaction" to "relate mental states to the world by moving muscles" —i.e., talking, writing and doing, and his "mind to world direction of fit" and "world to mind direction of fit" by "cause originates in the mind" and "cause originates in the world" S1 is only upwardly causal (world to mind) and contentless (lacking representations or information) while S2 has content and is downwardly causal (mind to world). I have adopted my terminology in this table.

I have made detailed explanations of this table in my other writings.

FROM THE ANALYSIS OF LANGUAGE GAMES

	Disposition*	Emotion	Memory	Perception	Desire	PI**	IA***	Action/Word
Cause Originates From****	World	World	World	World	Mind	Mind	Mind	Mind
Causes Changes In*****	None	Mind	Mind	Mind	None	World	World	World
Causally Self Reflexive******	No	Yes	Yes	Yes	No	Yes	Yes	Yes
True or False (Testable)	Yes	T only	T only	T only	Yes	Yes	Yes	Yes
Public Conditions of Satisfaction	Yes	Yes/No	Yes/No	No	Yes/No	Yes	No	Yes
Describe A Mental State	No	Yes	Yes	Yes	No	No	Yes/No	Yes
Evolutionary Priority	5	4	2,3	1	5	3	2	2
Voluntary Content	Yes	No	No	No	No	Yes	Yes	Yes
Voluntary Initiation	Yes/No	No	Yes	No	Yes/No	Yes	Yes	Yes
Cognitive System *******	2	1	2/1	1	2/1	2	1	2
Change Intensity	No	Yes	Yes	Yes	Yes	No	No	No
Precise Duration	No	Yes	Yes	Yes	No	No	Yes	Yes
Time, Place (H+N, T+T) ********	TT	HN	HN	HN	TT	TT	HN	HN
Special Quality	No	Yes	No	Yes	No	No	No	No
Localized in Body	No	No	No	Yes	No	No	No	Yes
Bodily Expressions	Yes	Yes	No	No	Yes	Yes	Yes	Yes
Self Contradictions	No	Yes	No	No	Yes	No	No	No
Needs a Self	Yes	Yes/No	No	No	Yes	No	No	No
Needs Language	Yes	No	No	No	No	No	No	Yes/No

FROM DECISION RESEARCH

	Disposition*	Emotion	Memory	Perception	Desire	PI**	IA***	Action/Word
Subliminal Effects	No	Yes/No	Yes	Yes	No	No	No	Yes/No
Associative/Rule Based	RB	A/RB	A	A	A/RB	RB	RB	RB
Context Dependent/Abstract	A	CD/A	CD	CD	CD/A	A	CD/A	CD/A
Serial/Parallel	S	S/P	P	P	S/P	S	S	S
Heuristic/Analytic	A	H/A	H	H	H/A	A	A	A
Needs Working Memory	Yes	No	No	No	No	Yes	Yes	Yes
General Intelligence Dependent	Yes	No	No	No	Yes/No	Yes	Yes	Yes
Cognitive Loading Inhibits	Yes	Yes/No	No	No	Yes	Yes	Yes	Yes
Arousal Facilitates or Inhibits	I	F/I	F	F	I	I	I	I

Public Conditions of Satisfaction of S2 are often referred to by Searle and others as COS, Representations, truthmakers or meanings (or COS2 by myself), while the automatic results of S1 are designated as presentations by others (or COS1 by myself).
*   Aka Inclinations, Capabilities, Preferences, Representations, possible actions etc.
**   Searle's PriorIntentions
***   Searle's Intention In Action
****   Searle's Direction of Fit
*****   Searle's Direction of Causation
****** (Mental State instantiates--Causes or Fulfills Itself). Searle formerly called this causally self- referential.
******* Tversky/Kahneman/Frederick/Evans/Stanovich defined cognitive systems.
******** Here and Now or There and Then

The most profound spiritual autobiography of all time? - a review of "The Knee of Listening" by Adi Da (Franklin Jones) (1995) (review revised 2019)

Michael Starks

ABSTRACT

A brief review of the life and spiritual autobiography of the unique American mystic Adi Da (Franklin Jones). The sticker on the cover of some editions says `The most profound spiritual autobiography of all time` and this might well be true. I am in my 70's and have read many books by spiritual teachers and on spirituality, and this is one of the greatest. Certainly, it is by far the fullest and clearest account of the process of enlightenment I have ever seen. Even if you have no interest at all in the most fascinating of all human psychological processes, it is an amazing document that reveals a great deal about religion, yoga, and human psychology and probes the depths and limits of human possibilities. I describe it in some detail and compare his teaching with that of the Contemporary Indian mystic Osho.

Those wishing a comprehensive up to date framework for human behavior from the modern two systems view may consult my books Talking Monkeys 3rd ed (2019), The Logical Structure of Philosophy, Psychology, Mind and Language in Ludwig Wittgenstein and John Searle 2nd ed (2019), Suicide by Democracy 4th ed (2019), The Logical Structure of Human Behavior (2019), The Logical Structure of Consciousness (2019, Understanding the Connections between Science, Philosophy, Psychology, Religion, Politics, and Economics (2019), and Suicidal Utopian Delusions in the 21st Century 5th ed (2019).

There are many editions of the spiritual autobiography of the unique American mystic Adi Da (Franklin Jones). The first edition was 1972 and new editions with more material and much advertising about the group continue to appear. The latest one I have seen (2004) is about 3 times the size and weight of the 1995 editon I prefer, as the hundreds of pages of new material are opaque prose and advertising. So, I recommend one of the earlier paperpack editions such as the 1995 one to which my page citations refer.

A brief review of the life and spiritual autobiography of the unique American mystic Adi Da (Franklin Jones). The sticker on the cover of some editions says `The most profound spiritual autobiography of all time` and this might well be true. I am in my 70's and have read many books by spiritual teachers and on spirituality, and this is one of the greatest ones. Certainly, it is by far the fullest and clearest account of the process of enlightenment I have ever seen. Even if you have no interest at all in the most fascinating of all human psychological processes, it is an amazing document that reveals a great deal about religion, yoga, and human psychology and probes the depths and limits of human possibilities.

As I have read and experienced alot in various religious traditions, I naturally compare his writings with those of others, particularly with the great Indian mystic Osho. Though they clearly agree on the major points of how to proceed on the path, letting go of the attachment to the spiritual quest etc, their styles are vastly different. Both are highly intelligent and well read (Osho could speed read and read a huge number of books) and were at home in the spiritual literature of the major religious traditions. However, like so much of the spiritual literature, most of Da's books are essentially unreadable as he struggles to express in language the ineffable realms of the enlightened mind. Even in this, by far his most readable book, he often veers off into pages of opacity as he tries to explain the unexplainable. A great pity he seems never to have read Wittgenstein –the greatest natural psychologist of all time—who showed that we must abandon the attempts at explanation and accept descriptions of our innate psychological functions in language, which is the mind.

Osho by contrast is the clearest, most jargon free expositor of the spiritual life who has ever lived. He wrote very little and nearly all of his more than 200 books are transcriptions of spontaneous talks he gave-- with no notes or preparation. They are nonetheless unexcelled masterpieces of spiritual literature. His amazing àutobiography` (actually compiled after his death) has been published by St. Martins and the full version, as well as all his books (many also available on DVD), are available online many places. Unfortunately, he has very little to say about the exact details of his spiritual progress.

As Da lived most of his later life in seclusion on an island in Fiji, it was not easy to get to hear him but the Dawn Horse Press sells a few videos on their web page. Da is not a very engaging or facile speaker, unlike Osho who is by turns amusing, shattering and hypnotic. But, as both of them understand, it's what the master is and not he says that is important.

Both of them were utterly honest and uncompromising in their life and teachings and Da omits nothing of relevance, including his youthful adventures with sex and drugs as well as his exposure to LSD, psilocybin and mescaline as a volunteer in government experiments. However, as with many or perhaps all of those destined to become enlightened, he was different from birth and experienced the Shakti energy (which he calls the Bright) from childhood. And, when he entered college, he said his primary interest was to discover what living beings are and what is living consciousness. Clearly not your typical freshman.

A major problem in describing advanced spiritual states is that no criteria or language for them exists in common discourse so mystics have to try to bend language in mostly vain attempts to capture their experiences. It is far worse than trying to describe seeing to a congenitally blind person since they at least have the cognitive structures and experience of the world. But mystics are quite rare and most of them have left little or no description of their mental states.

Unlike Osho, who rejected miracles, paranormal phenomena and all the other nonsense that commonly accompanies religion, Da seems to lack any science background at all and embraces precognition (p120), reincarnation (p555),`meditating` other persons, living on air (p287) etc., and regards the phenomena that I would say are happening in his brain as being `out there`. From comments included in newer editions it is clear that many of his disciples believe he can perform miracles like stopping a raging forest fire at their California retreat. Nevertheless, most of the time he is amazingly levelheaded, going thru over a decade of stress and psychic terrors that would drive most from the spiritual path. Millions of years of evolution have solidified the ego and it does not leave peacefully.

Interwoven with the spellbinding account of his spiritual progress are the details of the mind's interaction with the body, described in the East in terms of various forms of Yoga (eg., p95-9, 214-21, 249,281-3, 439-40 in the 1995 editionI recommend). These few pages are worth more than a whole shelf of yoga books if you want to get to the heart of the mind/body relation in spirituality.

Unlike most who have become enlightened, he had a thorough grounding in Christian practice and made a major effort to become a protestant, and then Greek Orthodox minister. Even years later, after he was far along the path with Muktananda, he had an amazing and totally unexpected series of visitations from Mary and Jesus that went on for weeks (p 301-3 et seq.).
Regarding drugs, as is nearly universal among spiritual teachers, he notes that although they may remove certain barriers at times, they do not provide a

shortcut to understanding. However, nearly everyone is now aware that they put many on the path to higher consciousness throughout human history, especially in the last few decades.

He describes in detail the many stages in his ego death or self realization (eg, p72-4, 198-200, 219,20, 238-9, 245, 249, 258-9, 281, 355-65, 368-72, 406). Along the way, he realized the ultimate disutility of all practices and all traditions (337-9) including yoga (281-3), which are all attached to seeking and goals, ultimately winding up in the present. He discovered, as have many others, that seeking and meditation became obstacles and gave them up for devotion to his guru Muktananda (p420-22). His detailed accounts of his interactions with the famous Swami Muktananda and his ultimate realization of his limitations are of rare insight and honesty. He constantly encounters his attachment to his ego (Narcissus-- eg, p108-110) and asks himself--`Avoiding Relationship? ` by which he seems to mean avoiding the divine or ego death by preoccupation with spiritual seeking.

After enlightenment, he teaches the 'only by me revealed and given Way of the heart`, finding all other paths to be `remedial` and 'egoic' and merely pursuing God or reality (p359 +), but after a careful reading of this and several other books I never got any idea what that way consists in. Undoubtedly being in his presence helps alot but in other places he has complained about the fact that his disciples just won't let it happen and one wonders if even one has been able to follow him. Of course, the same considerations apply to all traditions and teachers and though some of Osho's friends (he disavowed the master/disciple relationship) have claimed enlightenment, nobody of his status has emerged. It looks like you have to have the right genes and the right environment and a very advanced and preferably enlightened guru to stimulate you. I suspect that the time has passed when an enlightened one could start a movement that transforms much of the world. The world desperately needs higher consciousness and I hope that someone comes up with an easier way very soon, but I think it's quite unlikely.

Do our automated unconscious behaviors reveal our real selves and hidden truths about the universe? -- A review of David Hawkins 'Power vs Force--the hidden determinants of human behavior –author's official authoritative edition' 412p (2012) (original edition 1995) (review revised 2019)

Michael Starks

ABSTRACT

I am very used to strange books and special people, but Hawkins stands out due to his use of a simple technique for testing muscle tension as a key to the "truth" of any kind of statement whatsoever—i.e., not just to whether the person being tested believes it, but whether it is really true! What is well known is that people will show automatic, unconscious physiological and psychological responses to just about anything they are exposed to—images, sounds, touch, odors, ideas, people. So, muscle reading to find out their true feelings is not radical at all, unlike using it as a dousing stick (more muscle reading) to do "paranormal science".

Hawkins describes the use of decreasing tension in the muscles of an arm in response to increases in cognitive load thus causing the arm to drop in response to the constant pressure of someone's fingers. He seems unaware that there is a long established and vast ongoing research effort in social psychology referred to by such phrases as 'implicit cognition', 'automaticity' etc., and that his use of 'kinesiology' is one tiny section. In addition to muscle tone (infrequently used) social psychologists measure EEG, galvanic skin response and most frequently verbal responses to words, sentences, images or situations at times varying from seconds to months after the stimulus. Many, such as Bargh and Wegner, take the results to mean we are automatons who learn and act largely without awareness via S1 (automated System 1) and many others such as Kihlstrom and Shanks say these studies are flawed and we are creatures of S2 (deliberative System 2). Though Hawkins seems to have no idea, as in other areas of the descriptive psychology of higher order thought, the situation regarding "automaticity" is still as chaotic as it was when Wittgenstein described the reasons for the sterility and barrenness of psychology in the 30's. Nevertheless, this book is an easy read and some therapists and spiritual teachers may find it of use.

Those wishing a comprehensive up to date framework for human behavior from the modern two systems view may consult my books Talking Monkeys 3rd ed (2019), The Logical Structure of Philosophy, Psychology, Mind and Language in Ludwig Wittgenstein and John Searle 2nd ed (2019), Suicide by Democracy 4th ed (2019), The Logical Structure of Human Behavior (2019), The Logical Structure of Consciousness (2019, Understanding the Connections between Science, Philosophy, Psychology, Religion, Politics, and Economics (2019), and Suicidal Utopian Delusions in the 21st Century 5th ed (2019).

I am very used to strange books and special people, but Hawkins stands out due to his use of a simple technique for testing muscle tension as a key to the "truth" of any kind of statement whatsoever—i.e., not just to whether the person being tested believes it but, whether it is really true! How could any sane person believe this? As a person with over 50 years adult experience with science, psychology, philosophy, religion and life I do not find it at all credible that it is even highly reliable about the person's beliefs and there is no chance of getting to know reality this way. What is well known is that people will show automatic, unconscious physiological and psychological responses to just about anything they are exposed to—images, sounds, touch, odors, ideas, people. So, muscle reading to find out their true feelings is not radical at all, unlike using it as a dousing stick (more muscle reading) to do "paranormal science".

Kinesiology, also known as human kinetics, is the study of human movement. Kinesiology studies physiological, mechanical (muscle tone), and psychological mechanisms as indices of people's mental and physical status and often uses movement exercises as therapy. However, Hawkins (without saying so) is using the term to refer to a very narrow application of kinesiology—the use of decreasing tension in the muscles of an arm in response to increases in cognitive load (i.e., mention of some person, event or object), which causes the subject to be distracted by intellectual or emotional issues, thus decreasing the muscle tension and causing the arm to drop in response to the constant pressure of someone's fingers. Hawkins seems unaware that there is a long established and vast ongoing research effort in social psychology referred to by such phrases as 'implicit cognition', 'automaticity' etc., and that his use of 'kinesiology' is one tiny section. In addition to muscle tone (actually infrequently used) social psychologists measure EEG, galvanic skin response and most frequently verbal responses to words, sentences, images or situations at times varying from seconds to months after the stimulus.

It was just by chance that I read Hawkins book after reading several books and dozens of recent papers on implicit cognition and was greatly surprised that he uses it as a key to the universe--i.e., the 'ultimate nature of reality' and I am sure the hundreds of active researchers would be equally amazed. I relate his spiritual practice to contemporary work on implicit cognition.

A major issue in most contemporary research on implicit social cognition is the degree to which it is automatic ('unconscious') and what constitutes 'evidence' for this. Hundreds of papers and dozens of books have appeared in just the last few years with massive confusion and often acrimonious debates. Many, such as Bargh and Wegner, take the results to mean we are automatons who learn and act largely without awareness via S1 and many others such as Kihlstrom and Shanks say these studies are flawed and we are creatures of S2.

Though Hawkins seems to have no idea, as in other areas of the descriptive psychology of higher order thought, the situation regarding "automaticity" is still as chaotic as it waswhen Wittgenstein described the reasons for the sterility and barrenness of psychology in the 30's.

Often the issue is stated by researchers and philosophers in terms of System 1 and System 2 functioning --a very useful, even indispensable division of behavior (intentionality) into our primitive reptilian automated, nonreflective S1 and our higher cortical primate conscious deliberative functions of S2. As noted in my other reviews, this division was pioneered by philosopher Ludwig Wittgenstein in the 1930's, though nobody has realized it.

I am quite familiar with mediation and the phenomena of enlightenment (see my review of Adi Da's autobiography 'The Knee of Listening') and am willing to accept Hawkins' claim to be in this rarefied group (it is often said that we know of less than 1000 enlightened persons in all of human history). I can also accept that he may have been a very effective 'therapist' who helped many persons and clearly, he is highly intelligent. This does not make me accept his many questionable or clearly false statements about the facts of the world. I am also (on the basis of a lifetime of study of science and philosophy) very skeptical about the relevance of chaos, attractors, complexity theory, computation, etc. to the study of human behavior (see my reviews and books on academia.edu, philpapers.org, researchgate.net, vixra.org, libgen.io, b-ok.org, Amazon etc.), claims which are often made by scientists as well. Implicit cognition research involves the usual horrific mixing of factual true or false scientific issues about causal brain functions (the S1 mind), with those about how language works (i.e., the mind, which as Wittgenstein showed us ¾ of a century ago, is public behavior --the S2 mind)—other topics I have covered extensively in my reviews.

So, Hawkins makes much of his muscle reading and I'm sure it often works well but there is a major logical error here. Regardless of what it says about the beliefs of the person being tested, it clearly says nothing whatever about the world itself. So, I respect Hawkins and his therapeutic work but, with the vast array of approaches to spiritual and emotional healing, there are lots of choices. And it is one thing to be treated by an enlightened master-whose very presence (or even the thought of them) can be galvanizing, and quite another to be treated by an ordinary person. By far the best source of books, audios and videos of an enlightened master at work are those of Osho (Bhagwan Shree Rajneesh) which are available to buy or free on the net on various sites. He therapized thousands at a time on occasion and created the most remarkable therapeutic community of all time around him. Though he is gone, his therapists still practice worldwide, and his works can be transformative.

Hawkins has other books which have many favorable reviews so those deeply interested may consult them.

The Transient Suppression of the Worst Devils of our Nature—a review of Steven Pinker's 'The Better Angels of Our Nature: Why Violence Has Declined'(2012)(review revised 2019)

Michael Starks

ABSTRACT

This is not a perfect book, but it is unique, and if you skim the first 400 or so pages, the last 300 (of some 700) are a pretty good attempt to apply what's known about behavior to social changes in violence and manners over time. The basic topic is: how does our genetics control and limit social change? Surprisingly he fails to describe the nature of kin selection (inclusive fitness) which explains much of animal and human social life. He also (like nearly everyone) lacks a clear framework for describing the logical structure of rationality (LSR—John Searle's preferred term) which I prefer to call the Descriptive Psychology of Higher Order Thought (DPHOT). He should have said something about the many other ways of abusing and exploiting people and the planet, since these are now so much more severe as to render other forms of violence nearly irrelevant. Extending the concept of violence to include the global long-term consequences of replication of someone's genes, and having a grasp of the nature of how evolution works (i.e., kin selection) will provide a very different perspective on history, current events, and how things are likely to go in the next few hundred years. One might start by noting that the decrease in physical violence over history has been matched (and made possible) by the constantly increasing merciless rape of the planet (i.e., by people's destruction of their own descendant's future). Pinker (like most people most of the time) is often distracted by the superficialities of culture when it's biology that matters. See my recent reviews of Wilson's 'The Social Conquest of Earth' and Nowak and Highfield's 'SuperCooperators' here and on the net for a brief summary of the vacuity of 'true altruism' (group selection), and the operation of kin selection and the uselessness and superficiality of describing behavior in cultural terms.

This is the classic nature/nurture issue and nature trumps nurture --infinitely. What really matters is the violence done to the earth by the relentless increase in population and resource destruction (due to medicine and technology and conflict suppression by police and military). About 200,000 more people a day (another Las Vegas every 10 days, another Los Angeles every month), the 6 tons or so of topsoil going into the sea/person/year –about 1% of the world's total disappearing yearly, etc. mean that unless some miracle happens the biosphere and civilization will largely collapse during next two centuries, and there will be starvation, misery and violence of every kind on a staggering scale. People's manners, opinions and tendencies to commit violent acts are of no relevance unless they can do something to avoid this catastrophe, and I don't see how that is going to happen. There is no space for arguments, and no point either (yes I'm a fatalist), so I'll just make a few comments as though they were facts. Don't imagine I have a personal stake in promoting one group at the expense of others. I am 78, have no descendants and no close relatives and do not identify with any political, national or religious group and regard the ones I belong to by default as just as repulsive as all the rest.

Parents are the worst Enemies of Life on Earth and, taking the broad view of things, women are as violent as men when one considers the fact that women's violence (like most of that done by men) is largely done in slow motion, at a distance in time and space and mostly carried out by proxy -by their descendants and by men. Increasingly, women bear children regardless of whether they have a mate and the effect of stopping one woman from breeding is on average much greater than stopping one man, since they are the reproductive bottleneck. One can take the view that people and their offspring richly deserve whatever misery comes their way and (with rare exceptions) the rich and famous are the worst offenders. Meryl Streep or Bill Gates or J.K Rowling and each of their kids may destroy 50 tons of topsoil each per year for generations into the future, while an Indian farmer and his may destroy 1 ton. If someone denies it that's fine, and to their descendants I say "Welcome to Hell on Earth"(WTHOE).

The emphasis nowadays is always on Human Rights, but it is clear that if civilization is to stand a chance, Human Responsibilities must replace Human Rights. Nobody gets rights without being a responsible citizen and the first thing this means is minimal environmental destruction. The most basic responsibility is no children unless your society asks you to produce them. A society or a world that lets people breed at random will always be exploited by selfish genes until it collapses (or reaches a point where life is so horrific it's not worth living). If society continues to maintain Human Rights as primary, to their descendants one can say with confidence "WTHOE".

Those wishing a comprehensive up to date framework for human behavior from the modern two systems view may consult my books Talking Monkeys 3rd ed (2019), The Logical Structure of Philosophy, Psychology, Mind and

Language in Ludwig Wittgenstein and John Searle 2nd ed (2019), Suicide by Democracy 4th ed (2019), The Logical Structure of Human Behavior (2019), The Logical Structure of Consciousness (2019, Understanding the Connections between Science, Philosophy, Psychology, Religion, Politics, and Economics (2019), and Suicidal Utopian Delusions in the 21st Century 5th ed (2019).

This is not a perfect book, but it is unique, and if you skim the first 400 or so pages, the last 300 (of some 700) are a pretty good attempt to apply what's known about behavior to social changes in violence and manners over time. The basic topic is: how does our genetics control and limit social change? Surprisingly he fails to describe the nature of kin selection (inclusive fitness) which explains much of animal and human social life. He also (like nearly everyone) lacks a clear framework for describing the logical structure of rationality (LSR—John Searle's preferred term) which I prefer to call the Descriptive Psychology of Higher Order Thought (DPHOT). Mostly the criticisms given by others are nit-picking and irrelevant and, as Pinker has said, he could not write a coherent book about "bad things", nor could he give every possible reference and point of view, but he should have said at least something about the many other ways of abusing and exploiting people and the planet, since these are now so much more severe as to render other forms of violence irrelevant.

Extending the concept of violence to include the global long-term consequences of replication of someone's genes, and having a grasp of the nature of how evolution works (i.e., kin selection) will provide a very different perspective on history, current events, and how things are likely to go in the next few hundred years. One might start by noting that the decrease in physical violence over history has been matched (and made possible) by the constantly increasing merciless rape of the planet (i.e., by people's destruction of their own descendant's future). Pinker (like most people most of the time) is often distracted by the superficialities of culture when it's biology that matters. See my recent reviews of Wilson's 'The Social Conquest of Earth' and Nowak and Highfield's 'SuperCooperators' for a brief summary of the vacuity of altruism and the operation of kin selection and the uselessness and superficiality of describing behavior in cultural terms.

This is the classic nature/nurture issue and nature trumps nurture --infinitely. What really matters is the violence done to the earth by the relentless increase in population and resource destruction (due to medicine and technology and conflict suppression by police and military). About 200,000 more people a day (another Las Vegas every 10 days, another Los Angeles every month), the 6 tons or so of topsoil going into the sea/person/year etc. mean that unless some miracle happens the biosphere and civilization will largely collapse in the next two centuries and there will be starvation, misery and violence of every kind on a staggering scale.

People's manners, opinions and tendencies to commit violent acts are of no relevance unless they can do something to avoid this catastrophe, and I don't see how that is going to happen. There is no space for arguments, and no point either (yes, I'm a fatalist), so I'll just make a few comments as though they were facts. Don't imagine I have a personal stake in promoting one group at the expense of others. I am 75, have no descendants and no close relatives and do not identify with any political, national or religious group and regard the ones I belong to by default as just as repulsive as all the rest.

Parents are the worst Enemies of Life on Earth and, taking the broad view of things, women are as violent as men when one considers the fact that women's violence (like most of that done by men) is largely done in slow motion, at a distance in time and space and mostly carried out by proxy -by their descendants and by men. Increasingly, women bear children regardless of whether they have a mate and the effect of stopping one woman from breeding is on average much greater than stopping one man, since they are the reproductive bottleneck. One can take the view that people and their offspring richly deserve whatever misery comes their way and (with rare exceptions) the rich and famous are the worst offenders. Meryl Streep or Bill Gates or J.K.Rowling and each of their kids may destroy 50 tons of topsoil each per year for generations into the future, while an Indian farmer and his may destroy 1 ton. If someone denies it that's fine, and to their descendants I say "Welcome to Hell on Earth"(WTHOE).

The emphasis nowadays is always on Human Rights, but it is clear that if civilization is to stand a chance, Human Responsibilities must replace Human Rights. Nobody gets rights (i.e., privileges) without being a responsible citizen and the first thing this means is minimal environmental destruction. The most basic responsibility is no children unless your society asks you to produce them. A society or a world that lets people breed at random will always be exploited by selfish genes until it collapses (or reaches a point where life is so horrific it's not worth living). If society continues to maintain Human Rights as primary, that's fine and to their descendants one can say with confidence "WTHOE".

"Helping" has to be seen from a global long-term perspective. Almost all "help" that's given by individuals, organizations or countries harms others and the world in the long run and must only be given after very careful consideration. If you want to hand out money, food, medicine, etc., you need to ask what the long-term environmental consequences are. If you want to please everyone all the time, again to your descendants I say "WTHOE".

Dysgenics: endless trillions of creatures beginning with bacteria-like forms over 3 billion years ago have died to create us and all current life and this is called eugenics, evolution by natural selection or kin selection (inclusive fitness). We all have "bad genes" but some are worse than others. It is estimated that up to 50% of all human conceptions end in spontaneous abortion due to "bad genes". Civilization is dysgenic. This problem is currently trivial compared to overpopulation but getting worse by the day. Medicine, welfare, democracy, equality, justice, human rights and "helping" of all kinds have global long term environmental and dysgenic consequences which will collapse society even if population growth stops. Again, if the world refuses to believe it or doesn't want to deal with it that's fine and to their (and everyone's) descendants we can say "WTHOE".

Beware the utopian scenarios that suggest doomsday can be avoided by judicious application of technologies. As they say you can fool some of the people all of the time and all of the people some of the time but you can't fool mother nature any of the time. I leave you with just one example. Famous scientist Raymond Kurzweil (see my review of 'How to create a Mind') proposed nanobots as the saviors of humankind. They would make anything we needed and clean every mess. They would even make ever better versions of themselves. They would keep us as pets. But think of how many people treat their pets, and pets are overpopulating and destroying and becoming dysgenic almost as fast as humans (e.g. domestic and feral cats alone kill perhaps 100 billion wild animals a year). Pets only exist because we destroy the earth to feed them and we have spay and neuter clinics and euthanize the sick and unwanted ones. We practice rigorous population control and eugenics on them deliberately and by omission, and no form of life can evolve or exist without these two controls—not even bots. And what's to stop nanobots from evolving? Any change that facilitated reproduction would automatically be selected for and any behavior that wasted time or energy (i.e., taking care of humans) would be heavily selected against. What would stop the AI controlled bots program from mutating into a homicidal form and exploiting all earth's resources causing global collapse? There is no free lunch for bots either and to them too we can confidently say "WTHOE".

This is where any thoughts about the world and human behavior must lead an educated person but Pinker says nothing about it. So, the first 400 pages of this book can be skipped and the last 300 read as a nice summary of EP (evolutionary psychology) as of 2011. However, as in his other books and nearly universally in the behavioral sciences, there is no clear broad framework for intentionality as pioneered by Wittgenstein, Searle and many others. I have presented such a framework in my many reviews of works by and about these two natural psychological geniuses and will not repeat it here.

The Dead Hands of Group Selection and Phenomenology -- A Review of Individuality and Entanglement by Herbert Gintis 357p (2017)(review revised 2019)

Michael Starks

ABSTRACT

Since Gintis is a senior economist and I have read some of his previous books with interest, I was expecting some more insights into behavior. Sadly, he makes the dead hands of group selection and phenomenology into the centerpieces of his theories of behavior, and this largely invalidates the work. Worse, since he shows such bad judgement here, it calls into question all his previous work. The attempt to resurrect group selection by his friends at Harvard, Nowak and Wilson, a few years ago was one of the major scandals in biology in the last decade, and I have recounted the sad story in my article 'Altruism, Jesus and the End of the World—how the Templeton Foundation bought a Harvard Professorship and attacked Evolution, Rationality and Civilization -- A review of E.O. Wilson 'The Social Conquest of Earth' (2012) and Nowak and Highfield 'SuperCooperators' (2012).' Unlike Nowak, Gintis does not seem to be motivated by religious fanaticism, but by the strong desire to generate an alternative to the grim realities of human nature, made easy by the (near universal) lack of understanding of basic human biology and blank slateism of behavioral scientists, other academics, and the general public.

Gintis rightly attacks (as he has many times before) economists, sociologists and other behavioral scientists for not having a coherent framework to describe behavior. Of course, the framework needed to understand behavior is an evolutionary one. Unfortunately, he fails to provide one himself (according to his many critics and I concur), and the attempt to graft the rotten corpse of group selection onto whatever economic and psychological theories he has generated in his decades of work, merely invalidates his entire project.

Although Gintis makes a valiant effort to understand and explain the genetics, like Wilson and Nowak, he is far from an expert, and like them, the math just blinds him to the biological impossibilities and of course this is the norm in science. As Wittgenstein famously noted on the first page of Culture and Value "There is no religious denomination in which the misuse of metaphysical expressions has been responsible for so much sin as it has in mathematics."

It has always been crystal clear that a gene that causes behavior which decreases its own frequency cannot persist, but this is the core of the notion of group selection. Furthermore, it has been well known and often demonstrated that group selection just reduces to inclusive fitness (kin selection), which, as Dawkins has noted, is just another name for evolution by natural selection. Like Wilson, Gintis has worked in this arena for about 50 years and still has not grasped it, but after the scandal broke, it took me only 3 days to find, read and understand the most relevant professional work, as detailed in my article. It is mind boggling to realize that Gintis and Wilson were unable to accomplish this in nearly half a century.

I discuss the errors of group selection and phenomenology that are the norm in academia as special cases of the near universal failure to understand human nature that are destroying America and the world.

Those wishing a comprehensive up to date framework for human behavior from the modern two systems view may consult my books Talking Monkeys 3rd ed (2019), The Logical Structure of Philosophy, Psychology, Mind and Language in Ludwig Wittgenstein and John Searle 2nd ed (2019), Suicide by Democracy 4th ed (2019), The Logical Structure of Human Behavior (2019), The Logical Structure of Consciousness (2019, Understanding the Connections between Science, Philosophy, Psychology, Religion, Politics, and Economics (2019), and Suicidal Utopian Delusions in the 21st Century 5th ed (2019).

Since Gintis is a senior economist and I have read some of his previous books with interest, I was expecting some more insights into behavior. Sadly, he makes the dead hands of group selection and phenomenology into the centerpieces of his theories of behavior, and this largely invalidates the work. Worse, since he shows such bad judgement here, it calls into question all his previous work. The attempt to resurrect group selection by his friends at Harvard, Nowak and Wilson, a few years ago was one of the major scandals in biology in the last decade, and I have recounted the sad story in my article 'Altruism, Jesus and the End of the World—how the Templeton Foundation bought a Harvard Professorship and attacked Evolution, Rationality and Civilization -- A review of E.O. Wilson 'The Social Conquest of Earth' (2012) and Nowak and Highfield 'SuperCooperators' (2012).' Unlike Nowak, Gintis does not seem to be motivated by religious fanaticism, but by the strong desire to generate an alternative to the grim realities of human nature, made easy by the (near universal) lack of understanding of basic human biology and blank slateism of behavioral scientists, other academics, and the general public.

Gintis rightly attacks (as he has many times before) economists, sociologists and other behavioral scientists for not having a coherent framework to describe behavior. Of course, the framework needed to understand behavior is an evolutionary one. Unfortunately, he fails to provide one himself (according to his many critics and I concur), and the attempt to graft the rotten corpse of group selection onto whatever economic and psychological theories he has generated in his decades of work, merely invalidates his entire project.

Although Gintis makes a valiant effort to understand and explain the genetics, like Wilson and Nowak, he is far from an expert, and like them, the math just blinds him to the biological impossibilities and of course this is the norm in science. As Wittgenstein famously noted on the first page of Culture and Value "There is no religious denomination in which the misuse of metaphysical expressions has been responsible for so much sin as it has in mathematics."

It has always been crystal clear that a gene that causes behavior which decreases its own frequency cannot persist, but this is the core of the notion of group selection. Furthermore, it has been well known and often demonstrated that group selection just reduces to inclusive fitness (kin selection), which, as Dawkins has noted, is just another name for evolution by natural selection. Like Wilson, Gintis has worked in this arena for about 50 years and still has not grasped it, but after the Wilson scandal broke, it took me only 3 days to find, read and understand the most relevant professional work, as detailed in my article. It is mind boggling to realize that Gintis and Wilson were unable to accomplish this in nearly half a century.

In the years after the Nowak, Wilson, Tarnita paper was published in Nature, several population geneticists recounted chapter and verse on the subject, again showing conclusively that it is all a storm in a teacup. It is most unfortunate that Gintis, like his friends, failed to ask a competent biologist about this and regards as misguided the 140 some well known biologists who a signed a letter protesting the publication of this nonsense in Nature. I refer those who want the gory details to my paper, as it's the best account of the melee that I am aware of. For a summary of the tech details see Dawkins Article 'The Descent of Edward Wilson' http://www.prospectmagazine.co.uk/magazine/edward-wilson-social-conquest-earth-evolutionary-errors-origin-species. As Dawkins wrote 'For Wilson not to acknowledge that he speaks for himself against the great majority of his professional colleagues is—it pains me to say this of a lifelong hero —an act of wanton arrogance'. Sadly, Gintis has assimilated himself to such inglorious company. There are also some nice Dawkins youtubes such as https://www.youtube.com/watch?v=lBweDk4ZzZ4.

Gintis has also failed to provide the behavioral framework lacking in all the social sciences. One needs to have a logical structure for rationality, an understanding of the two systems of thought (dual process theory), of the division between scientific issues of fact and philosophical issues of how language works in the context at issue, and of how to avoid reductionism and scientism, but he, like nearly all students of behavior, is largely clueless. He, like them, is enchanted by models, theories, and concepts, and the urge to explain, while Wittgenstein showed us that we only need to describe, and that theories, concepts etc., are just ways of using language (language games) which have value only insofar as they have a clear test (clear truthmakers, or as eminent philosopher John Searle likes to say, clear Conditions of Satisfaction (COS)).

Those wishing a comprehensive up to date framework for human behavior from the modern two systems view may consult my books Talking Monkeys 3rd ed (2019), The Logical Structure of Philosophy, Psychology, Mind and Language in Ludwig Wittgenstein and John Searle 2nd ed (2019), Suicide by Democracy 4th ed (2019), The Logical Structure of Human Behavior (2019), The Logical Structure of Consciousness (2019, Understanding the Connections between Science, Philosophy, Psychology, Religion, Politics, and Economics (2019), and Suicidal Utopian Delusions in the 21st Century 5th ed (2019).

After half a century in oblivion, the nature of consciousness (intentionality, behavior) is now the hottest topic in the behavioral sciences and philosophy. Beginning with the pioneering work of Ludwig Wittgenstein from the 1930's (the Blue and Brown Books) to 1951, and from the 50's to the present by his successors Searle, Moyal-Sharrock, Read, Hacker, Stern, Horwich, Winch, Finkelstein etc., I have created the following table as an heuristic for furthering this study. The rows show various aspects or ways of studying and the columns show the involuntary processes and voluntary behaviors comprising the two systems (dual processes) of the Logical Structure of Consciousness (LSC), which can also be regarded as the Logical Structure of Rationality (LSR- Searle), of behavior (LSB), of personality (LSP), of Mind (LSM), of language (LSL), of reality (LSOR), of Intentionality (LSI) -the classical philosophical term, the Descriptive Psychology of Consciousness (DPC), the Descriptive Psychology of Thought (DPT) —or better, the Language of the Descriptive Psychology of Thought (LDPT), terms introduced here and in my other very recent writings.

The ideas for this table originated in the work by Wittgenstein, a much simpler table by Searle, and correlates with extensive tables and graphs in the three recent books on Human Nature by P.M.S Hacker. The last 9 rows come principally from decision research by Johnathan St. B.T. Evans and colleagues as revised by myself.

System 1 is involuntary, reflexive or automated "Rules" R1 while Thinking (Cognition) has no gaps and is voluntary or deliberate "Rules" R2 and Willing (Volition) has 3 gaps (see Searle).

I suggest we can describe behavior more clearly by changing Searle's "impose conditions of satisfaction on conditions of satisfaction" to "relate mental states to the world by moving muscles"—i.e., talking, writing and doing, and his "mind to world direction of fit" and "world to mind direction of fit" by "cause originates in the mind" and "cause originates in the world" S1 is only upwardly causal (world to mind) and contentless (lacking representations or information) while S2 has content and is downwardly causal (mind to world). I have adopted my terminology in this table.

I have made detailed explanations of this table in my other writings.

FROM THE ANALYSIS OF LANGUAGE GAMES

	Disposition*	Emotion	Memory	Perception	Desire	PI**	IA***	Action/Word
Cause Originates From****	World	World	World	World	Mind	Mind	Mind	Mind
Causes Changes In*****	None	Mind	Mind	Mind	None	World	World	World
Causally Self Reflexive******	No	Yes	Yes	Yes	No	Yes	Yes	Yes
True or False (Testable)	Yes	T only	T only	T only	Yes	Yes	Yes	Yes
Public Conditions of Satisfaction	Yes	Yes/No	Yes/No	No	Yes/No	Yes	No	Yes
Describe A Mental State	No	Yes	Yes	Yes	No	No	Yes/No	Yes
Evolutionary Priority	5	4	2,3	1	5	3	2	2
Voluntary Content	Yes	No	No	No	No	Yes	Yes	Yes
Voluntary Initiation	Yes/No	No	Yes	No	Yes/No	Yes	Yes	Yes
Cognitive System *******	2	1	2/1	1	2/1	2	1	2
Change Intensity	No	Yes	Yes	Yes	Yes	No	No	No
Precise Duration	No	Yes	Yes	Yes	No	No	Yes	Yes
Time, Place (H+N, T+T) ********	TT	HN	HN	HN	TT	TT	HN	HN
Special Quality	No	Yes	No	Yes	No	No	No	No
Localized in Body	No	No	No	Yes	No	No	No	Yes
Bodily Expressions	Yes	Yes	No	No	Yes	Yes	Yes	Yes
Self Contradictions	No	Yes	No	No	Yes	No	No	No
Needs a Self	Yes	Yes/No	No	No	Yes	No	No	No
Needs Language	Yes	No	No	No	No	No	No	Yes/No

FROM DECISION RESEARCH

	Disposition*	Emotion	Memory	Perception	Desire	PI**	IA***	Action/Word
Subliminal Effects	No	Yes/No	Yes	Yes	No	No	No	Yes/No
Associative/Rule Based	RB	A/RB	A	A	A/RB	RB	RB	RB
Context Dependent/Abstract	A	CD/A	CD	CD	CD/A	A	CD/A	CD/A
Serial/Parallel	S	S/P	P	P	S/P	S	S	S
Heuristic/Analytic	A	H/A	H	H	H/A	A	A	A
Needs Working Memory	Yes	No	No	No	No	Yes	Yes	Yes
General Intelligence Dependent	Yes	No	No	No	Yes/No	Yes	Yes	Yes
Cognitive Loading Inhibits	Yes	Yes/No	No	No	Yes	Yes	Yes	Yes
Arousal Facilitates or Inhibits	I	F/I	F	F	I	I	I	I

Public Conditions of Satisfaction of S2 are often referred to by Searle and others as COS, Representations, truthmakers or meanings (or COS2 by myself), while the automatic results of S1 are designated as presentations by others (or COS1 by myself).

*   Aka Inclinations, Capabilities, Preferences, Representations, possible actions etc.
**   Searle's Prior Intentions
***   Searle's Intention In Action
****   Searle's Direction of Fit
*****   Searle's Direction of Causation
****** (Mental State instantiates--Causes or Fulfills Itself). Searle formerly called this causally self- referential.
******* Tversky/Kahneman/Frederick/Evans/Stanovich defined cognitive systems.
******** Here and Now or There and Then

It is of interest to compare this with the various tables and charts in Peter

Hacker's recent 3 volumes on Human Nature. One should always keep in mind Wittgenstein's discovery that after we have described the possible uses (meanings, truthmakers, Conditions of Satisfaction) of language in a particular context, we have exhausted its interest, and attempts at explanation (i.e., philosophy) only get us further away from the truth. He showed us that there is only one philosophical problem—the use of sentences (language games) in an inappropriate context, and hence only one solution— showing the correct context.

Gintis starts making dubious, vague or downright bizarre claims early in the book. It begins on the first page of the overview with meaningless quotes from Einstein and Ryle. On pxii the paragraph beginning 'Third Theme' about entangled minds needs rewriting to specify that language games are functions of System 2 and that's how thinking, believing etc. work (what they are), while the Fourth Theme which tries to explain behavior as due to what people 'consciously believe' is right. That is, with 'nonconsequentialism' he's trying to 'explain' behavior as 'altruistic' group selection mediated by conscious linguistic System 2. But if we take an evolutionary long term view, it's clearly due to reciprocal altruism, attempting to serve inclusive fitness, which is mediated by the unconscious operation of System 1. Likewise, for the Fifth Theme and the rest of the Overview. He favors Rational Choice but has no idea this is a language game for which the exact context must be specified, nor that both System 1 and System 2 are 'rational' but in quite different ways. This is the classic error of most descriptions of behavior, which Searle has called The Phenomenological Illusion, Pinker the Blank Slate and Tooby and Cosmides 'The Standard Social Science Model' and I have discussed it extensively in my other reviews and articles. As long as one does not grasp that most of our behavior is automated by nonlinguistic System 1, and that our conscious linguistic System 2 is mostly for rationalization of our compulsive and unconscious choices, it is not possible to have more than a very superficial view of behavior, i.e., the one that is nearly universal not only among academics but politicians, billionaire owners of high tech companies, movie stars and the general public. Consequently, the consequences reach far beyond academia, producing delusional social policies that are bringing about the inexorable collapse of industrial civilization. See my 'Suicide by Democracy-an Obituary for America and the World'. It is breathtaking to see America and the European democracies helping citizens of the third world destroy everyone's future.

On pxiii one can describe the 'nonconsequentialist' (i.e., apparently 'true' altruistic or self- destructive behavior) as actually performing reciprocal altruism, serving inclusive fitness due to genes evolved in the EEA

(Environment of Evolutionary Adaptation—i.e., that of our very distant ancestors), which stimulates the dopaminergic circuits in the ventral tegmentum and the nucleus accumbens, with the resulting release of dopamine which makes us feel good—the same mechanism that appears to be involved in all addictive behavior from drug abuse to soccer moms.

And more incoherent babble such as "In the context of such environments, there is a fitness benefit to the 'epigenetic transmission' of such 'information' concerning the 'current state' of the 'environment', i.e., transmission through non-genetic 'channels'. This is called 'cultural transmission'" [scare quotes mine]. Also, that 'culture' is 'directly encoded' in the brain (p7), which he says is the main tenet of gene-culture coevolution, and that democratic institutions and voting are altruistic and cannot be explained in terms of self-interest (p17-18). The major reason for these peculiar views does not really come out until p186 when he finally makes it clear that he is a group selectionist. Since there is no such thing as group selection apart from inclusive fitness, it's no surprise that this is just another incoherent account of behavior—i.e., more or less what Tooby and Cosmides famously termed The Standard Social Science Model or Pinker 'The Blank Slate'.

What he calls 'altruistic genes' on p188 should be called 'inclusive fitness genes' or 'kin selection genes'. Gintis is also much impressed with the idea of gene-culture coevolution, which only means that culture may itself be an agent of natural selection, but he fails to grasp that this can only happen within the context of natural selection (inclusive fitness). Like nearly all social scientists (and scientists, philosophers etc.), it never crosses his mind that 'culture', 'coevolution',' symbolic',' 'epigenetic', 'information', 'representation' etc., are all families of complex language games, whose COS (Conditions Of Satisfaction, tests for truth) are exquisitely sensitive to context. Without a specific context, they don't mean anything. So, in this book, as in most of the literature on behavior, there is much talk that has the appearance of sense without sense (meaning or clear COS).

His claim on pxv, that most of our genes are the result of culture, is clearly preposterous as e.g., it is well known that we are about 98% chimpanzee. Only if he means those relating to language can we accept the possibility that some of our genes have been subject to cultural selection and even these merely modified ones that already existed—i.e., a few base pairs were changed out of hundreds of thousands or millions in each gene.

He is much taken with the 'rational actor' model of economic behavior. but again, is unaware that the automaticities of S1 underlie all 'rational' behavior and the conscious linguistic deliberations of S2 cannot take place without them. Like many, perhaps the vast majority of current younger students of behavior, I see all human activities as easily comprehensible results of the working of selfish genetics in a contemporary context in which police surveillance and a temporary abundance of resources, gotten by raping the earth and robbing our own descendants, leads to relative temporary tranquility. In this connection, I suggest my review of Pinker's recent book—The Transient Suppression of the Worst Devils of Our Nature—A Review of The Better Angels of Our Nature'.

Many behaviors look like true altruism, and some are (i.e., they will decrease the frequency of the genes that bring them about – i.e, lead to the extinction of their own descendants), but the point which Gintis misses is that these are due to a psychology which evolved long ago in small groups on the African plains in the EEA and made sense then (i.e., it was inclusive fitness, when everyone in our group of a few dozen to a few hundred were our close relatives), and so we often continue with these behaviors even though they no longer make sense (i.e., they serve the interests of unrelated or distantly related persons which decreases our genetic fitness by decreasing the frequency of the genes that made it possible). This accounts for his promoting the notion that many behaviors are 'truly altruistic', rather than selfish in origin (such as in sect. 3.2). He even notes this and calls it 'distributed effectivity' (p60-63) in which people behave in big elections as though they were small ones, but he fails to see this is not due to any genes for 'true altruism' but to genes for reciprocal altruism (inclusive fitness), which is of course selfish. Thus, people behave as though their actions (e.g., their votes) were consequential, even though it is clear that they are not. E.g., one can find on the net that the chances of any one person's vote deciding the outcome of an American presidential election is in the range of millions to tens of millions to one. And of course, the same is true of our chances of winning a lottery, yet our malfunctioning EEA psychology makes lotteries and voting hugely popular activities.

He also seems unaware of the standard terminology and ways of describing behavior used in evolutionary psychology (EP). E.g., on pg. 75 Arrow's description of norms of social behavior are described in economic terms rather than as EP from the EEA trying to operate in current environments, and at the bottom of the page, people act not as 'altruistic' punishers (i.e., as 'group selectionists') but as inclusive fitness punishers. On p 78, to say that subjects act 'morally' or in accord with a norm 'for its own sake', is again to embrace the group selectionist/phenomenological illusion, and clearly it is groups of genes that are trying to increase their inclusive fitness via well-known EP mechanisms like cheater detection and punishment. Again, on p88, what he describes as other-regarding unselfish actions can just as easily be described as self-regarding attempts at reciprocal altruism which go astray in a large society.

Naturally, he often uses standard economics jargon such as 'the subjective prior must be interpreted as a conditional probability', which just means a belief in the likelihood of a particular outcome (p90-91), and 'common subjective priors' (shared beliefs) p122. Much of the book and of behavior concerns what is often called 'we intentionality' or the construction of social reality, but the most eminent theorist in this arena, John Searle, is not discussed, his now standard terminology such as COS and DIRA (desire independent reasons for action) does not appear, he is not in the index, and only one of his many works, and that over 20 years old, is found in the bibliography.

On p97 he comments favorably on Bayesian updating without mentioning that it is notorious for lacking any meaningful test for success (i.e., clear COS), and commonly fails to make any clear predictions, so that no matter what people do, it can be made to describe their behavior after the fact.

However, the main problem with chapter 5 is that 'rational' and other terms are complex language games that have no meaning apart from very specific contexts, which are typically lacking here. Of course, as Wittgenstein showed us, this is the core problem of all discussion of behavior and Gintis has most of the behavioral science community (or at least most of those over 40) as coconspirators. Likewise, throughout the book, such as chapter 6, where he discusses 'complexity theory', 'emergent properties', 'macro and micro levels', and 'nonlinear dynamical systems' and the generation of 'models' (which can mean almost anything and 'describe' almost anything), but it's only prediction that counts (i.e., clear COS).

In spite of his phenomenological illusion (i.e., the near universal assumption that our conscious deliberations describe and control behavior—at odds with almost all the research in social psychology for the last 40 years), he also shares the reductionist delusion, wondering why the social sciences have not got a core analytical theory and have not coalesced. This of course is a frequent subject in the social sciences and philosophy and the reason is that psychology of higher order thought is not describable by causes, but by reasons, and one cannot make psychology disappear into physiology nor physiology into biochemistry nor it into physics etc. They are just different and indispensable levels of description. Searle writes about it often and Wittgenstein famously described it 80 years ago in the Blue Book.

"Our craving for generality has [as one] source ... our preoccupation with the method of science. I mean the method of reducing the explanation of natural phenomena to the smallest possible number of primitive natural laws; and, in mathematics, of unifying the treatment of different topics by using a generalization. Philosophers constantly see the method of science before their eyes, and are irresistibly tempted to ask and answer in the way science does. This tendency is the real source of metaphysics, and leads the philosopher into complete darkness. I want to say here that it can never be our job to reduce anything to anything, or to explain anything. Philosophy really is "purely descriptive."

He is also quite out of touch with the contemporary world, thinking that people are going to be nice because they have internalized altruism (i.e., group selection), and with demographic realities, when he opines that population growth is under control, when in fact predictions are for another 4 billion by 2100 (p133), violence is increasing and the outlook is grim indeed.

He sees a need to "carve an academic niche for sociology" (p148), but the whole discussion is typical gibberish (no clear COS), and all one really needs (or can give) is a clear description of the language games (the mind at work) we play in social situations, and how they show how our attempts at inclusive fitness work or go astray in contemporary contexts. Over and over he pushes his fantasy that "inherently ethical behavior" (i.e., group selectionist altruism) explains our social behavior, ignoring the obvious facts that it's due to temporary abundance of resources, police and surveillance, and that always when you take these away, savagery quickly emerges (e.g., p151). It's easy to maintain such delusions when one lives in the ivory tower world of abstruse theories, inattentive to the millions of scams, robberies, rapes, assaults, thefts and murders taking place every day.

Again, and again, (e.g., top p170) he ignores the obvious explanations for our 'rationality', which is natural selection –i.e., inclusive fitness in the EEA leading to ESS (Evolutionarily Stable Strategies), or at least they were more or less stable in small groups 100,000 to 3 million years ago.

Chapter 9 on the Sociology of the Genome is inevitably full of mistakes and incoherence—e.g., there are not special 'altruistic genes', rather, all genes serve inclusive fitness or they disappear (p188). The problem is that the only way to really get selfish genetics and inclusive fitness across is to have Gintis in a room for a day with Dawkins, Franks, Coyne etc., explaining why it is wrong. But as always, one has to have a certain level of education, intelligence, rationality and honesty for this to work, and if one is just a little bit short in several categories, it will not succeed. The same of course is true for much of human understanding, and so the vast majority will never get anything that is at all subtle. As with the Nowak, Wilson, Tarnita paper, I am sure that Dawkins, Franks and others would have been willing to go over this chapter and explain where it goes astray..

The major problem is that people just do not grasp the concept of natural selection by inclusive fitness, nor of subconscious motivations, and that many have 'religious' motivations for rejecting them. This includes not just the general public and non-science academics, but a large percentage of biologists and behavioral scientists. I recently came across a lovely review by Dawkins of a discussion of the selfish gene idea by top level professional biologists, in which he had to go over their work line by line to explain that they just did not grasp how it all works. But only a small number of people like him could do this, and the sea of confusion is vast, and so these delusions about human nature that destroy this book, and are destroying America and the world will, as the Queen said to Alice in a slightly different context, go on until they come to the end and then stop.

Altruism, Jesus and the End of the World—how the Templeton Foundation bought a Harvard Professorship and attacked Evolution, Rationality and Civilization. A review of E.O. Wilson 'The Social Conquest of Earth' (2012) and Nowak and Highfield 'SuperCooperators'(2012)(review revised 2019)

Michael Starks

ABSTRACT

Famous ant-man E.O. Wilson has always been one of my heroes --not only an outstanding biologist, but one of the tiny and vanishing minority of intellectuals who at least dares to hint at the truth about our nature that others fail to grasp, or insofar as they do grasp, studiously avoid for political expedience. Sadly, he is ending his long career in a most sordid fashion as a party to an ignorant and arrogant attack on science motivated at least in part by the religious fervor of his Harvard colleagues. It shows the vile consequences when universities accept money from religious groups, science journals are so awed by big names that they avoid proper peer review, and when egos are permitted to get out of control. It takes us into the nature of evolution, the basics of scientific methodology, how math relates to science, what constitutes a theory, and even what attitudes to religion and generosity are appropriate as we inexorably approach the collapse of industrial civilization.

Those wishing a comprehensive up to date framework for human behavior from the modern two systems view may consult my books Talking Monkeys 3rd ed (2019), The Logical Structure of Philosophy, Psychology, Mind and Language in Ludwig Wittgenstein and John Searle 2nd ed (2019), Suicide by Democracy 4th ed (2019), The Logical Structure of Human Behavior (2019), The Logical Structure of Consciousness (2019, Understanding the Connections between Science, Philosophy, Psychology, Religion, Politics, and Economics (2019), and Suicidal Utopian Delusions in the 21st Century 5th ed (2019).

Famous ant-man E.O. Wilson has always been one of my heroes--not only an outstanding biologist, but one of the tiny and vanishing minority of intellectuals who at least dares to hint at the truth about our nature that others fail to grasp, or insofar as they do grasp, studiously avoid for of political expedience. Sadly, he is ending his long career in a most sordid fashion as a party to an ignorant and arrogant attack on science motivated at least in part by the religious fervor of his Harvard colleagues. It shows the vile consequences when universities accept money from religious groups, science journals are so awed by big names that they avoid proper peer review, and when egos are permitted to get out of control. It takes us into the nature of evolution, the basics of scientific methodology, how math relates to science, what constitutes a theory, and even what attitudes to religion and generosity are appropriate as we inexorably approach the collapse of industrial civilization.

I found sections in 'Conquest' with the usual incisive commentary (though nothing really new or interesting if you have read his other works and are up on biology in general) in the often-stilted prose that is his hallmark, but was quite surprised that the core of the book is his rejection of inclusive fitness (which has been a mainstay of evolutionary biology for over 50 years) in favor of group selection. One assumes that coming from him and with the articles he refers to published by himself and Harvard mathematics colleague Nowak in major peer reviewed journals like Nature, it must be a substantial advance, in spite of the fact that I knew group selection was nearly universally rejected as having any major role in evolution.

I have read numerous reviews on the net and many have good comments but the one I most wanted to see was that by renowned science writer and evolutionary biologist Richard Dawkins. Unlike most by professionals, which are in journals only available to those with access to a university, it is readily available on the net, though apparently, he decided not to publish it in a journal as it is suitably scathing.

Sadly, one finds a devastating rejection of the book and the most acerbic commentary on a scientific colleague I have ever seen from Dawkins--exceeding anything in his many exchanges with late and unlamented demagogue and pseudoscientist Stephan Jay Gould. Although Gould was infamous for his personal attacks on his Harvard colleague Wilson, Dawkins notes that much of 'Conquest' reminds one uncomfortably of Gould's frequent lapses into "bland, unfocussed ecumenicalism". The same is more or less true of all Wilson's popular writing including his most recent book 'The Meaning of Human Existence'—another shameless self-promotion of his discredited ideas on Inclusive Fitness (IF).

Dawkins points out that the notorious 2010 paper by Nowak, Tarnita and Wilson in Nature was almost universally rejected by over 140 biologists who signed a letter and that there is not one word about this in Wilson's book. Nor have they corrected this in the subsequent 4 years of articles, lectures and several books. There is no choice but to agree with Dawkin's trenchant comment "For Wilson not to acknowledge that he speaks for himself against the great majority of his professional colleagues is--it pains me to say this of a lifelong hero --an act of wanton arrogance." In view of Nowak's subsequent behavior one must include him as well. I feel like one of the stunned people one sees on TV being interviewed after the nice man next door, who has been babysitting everyone's children for 30 years, is exposed as a serial killer.

Dawkins also points out (as he and others have done for many years) that inclusive fitness is entailed by (i.e., logically follows from) neo- Darwinism and cannot be rejected without rejecting evolution itself. Wilson again reminds us of Gould, who denounced creationists from one side of his mouth while giving them comfort by spewing endless ultraliberal Marxist-tinged gibberish about spandrels, punctuated equilibrium and evolutionary psychology from the other. The vagueness and mathematical opacity (to most of us) of the mathematics of group or multilevel selection is just what the soft-minded want to enable them to escape rational thinking in their endless antiscientific rants, and (in academia) postmodernist word salads.

Worse yet, Wilson's 'Conquest' is a poorly thought out and sloppily written mess full of nonsequiturs, vague ramblings, confusions and incoherence. A good review that details some of these is that by graduate student Gerry Carter which you can find on the net. Wilson is also out of touch with our current understanding of evolutionary psychology (EP) (see e.g., the last 300 pages of Pinker's 'The Better Angels of our Nature'). If you want a serious book length account of social evolution and some relevant EP from an expert see 'Principles of Social Evolution' by Andrew F.G. Bourke, or a not quite so serious and admittedly flawed and rambling account but a must read nevertheless by Robert Trivers—'The Folly of Fools: The Logic of Deceit and Self-Deception in Human Life' and older but still current and penetrating works such as 'The Evolution of Cooperation': Revised Edition by Robert Axelrod and 'The Biology of Moral Systems' by Richard Alexander.

After reading this book and its reviews, I dug into some of the scientific articles which responded to Nowak and Wilson and to Van Veelen's critiques of the Price equation upon which they heavily relied. The reviews noted that it has always been clear that the math of group or multilevel selection reduces to that of inclusive fitness (kin selection) and that it is not logically possible to select for behavior that does not benefit the genes that are unique to the actor and its immediate relatives. To put it bluntly, 'altruistic' behavior is always selfish in the end in the sense that it increases survival of the genes in the altruist. This to me is obvious from daily life and any scientists who claim otherwise have clearly lost their way. Yes, it does happen in the weirdness of modern life (i.e., so unlike the stone age society in which we evolved) that one sometimes sees a person give their life to protect a nonrelated person, but clearly, they will not do it again and (provided its done before they replicate) any tendency to do it will not be inherited either. Even if they have already replicated, they will on average leave behind fewer descendants than if they held back. This guarantees that any genetic tendency for 'true altruism'- i.e., behavior that decreases one's genes in the population-- will be selected against and no more than this very basic logic is needed to grasp evolution by natural selection, kin selection and inclusive fitness—all the mathematical niceties serving only to quantitate things and to clarify strange living arrangements in some of our relatives (e.g., ants, termites and mole rats).

The major focus of the group selectionist's ('groupies') attack was the famous Extended Price Equation that has been used to model inclusive fitness, published by Price about 40 years ago. The best papers debunking these attacks that I have found are those of Frank and Bourke and I will start with a few quotes from Frank 'Natural selection. IV. The Price equation' J. EVOL. BIOL. 25 (2012) 1002–1019.

"The critics confuse the distinct roles of general abstract theory and concrete dynamical models for particular cases. The enduring power of the Price equation arises from the discovery of essential invariances in natural selection. For example, kin selection theory expresses biological problems in terms of relatedness coefficients. Relatedness measures the association between social partners. The proper measure of relatedness identifies distinct biological scenarios with the same (invariant) evolutionary outcome. Invariance relations provide the deepest insights of scientific thought...Essentially, all modern discussions of multilevel selection and group selection derive from Price (1972a), as developed by Hamilton (1975). Price and Hamilton noted that the Price equation can be expanded recursively to represent nested levels of analysis, for example individuals living in groups... All modern conceptual insights about group selection derive from Price's recursive expansion of his abstract expression of selection... A criticism of these Price equation applications is a criticism of the central approach of evolutionary quantitative genetics. Such criticisms may be valid for certain applications, but they must be evaluated in the broader context of quantitative genetics theory...[and in a quote from Price ... 'Gene frequency change is the basic event in biological evolution. The following equation...which gives frequency change under selection from one generation to the next for a single gene or for any linear function of any number of genes at any number of loci, holds for any sort of dominance or epistasis, for sexual or asexual reproduction, for random or nonrandom mating, for diploid, haploid or polyploid species, and even for imaginary species with more than two sexes'...]... Path (contextual) analysis follows as a natural extension of the Price equation, in which one makes specific models of fitness expressed by regression. It does not make sense to discuss the Price equation and path analysis as alternatives... Critiques of the Price equation rarely distinguish the costs and benefits of particular assumptions in relation to particular goals. I use van Veelen's recent series of papers as a proxy for those critiques. That series repeats some of the common misunderstandings and adds some new ones.

Nowak recently repeated van Veelen's critique as the basis for his commentary on the Price equation (van Veelen, 2005; Nowak et al., 2010; van Veelen et al., 2010; Nowak& Highfield, 2011; van Veelen, 2011; van Veelen et al., 2012... This quote from van Veelen et al. (2012) demonstrates an interesting approach to scholarship. They first cite Frank as stating that dynamic insufficiency is a drawback of the Price equation. They then disagree with that point of view and present as their own interpretation an argument that is nearly identical in concept and phrasing to my own statement in the very paper that they cited as the foundation for their disagreement... The recursive form of the full Price equation provides the foundation for all modern studies of group selection and multilevel analysis. The Price equation helped in discovering those various connections, although there are many other ways in which to derive the same relations... Kin selection theory derives much of its power by identifying an invariant informational quantity sufficient to unify a wide variety of seemingly disparate processes (Frank, 1998, Chapter 6). The interpretation of kin selection as an informational invariance has not been fully developed and remains an open problem. Invariances provide the foundation of scientific understanding: 'It is only slightly overstating the case to say that physics is the study of symmetry' (Anderson, 1972). Invariance and symmetry mean the same thing (Weyl, 1983). Feynman (1967) emphasized that invariance is The Character of Physical Law. The commonly observed patterns of probability can be unified by the study of invariance and its association with measurement (Frank & Smith, 2010, 2011). There has been little effort in biology to pursue similar understanding of invariance and measurement (Frank, 2011; Houle et al.,2011)."

I hope it is becoming clear why I chose the title I did for this article. To attack the Price equation and inclusive fitness is to attack not only quantitative genetics and evolution by natural selection, but the universally used concepts of covariance, invariance and symmetry, which are basic to science and to rationality. Furthermore, the clearly voiced religious motivation of Nowak invites us to consider to what extent such Christian virtues as true (permanently genetically self-diminishing) altruism and the brotherhood of man (woman, child, dog etc.) can be part of a rational program for survival in the near future. My take is that true altruism is a luxury for those who don't mind being evolutionary dead ends and that even in it's 'make believe' inclusive fitness version, one will be hard pressed to find it when the wolf is at the door (i.e., the likely universal scenario for the 11 billion in the next century).

There is much more in this gem, which goes into exquisite logical and mathematical detail (and likewise his many other papers-you can get all 7 in this series in one pdf) but this will give the flavor. Another amusing episode concerns tautology in math. Frank again: 'Nowak & Highfield (2011) and van Veelen et al. (2012) believe their arguments demonstrate that the Price equation is true in the same trivial sense, and they call that trivial type of truth a mathematical tautology. Interestingly, magazines, online articles and the scientific literature have for several years been using the phrase mathematical tautology for the Price equation, although Nowak & Highfield (2011) and van Veelen et al. (2012) do not provide citations to previous literature. As far as I know, the first description of the Price equation as a mathematical tautology was in the study of Frank (1995).'

Unlike Frank, Lamm and others, the 'groupies' have not shown any understanding of the philosophy of science (the descriptive psychology of higher order thought, as I like to call it) in these recent books and articles, nor in any of Wilson's numerous popular books and articles over the last half century, so I would not expect them to have studied Wittgenstein (the most penetrating philosopher of mathematics) who famously remarked that in math 'everything is syntax, nothing is semantics'. Wittgenstein exposes a nearly universal misunderstanding of the role of math in science. All math (and logic) is a tautology that has no meaning or use until it is connected to our life with words. Every equation is a tautology until numbers and words and the system of conventions we call evolutionary psychology are employed. Amazingly Lamm in his recent excellent article 'A Gentle Introduction to The Price Equation' (2011) notes this:

"The Price equation deals with any selection process. Indeed, we can define selection using it. It says nothing in particular about biological or genetic evolution, and is not tied to any particular biological scenario. This gives it immense power, but also means that it is quite possible to apply it incorrectly to the real world. This leads us to the second and final observation. The Price equation is analytic [true by definition or tautologous]. It is not a synthetic proposition [an empirical issue as to its truth or falsity]. We derived it based on straightforward definitions, and universal mathematical principles. The equation simply provides a useful way of interpreting the meaning of the straightforward definitions we started from. This however is not the case once you put the equation into words, thereby interpreting the mathematical relationships. If you merely say: _I define 'selection' to be the covariance blah blah blah, you might be safe. If you say: _the covariance blah blah blah is selection, you are making a claim with empirical content. More fundamentally, the belief that the rules of probability theory and statistics, or any other mathematical manipulation, describe the actual world is synthetic."

In this regard, also recommended is Helantera and Uller's 'The Price Equation and Extended Inheritance' Philos Theor Biol (2010) 2: e101.

"Here we use the Price Equation as a starting point for a discussion of the differences between four recently proposed categories of inheritance systems; genetic, epigenetic, behavioral and symbolic. Specifically, we address how the components of the Price Equation encompass different non-genetic systems of inheritance in an attempt to clarify how the different systems are conceptually related. We conclude that the four classes of inheritance systems do not form distinct clusters with respect to their effect on the rate and direction of phenotypic change from one generation to the next in the absence or presence of selection. Instead, our analyses suggest that different inheritance systems can share features that are conceptually very similar, but that their implications for adaptive evolution nevertheless differ substantially as a result of differences in their ability to couple selection and inheritance."

So, it should be clear that there is no such thing as sidestepping the Price equation and that like any equation, it has limitless applications if one only connects it to the world with suitable words.

As Andy Gardner put it in his article on Price (Current Biology 18#5 R198) (Also see his 'Adaptation and Inclusive Fitness' Current Biology 23, R577–R584, July 8, 2013)

"Such ideas were rather confused until Price, and later Hamilton, showed that the Price equation can be expanded to encompass multiple levels of selection acting simultaneously (Box 2). This allows selection at the various levels to be explicitly defined and separated, and provides the formal basis of group selection theory. Importantly, it allows the quantification of these separate forces and yields precise predictions for when group-beneficial behavior will be favoured. It turns out that these predictions are always consistent with Hamilton's rule, $rb - c > 0$.

Furthermore, because kin selection and group selection theory are both based upon the same Price equation, it is easy to show that the two approaches are mathematically exactly equivalent, and are simply alternative ways of carving up the total selection operating upon the social character. Irrespective of the approach taken, individual organisms are expected to maximize their inclusive fitness — though this result follows more easily from a kin selection analysis, as it makes the key element of relatedness more explicit."

Consequently, to have the 'groupies' attacking the Price equation is bizarre. And here is Bourke's recent summary of inclusive fitness vs 'groupism': (haplodiploid and eusocial refer to the social insects which provide some of the best tests).

"Recent critiques have questioned the validity of the leading theory for explaining social evolution and eusociality, namely inclusive fitness (kin selection) theory. I review recent and past literature to argue that these critiques do not succeed. Inclusive fitness theory has added fundamental insights to natural selection theory. These are the realization that selection on a gene for social behaviour depends on its effects on co-bearers, the explanation of social behaviours as unalike as altruism and selfishness using the same underlying parameters, and the explanation of within-group conflict in terms of non-coinciding inclusive fitness optima. A proposed alternative theory for eusocial evolution assumes mistakenly that workers' interests are subordinate to the queen's, contains no new elements and fails to make novel predictions. The haplodiploidy hypothesis has yet to be rigorously tested and positive relatedness within diploid eusocial societies supports inclusive fitness theory. The theory has made unique, falsifiable predictions that have been confirmed, and its evidence base is extensive and robust. Hence, inclusive fitness theory deserves to keep its position as the leading theory for social evolution."

However inclusive fitness (especially via the Extended Price Equation) explains much more than ant society, it explains how multicellular organisms came into being.

"The third insight of inclusive fitness theory is the demonstration that conflict between members of a society is potentially present if they are unequally related to group offspring, since differential relatedness leads to unequal inclusive fitness optima. From this has sprung an understanding of an immense range of kin-selected conflicts, including conflicts within families and eusocial societies and intragenomic conflicts that follow the same underlying logic. The corollary of this insight is that societies are stable to the extent that the inclusive fitness optima of their members coincide. This in turn provides the rationale for the entire 'major transitions' view of evolution, whereby the origin of novel types of group in the history of life (e.g. genomes within cells, multicellular organisms and eusocial societies) can be explained as the result of their previously independent constituent units achieving a coincidence of inclusive fitness optima through grouping. From this standpoint, a multicellular organism is a eusocial society of cells in which the members of the society happen to be physically stuck together; the more fundamental glue, however, is the clonal relatedness that (barring mutations) gives each somatic cell within the organism a common interest in promoting the production of gametes…Nowak et al. argued that their perspective assumes a 'gene-centred approach' that 'makes inclusive fitness theory unnecessary'. This is puzzling, because entirely lacking from their perspective is the idea, which underpins each of inclusive fitness theory's insights, of the gene as a self-promoting strategist whose evolutionary interests are conditional on the kin class in which it resides…In their model of the evolution of eusociality, Nowak et al. deduced that the problem of altruism is illusory. They wrote that 'There is no paradoxical altruism that needs to be explained' because they assumed that potential workers (daughters of a colony-founding female or queen) are 'not independent agents' but rather can be seen 'as "robots" that are built by the queen' or the 'extrasomatic projection of [the queen's] personal genome'. If this claim were correct, then only the queen's interests would need to be addressed and one could conclude that worker altruism is more apparent than real. But it is incorrect, for two reasons. One is that, as has repeatedly been argued in response to previous 'parental manipulation' theories of the origin of eusociality, the inclusive fitness interests of workers and the mother queen do not coincide, because the two parties are differentially related to group offspring. The second is that worker behaviours such as eating of the queen's eggs, egg-laying in response to perceived declines in queen fecundity, sex-ratio manipulation by destruction of the queen's offspring and lethal aggression towards the queen all demonstrate that workers can act in their own interests and against those of the queen. In the light of this proven lack of worker passivity, workers' reproductive self-sacrifice is paradoxical at first sight and this is the genuine problem of altruism that inclusive fitness theory has solved. (c) Alternative theory of eusocial evolution Nowak et al. [38] presented an 'alternative theory of eusocial evolution' (as alluded to in §2b), backed up by a 'mathematical model for the origin of eusociality'. However, these do not represent true alternative theories, either alone or in combination, because they do not make any points or predictions that have not been made within inclusive fitness theory"

Speaking of various steps in a scheme suggested by Nowak et al, Bourke says:

"These steps constitute a reasonable scenario for the origin and elaboration of insect eusociality, but neither the sequence of steps nor the individual elements differ substantially from those that have been proposed to occur within the inclusive fitness framework...The alternative theory of eusocial evolution of Nowak et al. also exhibits two important weaknesses. To begin with, by allowing groups to form in multiple ways in step (i) (e.g. subsocially through parent–offspring associations but also by any other means, including 'randomly by mutual local attraction'), their scenario ignores two critical points that are inconsistent with it but consistent with inclusive fitness theory. First, the evidence is that, in almost all eusocial lineages, eusociality has originated in social groups that were ancestrally subsocial and therefore characterized by high within-group relatedness. Second, the evidence is that the origin of obligate or complex eusociality, defined as involving adult workers irreversibly committed to a worker phenotype, is associated with ancestral lifetime parental monogamy and hence, again, with predictably high within-group relatedness...In sum, Nowak et al. make a case for considering the effect of the population-dynamic context in which eusocial evolution occurs. But their alternative theory and its associated model add no fundamentally new elements on top of those identified within the inclusive fitness framework and, relative to this framework, exhibit substantial shortcomings...More fundamentally, as has long been recognized and repeatedly stressed , the haplodiploidy hypothesis is not an essential component of inclusive fitness theory, since Hamilton's rule for altruism can hold without the relatedness asymmetries caused by haplodiploidy being present. Highlighting the status of the haplodiploidy hypothesis to criticize inclusive fitness theory therefore misses the target. It also overlooks the fact that all diploid eusocial societies identified since the haplodiploidy hypothesis was proposed have turned out to be either clonal or family groups and so, as predicted by inclusive fitness theory, to exhibit positive relatedness. This is true of ambrosia beetle, social aphids, polyembryonic wasps, social shrimps and mole-rats. It is even true of a newly discovered eusocial flatworm. In short, the diploid eusocial societies, far from weakening inclusive fitness theory, serve to strengthen it...More broadly, the theory uniquely predicts the absence of altruism (involving lifetime costs to direct fitness) between non-relatives, and indeed no such cases have been found except in systems clearly derived from ancestral societies of relatives. Finally, inclusive fitness theory is unique in the range of social phenomena that it has successfully elucidated, including phenomena as superficially dissimilar as the

origin of multicellularity and the origin of eusociality, or intragenomic conflicts and conflicts within eusocial societies. Overall, no other theory comes close to matching inclusive fitness theory's record of successful explanation and prediction across such a range of phenomena within the field of social evolution. The challenge to any approach purporting to replace inclusive fitness theory is to explain the same phenomena without using the insights or concepts of the theory...Recent critiques of inclusive fitness theory have proved ineffective on multiple fronts. They do not demonstrate fatal or unrecognized difficulties with inclusive fitness theory. They do not provide a distinct replacement theory or offer a similarly unifying approach. They do not explain previously unexplained data or show that explanations from inclusive fitness theory are invalid. And they do not make new and unique predictions. The latest and most comprehensive critique of inclusive fitness theory, though broad-ranging in the scope of its criticism, suffers from the same faults. Certainly, relatedness does not explain all variation in social traits. In addition, the long-standing message from inclusive fitness theory is that particular combinations of non-genetic (e.g. ecological) and genetic factors are required for the origin of eusociality. Nonetheless, relatedness retains a unique status in the analysis of eusocial evolution because no amount of ecological benefit can bring about altruism if relatedness is zero."
Andrew F. G. Bourke 'The validity and value of inclusive fitness theory' Proc. R. Soc. B 2011 278, doi: 10.1098/rspb.2011.1465 14 September (2011)

One thing rarely mentioned by the groupies is the fact that, even were 'group selection' possible, selfishness is at least as likely (probably far more likely in most contexts) to be group selected for as altruism. Just try to find examples of true altruism in nature –the fact that we can't (which we know is not possible if we understand evolution) tells us that its apparent presence in humans is an artefact of modern life, concealing the facts, and that it can no more be selected for than the tendency to suicide (which in fact it is). One might also benefit from considering a phenomenon never (in my experience) mentioned by groupies-- cancer. No group has as much in common as the (originally) genetically identical cells in our own bodies-a 100 trillion cell clone-- but we all born with thousands and perhaps millions of cells that have already taken the first step on the path to cancer and generate millions to billions of cancer cells in our life. If we did not die of other things first, we (and perhaps all multicellular organisms) would all die of cancer. Only a massive and hugely complex mechanism built into our genome that represses or derepresses trillions of genes in trillions of cells, and kills and creates billions of cells a second, keeps the majority of us alive long enough to reproduce. One might take this to imply that a just, democratic and enduring society for any kind of entity on any planet in any universe is only a dream, and that no being or power could make it otherwise. It is not only 'the laws' of physics that are universal and inescapable, or perhaps we should say that inclusive fitness is a law of physics.

In a bizarre twist, it was apparently such thoughts that drove Price (creator of the Price equation and a devout Christian) to suicide. Regarding the notion of 'theory', it is a classic Wittgensteinian language game—a group of uses loosely linked but having critical differences.

When it was first proposed, evolution by natural selection was indeed highly theoretical, but as time passed it became inextricably linked to so many observations and experiments that its basic ideas were no longer any more theoretical than that vitamins play critical roles in human nutrition. For the 'Theory of Deity' however it is not clear what would count as a definitive test. Perhaps the same is true of String Theory.

Many besides groupies note the pleasant nature of much human interaction and see a rosy future ahead-- but they are blind. It is crushingly obvious that the pleasantry is a transient phase due to abundant resources produced by the merciless rape of the planet, and as they are exhausted in the next two centuries or so, there will be misery and savagery worldwide as the (likely) permanent condition. Not just movie stars, politicians and the religious are oblivious to this, but even very bright academics who should know better. In his recent book 'The Better Angels of Our Nature' one of my most admired scholars Steven Pinker spends half the book showing how we have gotten more and more civilized, but he seems never to mention the obvious reasons why--the temporary abundance of resources coupled with massive police and military presence facilitated by surveillance and communication technologies. As industrial civilization collapses, it is inevitable that the Worst Devils of Our Nature will reappear. One sees it in the current chaos in the Middle East, Latin America and Africa, and even the world wars were Sunday picnics compared to what's coming. Perhaps half of the 12 billion then alive will die of starvation, disease and violence, and it could be many more. See my 'Suicide by Democracy' for a brief summary of doomsday.

Another unpleasant fact about altruism, generosity and helping, virtually never mentioned, is that if you take a global long-term view, in an overcrowded world with vanishing resources, helping one person hurts everyone else in some small way. Each meal, each pair of shoes create pollution and erosion and use up resources, and when you add 7.8 billion of them together (soon to be 11) it is clear that one person's gain is everyone else's loss. Every dollar earned or spent damages the world and if countries cared about the future they would reduce their GDP (gross destructive product) every year. Even were groupism true this would not change.

The facts that Wilson, Nowak et al have, for four years, persisted in publishing and making extravagant claims for grossly inadequate work is not the worst of this scandal. It turns out that Nowak's professorship at Harvard was purchased by the Templeton Foundation—well known for its pervasive sponsorship of lectures, conferences and publications attempting to reconcile religion and science. Nowak is a devout Catholic and it appears that a large gift to Harvard was contingent on Nowak's appointment. This made him Wilson's colleague and the rest is history.

However, Wilson was only too willing as he had long shown a failure to grasp Evolutionary theory—e.g., regarding kin selection as a division of group selection rather than the other way around. I noticed years ago that he co-published with David Wilson, a longtime supporter of group selection, and had written other papers demonstrating his lack of understanding. Any of the groupies could have gone to the experts to learn the error of their ways (or just read their papers). The grand old men of kin selection such as Hamilton, Williams and Trivers, and younger bloods like Frank, Bourke and many others, would have been happy to teach them. But Nowak has received something like $14 million in Templeton grants in a few years (for mathematics!) and who wants to give that up? He is quite outspoken in his intent to prove that the gentleness and kindness of Jesus is built into us and all the universe. Jesus is conveniently absent, but one can guess from the qualities of other enlightened ones and the history of the church that the real story of early Christianity would come as a shock. Recall that the bible was expurgated of anything that did not meet the party line (e.g., Gnosticism -check out the Nag-Hammadi manuscripts). And in any case, who would record the harsh realities of daily life?

Almost certainly, the Nowak, Tarnita, Wilson paper would never have been published (at least not by Nature) if it had been presented by two average biologists, but coming from two famous Harvard professors it clearly did not get the peer review that it should have.

Regarding Nowak and Highland's book 'SuperCooperators' I will let Dawkins do the honors:

I have read the book by Nowak and Highfield. Parts of it are quite good, but the quality abruptly, and embarrassingly, plummets in the chapter on kin selection, possibly under the influence of E O Wilson (who has been consistently

misunderstanding kin selection ever since Sociobiology, mistakenly regarding it as a subset of group selection). Nowak misses the whole point of kin selection theory, which is that it is not something additional, not something over and-above 'classical individual selection' theory. Kin selection is not something EXTRA, not something to be resorted to only if 'classical individual selection' theory fails. Rather, it is an inevitable consequence of neo-Darwinism, which follows from it deductively. To talk about Darwinian selection MINUS kin selection is like talking about Euclidean geometry minus Pythagoras' theorem. It is just that this logical consequence of neo-Darwinism was historically overlooked, which gave people a false impression that it was something additional and extra. Nowak's otherwise good book is tragically marred by this elementary blunder. As a mathematician, he really should have known better. It seems doubtful that he has ever read Hamilton's classic papers on inclusive fitness, or he couldn't have misunderstood the idea so comprehensively. The chapter on kin selection will discredit the book and stop it being taken seriously by those qualified to judge it, which is a pity.
http://whyevolutionistrue.wordpress.com/2011/03/16/new-book-shows-that-humans-are-genetically-nice-ergo-jesus/

A scathing review of 'SuperCooperators' also appeared from eminent game theorist/economist/political scientist (and Harvard alumnus) Herbert Gintis (who recounts the Templeton scandal therein), which is quite surprising considering his own love affair with group selection— see the review of his book with Bowles by Price www.epjournal.net – 2012. 10(1): 45-49 and my review of his most recent volume 'Individuality and Entanglement'(2017).

Regarding Wilson's subsequent books, 'The Meaning of Human Existence' is bland and likewise confused and dishonest, repeating several times the groupies party line four years after its thorough debunking, and 'A Window on Eternity'- is a meagre travel journal about the establishing of a national park in Mozambique. He carefully avoids mentioning that Africa will add 3 billion in the near future (the official UN projection), eliminating all of nature along with peace, beauty, decency, sanity and hope.

In the end, it is clear that this whole sad affair will be only the tiniest bump on the road and, like all things which exercise our attention now, will soon be forgotten as the horrors of unrestrained motherhood and the subjugation of the world by the Seven Sociopaths who rule China will bring society crashing down. But one can be sure that even when global warming has put Harvard beneath the sea and starvation, disease and violence are the daily norm, there will be those who insist that it is not due to human activities (the opinion of half the American public currently) and that overpopulation is not a problem (the view of 40%), there will be billions praying to their chosen deity for a rain of Big Macs from the sky, and that (assuming the enterprise of science has not collapsed, which is assuming a lot) someone somewhere will be writing a paper embracing group selection.

A Review of The Murderer Next Door by David Buss (2005)(review revised 2019)

Michael Starks

ABSTRACT

Though this volume is a bit dated, there are few recent popular books dealing specifically with the psychology of murder and it's a quick overview available for a few dollars, so still well worth the effort. It makes no attempt to be comprehensive and is somewhat superficial in places, with the reader expected to fill in the blanks from his many other books and the vast literature on violence. For an update see e.g., Buss, The Handbook of Evolutionary Psychology 2nd ed. V1 (2016) p 265, 266, 270–282, 388–389, 545–546, 547, 566 and Buss, Evolutionary Psychology 5th ed. (2015) p 26, 96–97,223, 293-4, 300, 309–312, 410 and Shackelford and Hansen, The Evolution of Violence (2014). He has been among the top evolutionary psychologists for several decades and covers a wide range of behavior in his works, but here he concentrates almost entirely on the psychological mechanisms that cause individual people to murder and their possible evolutionary function in the EEA (Environment of Evolutionary Adaptation—i.e., the plains of Africa during the last million years or so).

Buss starts by noting that as with other behaviors, 'alternative' explanations such as psychopathology, jealousy, social environment, group pressures, drugs and alcohol etc. do not really explain, since the question still remains as to why these produce homicidal impulses, i.e., they are the proximate causes and not the ultimate evolutionary (genetic) ones. As always, it inevitably boils down to inclusive fitness (kin selection), and so to the struggle for access to mates and resources, which is the ultimate explanation for all behavior in all organisms. Sociological data (and common sense) make it clear that younger poorer males are the most likely to kill. He presents his own and others homicide data from industrialized nations, and tribal cultures, conspecific killing in animals, archeology, FBI data and his own research into normal people's homicidal fantasies. Much archeological evidence continues to accumulate of murders, including that of whole groups, or of groups minus young females, in prehistoric times.

After surveying Buss's comments, I present a very brief summary of intentional psychology (the logical structure of rationality), which is covered extensively in my many other articles and books.

Those with a lot of time who want a detailed history of homicidal violence from an evolutionary perspective may consult Steven Pinker's 'The Better Angels of Our Nature Why Violence Has Declined'(2012), and my review of it, easily available on the net and in two of my recent books. Briefly, Pinker notes that murder has decreased steadily and dramatically by a factor of about 30 since our days as foragers. So, even though guns now make it extremely easy for anyone to kill, homicide is much less common. Pinker thinks this is due to various social mechanisms that bring out our 'better angels', but I think it's due mainly to the temporary abundance of resources from the merciless rape of our planet, coupled with increased police presence, with communication and surveillance and legal systems that make it far more likely to be punished. This becomes clear every time there is even a brief and local absence of the police.

Those wishing a comprehensive up to date framework for human behavior from the modern two systems view may consult my books Talking Monkeys 3rd ed (2019), The Logical Structure of Philosophy, Psychology, Mind and Language in Ludwig Wittgenstein and John Searle 2nd ed (2019), Suicide by Democracy 4th ed (2019), The Logical Structure of Human Behavior (2019), The Logical Structure of Consciousness (2019, Understanding the Connections between Science, Philosophy, Psychology, Religion, Politics, and Economics (2019), and Suicidal Utopian Delusions in the 21st Century 5th ed (2019).

Buss starts by noting that as with other behaviors, 'alternative' explanations such as psychopathology, jealousy, social environment, group pressures, drugs and alcohol etc. do not really explain, since the question still remains as to why these produce homicidal impulses, i.e., they are the proximate causes and not the ultimate evolutionary (genetic) ones. As always, it inevitably boils down to inclusive fitness (kin selection), and so to the struggle for access to mates and resources, which is the ultimate explanation for all behavior in all organisms. Sociological data (and common sense) make it clear that younger poorer males are the most likely to kill. He presents his own and others homicide data from industrialized nations, and tribal cultures, conspecific killing in animals, archeology, FBI data and his own research into normal people's homicidal fantasies. Much archeological evidence continues to accumulate of murders, including that of whole groups, or of groups minus young females, in prehistoric times.

On p 12 he notes that the war between each individual and the world over resources begins at conception, when it begins growing by robbing its mother of food and stressing her body, and when her system fights back with frequently fatal consequences for the conceptus. He does not tell us that estimates of spontaneous abortion are in the range of up to about 30% of all conceptions, so that as many as 80 million a year die, most so early that the mother does not even know she is pregnant, and perhaps her period is a bit late. This is part of nature's eugenics which we have not succeeded in defeating, though the overall dysgenic effect of civilization continues and each day the approx. 300,000 who are born are on average just slightly less mentally a physically fit than the approx. 100,000 who die, with a net increase in world population of ca. 200,000 and an ever larger 'unfit' population to destroy the earth (while being partly or wholly supported by their 'fit' neighbors).

On p13 he says that we don't know for sure that OJ Simpson was guilty but I would say that regardless of the trial we do know he was, as it's the only reasonable interpretation of the facts of the case, which include his bizarre behavior. Also, in the subsequent civil trial, where his multimillion dollar defense attorneys were not present to subvert justice, he was quickly convicted, which led to the attachment of his assets, which led to his armed robbery conviction and imprisonment.

He notes on p20 that there were about 100 million known murders worldwide in the last 100 years, with maybe as many as 300 million if all the unreported were included. I don't think he counts the 40 million by the Chinese Communist Party (which does not count the 60 million who starved to death under Mao), nor the ten of millions by Stalin. It is also to be kept in mind that America's murder rate is decreased by about 75% due to the world class medical system which saves most victims of attempts. I will add that Mexico has about 5X the murder rate of the USA and Honduras about 20X, and your descendants can certainly look forward to our rate moving in that direction due to America's fatal embrace of Diversity, Democracy and Equality. Ann Coulter in 'Adios America' (2015) notes that Hispanics have committed about 23,000 murders here in the last few decades. For now, nothing will be done, and crime here will reach the levels in Mexico as the border continues to dissolve and environmental collapse and approaching bankruptcy dissolve the economy. Inside Mexico in 2014 alone, 100 U.S. citizens were known to have been murdered and more than 130 kidnapped and others just disappeared, and if you add other foreigners and Mexicans it runs into the thousands. See my 'Suicide by Democracy' 4th ed (2019) for further details.

Even a tiny lightly traveled country like Honduras manages some 10 murders and 2 kidnappings a year of US citizens. And these are the best of times—it is getting steadily worse as unrestrained motherhood and resource depletion bring collapse ever closer. In addition to continued increases in crime of all kinds we will see the percentage of crimes solved drop to the extremely low levels of the third world. More resources are devoted to the solution of murders than any other crime and about 65% are solved in the USA, but in Mexico less than 2% are solved and as you get further from Mexico City the rate drops to near zero. Also note that the rate here used to be about 80%, but it has dropped in parallel with the increase in the Diverse. Also 65% is the average but if you could get statistics I am sure it would rise with the percent of Euro's in a city and drop as the percent of Diverse increases. In Detroit (83% black) only 30% are solved. If you keep track of who robs, rapes and murders, it's obvious that black lives matter lots more to Euros (those of European descent) than they do to other blacks. These are my observations.

Throughout history women have been at a major disadvantage when it came to murdering, but with the ready availability of guns we would expect this to change, but on p22 we find that about 87% of USA murderers are men and for same sex killing this rises to 95% and is about the same worldwide. Clearly something in the male psyche encourages violence as a route to fitness that is largely absent in women. Also relevant is that murders by acquaintances are more common than those by strangers.

On p37 he notes that with high likelihood of conviction (and I would say the higher likelihood the intended victim or others will be armed), murder is now a more costly strategy than formerly, but I think this depends entirely on who you are. In a largely Euro USA city, or among middle and upper class people, over 95% of murders might be solved, but in lower class areas maybe 20% might be, and for gang dominated areas even less than that. And in 3rd world countries the chances of justice are even lower, especially when committed by gang members, so it is a highly viable strategy, especially if planned ahead of time.

Next, he deals with violence and murder as a part of mating strategies, which they have clearly been throughout our evolution, and remain so especially among the lower classes and in third world countries. He notes the frequent murder of wives or lovers by men during or after breakups. He comments in passing on mate selection and infidelity, but there is minimal discussion as these topics are treated in great detail in his other writings and edited volumes. It is now well known that women tend to have affairs with sexy men that they would not select as a permanent partner (the sexy son theory) and to mate with them on their most fertile days. All these phenomena are viewed from an evolutionary perspective (i.e., what would the fitness advantage have been formerly).

There is very strong selection for behaviors that prevent a man from raising children fathered by someone else for the same reasons that 'group selection' is strongly selected against (see my essay on group selection 'Altruism, Jesus and the End of the World...'). However modern life provides ample opportunities for affairs, and genetic studies have shown that a high percentage of children are fathered by other than the putative partner of their mother, with the percentage increasing from a few percent to as much as 30% as one descends from upper to lower classes in various modern Western countries at various periods and undoubtedly higher than that in many 3rd world countries. In his book Sperm Wars: The Science of Sex (2006) Robin Baker summarizes: 'Actual figures range from 1 percent in high-status areas of the United States and Switzerland, to 5 to 6 percent for moderate-status males in the United States and Great Britain, to 10 to 30 percent for lower-status males in the United States, Great Britain and France'. One might suppose that in societies where both men and women are highly concentrated in cities and have mobile phones, this percentage is rising, especially in the third world where, use of birth control and abortion is erratic.

He finds that most men and women who murder their mates are young and the younger their mates are, the more likely they will be murdered. Like all behavior, this is hard to explain without an evolutionary perspective. One study found men in their 40's constituted 23% of mate murderers but men in their 50's only 7.7%, and 79% of female mate killers were between 16 and 39. It makes sense that the younger they are, the bigger the potential fitness loss to the male (decreased reproduction) and so the more intense the emotional response. As Buss puts it: "From Australia to Zimbabwe, the younger the woman, the higher the likelihood that she will be killed as a result of a sexual infidelity or leaving a romantic relationship. Women in the 15 to 24 year-old bracket are at the greatest risk." A high percentage are killed within two months of separation and most in the first year. One study found that 88% of them had been stalked prior to being killed. In some chapters there are quotes from people giving their feelings about their unfaithful mates and these typically include homicidal fantasies, which were more intense and went on for longer periods for men than for women.

He devotes some time to the increased risk of abuse and murder from having a stepparent with e.g., the risk to a girl of rape increasing about 10X if her father is a stepfather. It is now very well known that in a wide range of mammals, a new male encountering a female with young will attempt to kill them. One USA study found that if one or both parents are surrogates, this raises the child's chance of being murdered in the home between 40 and 100X (p174). A Canadian study found the beating death rate rose by 27X if one parent in a registered marriage was a stepparent while it rose over 200X if the surrogate was a live-in boyfriend. Child abuse rates in Canada rose 40X when there was a stepparent.

In humans, being without resources is a strong stimulus for women to eliminate their existing children in order to attract a new mate. A Canadian study found that even though single women were only 12% of all mothers, they committed over 50% of infanticides (p169). Since younger women lose less fitness from an infant death than older ones, it is not surprising that a cross-cultural study found that teenagers killed their infants at rates about 30X that of women in their twenties (p170).

He then briefly discusses serial killers and serial rapists, the most successful of all time being the Mongols of Genghis Khan, whose Y chromosomes are represented in about 8% of all the men in the territories they controlled, or some 20 million men (and an equal number of women) or about half a percent of all the people on earth, which makes them easily the most genetically fit of all the people who have ever lived in historical times.

Though this volume is a bit dated, there are few recent popular books dealing specifically with the psychology of murder and it's a quick overview available for a few dollars, so still well worth the effort. It makes no attempt to be comprehensive and is somewhat superficial in places, with the reader expected to fill in the blanks from his many other books and the vast literature on violence. For an update see e.g., Buss, The Handbook of Evolutionary Psychology 2nd ed. V1 (2016) p 265, 266, 270–282, 388–389, 545–546, 547, 566 and Buss, Evolutionary Psychology 5th ed. (2015) p 26, 96–97,223, 293-4, 300, 309–312, 410 and Shackelford and Hansen, The Evolution of Violence (2014) He has been among the top evolutionary psychologists for several decades and covers a wide range of behavior in his works, but here he concentrates almost entirely on the psychological mechanisms that cause individual people to murder and their possible evolutionary function in the EEA (Environment of Evolutionary Adaptation—i.e., the plains of Africa during the last million years or so).

Those with a lot of time who want a detailed history of homicidal violence from an evolutionary perspective may consult Steven Pinker's 'The Better Angels of Our Nature-Why Violence Has Declined'(2012) and my review of it easily available on the net and in two of my recent books. Briefly, Pinker notes that murder has decreased steadily and dramatically by a factor of about 30 since our days as foragers. So, even though guns now make it extremely easy for anyone to kill, homicide is much less common. Pinker thinks this is due to various social mechanisms that bring out our 'better angels', but I think it's due mainly to the temporary abundance of resources from the merciless rape of our planet, coupled with increased police presence, with communication and surveillance and legal systems that make it far more likely to be punished. This becomes clear every time there is even a brief and local absence of the police.

Others also take the view that we have a 'nice side' that is genetically innate and supports the favorable treatment of even those not closely related to us ('group selection'). This is hopelessly confused and I have done my small part to lay it to rest in 'Altruism, Jesus and the End of the World—how the Templeton Foundation bought a Harvard Professorship and attacked Evolution, Rationality and Civilization. A review of E.O. Wilson 'The Social Conquest of Earth' (2012) and Nowak and Highfield 'SuperCooperators'(2012)'.

Those wishing a comprehensive up to date framework for human behavior from the modern two systems view may consult my books Talking Monkeys 3rd ed (2019), The Logical Structure of Philosophy, Psychology, Mind and Language in Ludwig Wittgenstein and John Searle 2nd ed (2019), Suicide by Democracy 4th ed (2019), The Logical Structure of Human Behavior (2019), The Logical Structure of Consciousness (2019, Understanding the Connections between Science, Philosophy, Psychology, Religion, Politics, and Economics (2019), and Suicidal Utopian Delusions in the 21st Century 5th ed (2019).

I now present a very brief summary of intentional psychology (the logical structure of rationality) which is covered extensively in my many other articles and books. Impulsive violence will involve the automated subcortical functions of System 1, but is sometimes deliberated upon ahead of time via cortical System 2.

About a million years ago primates evolved the ability to use their throat muscles to make complex series of noises (i.e., speech) that by about 100,000 years ago had evolved to describe present events (perceptions, memory, reflexive actions with basic utterances that can be described as Primary Language Games (PLG's) describing System 1—i.e., the fast unconscious automated System One, true-only mental states with a precise time and location). We gradually developed the further ability to encompass displacements in space and time to describe memories, attitudes and potential events (the past and future and often counterfactual, conditional or fictional preferences, inclinations or dispositions) with the Secondary Language Games (SLG's) of System Two- slow conscious true or false propositional attitudinal thinking, which has no precise time and are abilities and not mental states. Preferences are Intuitions, Tendencies, Automatic Ontological Rules, Behaviors, Abilities, Cognitive Modules, Personality Traits, Templates, Inference Engines, Inclinations, Emotions, Propositional Attitudes, Appraisals, Capacities, Hypotheses.

Emotions are Type 2 Preferences (Wittgenstein RPP2 p148). "I believe", "he loves", "they think" are descriptions of possible public acts typically displaced in spacetime. My first-person statements about myself are true-only (excluding lying), while third person statements about others are true or false (see my review of Johnston - 'Wittgenstein: Rethinking the Inner').

Now that we have a reasonable start on the Logical Structure of Rationality (the Descriptive Psychology of Higher Order Thought) laid out, we can look at the table of Intentionality that results from this work, which I have constructed over the last few years. It is based on a much simpler one from Searle, which in turn owes much to Wittgenstein. I have also incorporated in modified form tables being used by current researchers in the psychology of thinking processes which are evidenced in the last 9 rows. It should prove interesting to compare it with those in Peter Hacker's 3 recent volumes on Human Nature. I offer this table as an heuristic for describing behavior that I find more complete and useful than any other framework I have seen and not as a final or complete analysis, which would have to be three dimensional with hundreds (at least) of arrows going in many directions with many (perhaps all) pathways between S1 and S2 being bidirectional. Also, the very distinction between S1 and S2, cognition and willing, perception and memory, between feeling, knowing, believing and expecting etc. are arbitrary--that is, as W demonstrated, all words are contextually sensitive and most have several utterly different uses (meanings or COS).

INTENTIONALITY can be viewed as personality or as the Construction of Social Reality (the title of Searle's well known book) and from many other viewpoints as well.

Beginning with the pioneering work of Ludwig Wittgenstein in the 1930's (the Blue and Brown Books) and from the 50's to the present by his successors Searle, Moyal-Sharrock, Read, Baker, Hacker, Stern, Horwich, Winch, Finkelstein, Coliva etc., I have created the following table as an heuristic for furthering this study. The rows show various aspects or ways of studying and the columns show the involuntary processes and voluntary behaviors comprising the two systems (dual processes) of the Logical Structure of Consciousness (LSC), which can also be regarded as the Logical Structure of Rationality (LSR), of behavior (LSB), of personality (LSP), of Mind (LSM), of language (LSL), of reality (LSOR), of Intentionality (LSI) -the classical philosophical term, the Descriptive Psychology of Consciousness (DPC) , the Descriptive Psychology of Thought (DPT) –or better, the Language of the Descriptive Psychology of Thought (LDPT), terms introduced here and in my other very recent writings.

I suggest we can describe behavior more clearly by changing Searle's "impose conditions of satisfaction on conditions of satisfaction" to "relate mental states to the world by moving muscles" —i.e., talking, writing and doing, and his "mind to world direction of fit" and "world to mind direction of fit" by "cause originates in the mind" and "cause originates in the world" S1 is only upwardly causal (world to mind) and contentless (lacking representations or information) while S2 has content and is downwardly causal (mind to world). I have adopted my terminology in this table.

I have made detailed explanations of this table in my other writings.

FROM THE ANALYSIS OF LANGUAGE GAMES

	Disposition*	Emotion	Memory	Perception	Desire	PI**	IA***	Action/Word
Cause Originates From****	World	World	World	World	Mind	Mind	Mind	Mind
Causes Changes In*****	None	Mind	Mind	Mind	None	World	World	World
Causally Self Reflexive******	No	Yes	Yes	Yes	No	Yes	Yes	Yes
True or False (Testable)	Yes	T only	T only	T only	Yes	Yes	Yes	Yes
Public Conditions of Satisfaction	Yes	Yes/No	Yes/No	No	Yes/No	Yes	No	Yes
Describe A Mental State	No	Yes	Yes	Yes	No	No	Yes/No	Yes
Evolutionary Priority	5	4	2,3	1	5	3	2	2
Voluntary Content	Yes	No	No	No	No	Yes	Yes	Yes
Voluntary Initiation	Yes/No	No	Yes	No	Yes/No	Yes	Yes	Yes
Cognitive System *******	2	1	2/1	1	2/1	2	1	2
Change Intensity	No	Yes	Yes	Yes	Yes	No	No	No
Precise Duration	No	Yes	Yes	Yes	No	No	Yes	Yes
Time, Place (H+N, T+T) ********	TT	HN	HN	HN	TT	TT	HN	HN
Special Quality	No	Yes	No	Yes	No	No	No	No
Localized in Body	No	No	No	Yes	No	No	No	Yes
Bodily Expressions	Yes	Yes	No	No	Yes	Yes	Yes	Yes
Self Contradictions	No	Yes	No	No	Yes	No	No	No
Needs a Self	Yes	Yes/No	No	No	Yes	No	No	No
Needs Language	Yes	No	No	No	No	No	No	Yes/No

FROM DECISION RESEARCH

	Disposition*	Emotion	Memory	Perception	Desire	PI**	IA***	Action/Word
Subliminal Effects	No	Yes/No	Yes	Yes	No	No	No	Yes/No
Associative/Rule Based	RB	A/RB	A	A	A/RB	RB	RB	RB
Context Dependent/Abstract	A	CD/A	CD	CD	CD/A	A	CD/A	CD/A
Serial/Parallel	S	S/P	P	P	S/P	S	S	S
Heuristic/Analytic	A	H/A	H	H	H/A	A	A	A
Needs Working Memory	Yes	No	No	No	No	Yes	Yes	Yes
General Intelligence Dependent	Yes	No	No	No	Yes/No	Yes	Yes	Yes
Cognitive Loading Inhibits	Yes	Yes/No	No	No	Yes	Yes	Yes	Yes
Arousal Facilitates or Inhibits	I	F/I	F	F	I	I	I	I

*   Aka Inclinations, Capabilities, Preferences, Representations, possible actions etc.
**   Searle's Prior Intentions
***   Searle's Intention In Action
****   Searle's Direction of Fit
*****   Searle's Direction of Causation
******   (Mental State instantiates--Causes or Fulfills Itself). Searle formerly called this causally self- referential.
*******   Tversky/Kahneman/Frederick/Evans/Stanovich defined cognitive systems.
******** Here and Now or There and Then

A detailed explanation of this table is given in my other writings.

One should always keep in mind Wittgenstein's discovery that after we have described the possible uses (meanings, truthmakers, Conditions of Satisfaction) of language in a particular context, we have exhausted its interest, and attempts at explanation (i.e., philosophy) only get us further away from the truth. It is critical to note that this table is only a highly simplified context-free heuristic and each use of a word must be examined in its context. The best examination of context variation is in Peter Hacker's recent 3 volumes on Human Nature, which provide numerous tables and charts that should be compared with this one.

Suicide by Democracy - an Obituary for America and the World

Michael Starks

ABSTRACT

America and the world are in the process of collapse from excessive population growth, most of it for the last century, and now all of it, due to 3rd world people. Consumption of resources and the addition of 4 billion more ca. 2100 will collapse industrial civilization and bring about starvation, disease, violence and war on a staggering scale. The earth loses at least 1% of its topsoil every year, so as it nears 2100, most of its food growing capacity will be gone. Billions will die and nuclear war is all but certain. In America, this is being hugely accelerated by massive immigration and immigrant reproduction, combined with abuses made possible by democracy. Depraved human nature inexorably turns the dream of democracy and diversity into a nightmare of crime and poverty. China will continue to overwhelm America and the world, as long as it maintains the dictatorship which limits selfishness. The root cause of collapse is the inability of our innate psychology to adapt to the modern world, which leads people to treat unrelated persons as though they had common interests. The idea of human rights is an evil fantasy promoted by leftists to draw attention away from the merciless destruction of the earth by unrestrained 3rd world motherhood. This, plus ignorance of basic biology and psychology, leads to the social engineering delusions of the partially educated who control democratic societies. Few understand that if you help one person you harm someone else—there is no free lunch and every single item anyone consumes destroys the earth beyond repair. Consequently, social policies everywhere are unsustainable and one by one all societies without stringent controls on selfishness will collapse into anarchy or dictatorship. The most basic facts, almost never mentioned, are that there are not enough resources in America or the world to lift a significant percentage of the poor out of poverty and keep them there. The attempt to do this is bankrupting America and destroying the world. The earth's capacity to produce food decreases daily, as does our genetic quality. And now, as always, by far the greatest enemy of the poor is other poor and not the rich. Without dramatic and immediate changes, there is no hope for preventing the collapse of America, or any country that follows a democratic system.

The saddest day in US history. President Johnson, with 2 Kennedy's and ex-President Hoover, gives America to Mexico -Oct 3rd 1965

153

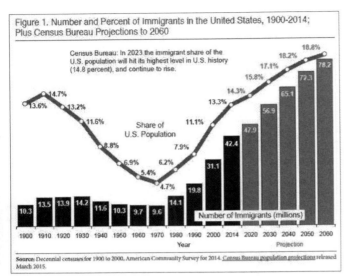

Figure 1. Number and Percent of Immigrants in the United States, 1900-2014; Plus Census Bureau Projections to 2060

PERCENT OF AMERICANS WHO ARE FOREIGN BORN -- the result of the "no significant demographic impact" immigration act of 1965—non-Europeans (the Diverse) were a 16% share, are now (2019) about 38% and will be about 60% by 2100, since they are now 100% of the population increase of about 2.4 million every year. Suicide by democracy.

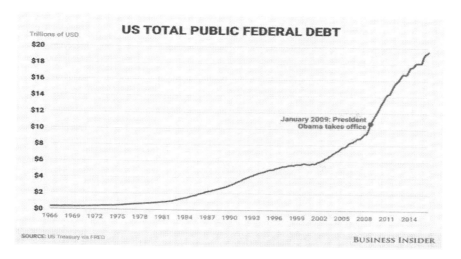

PART OF THE COST OF DIVERSITY and of aging, being the world's unpaid policeman, etc., (not counting future liabilities which are 5 to 10 times as much, barring major social changes).

Useful definitions for understanding American politics

DIVERSITY: 1. USA government program for handing over control to Mexico. 2. USA government program for providing free or heavily subsidized goods and services to those from other countries. 3. A means for turning America into a 3rd world Hellhole. 4. Multiculturalism, multiethnicism, multipartisanism, inclusivity, third world supremacy.

RACIST: 1. Person opposed to diversity in above sense. 2. Person of different ethnicity who disagrees with me on any issue. 3. Person of any ethnicity who disagrees with me on anything. Also, called 'bigot' 'hater' or 'nativist'.

WHITE SUPREMACIST: Anyone opposed to diversity in the above sense, i.e., anyone trying to prevent the collapse of America and of industrial civilization worldwide.

THIRD WORLD SUPREMACIST: Anyone in favor of diversity in above senses. Anyone working to destroy their descendant's future. AKA Democrats, Socialists, Neomarxists, Democratic Socialists, Marxists, Leftists, Liberals, Progressives, Communists, Maternalists, Leftist Fascists, Multiculturalists, Inclusivists, Human

Rightists.

HATE: 1. Any opposition to diversity in the above sense. 2. Expression of a desire to prevent the collapse of America and the world.

EURO: White or Caucasian or European: one whose ancestors left Africa over 50,000 years ago.
BLACK: African or Afro-American: one whose ancestors stayed in Africa or left in the last few hundred years (so there has not been time for evolution of any significant differences from Euros).

DIVERSE: Anyone who is not EURO (European, white, Caucasian).

HUMAN RIGHTS: An evil fantasy created by leftists to draw attention away from the merciless destruction of the earth by unrestrained 3rd world reproduction. Thus, temporary anomalies, such as democracy, equality, labor unions, women's rights, child rights, animal rights, etc. are due to high standards of living created by the rape of the planet and will disappear as civilization collapses and China rules the world.

I should first note that I have no investment in the outcome of any social or political movement. I am old, without kids or close relatives, and in the blink of an eye I will be gone (of course the most important thing to remember is that very soon we will all be gone and our descendants will face the horrific consequences of our stupidity and selfishness). I offer these comments in hope they will give perspective, since concise rational competent analyses of the perilous situation in America and the world are almost nonexistent. I have close friends of various ethnicities, several times given my only assets to an impoverished third world person (no I did not inherit anything significant, did not have rich relatives, a trust fund or a cushy job), have had third world friends, colleagues, girlfriends, wives and business partners, and helped anyone in any way I could regardless of race, age, creed, sexual preferences or national origin or position on the autism spectrum, and am still doing so. I have not voted in any kind of election, belonged to any religious, social or political group, listened to a political speech or read a book on politics in over 50 years, as I considered it pointless and demeaning to have my views carry the same weight as those of morons, lunatics, criminals and merely uneducated (i.e., about 95% of the population). I find nearly all political dialog to be superficial, mistaken and useless. This is my first and last social/political commentary.

The millions of daily articles, speeches, tweets and newsbites rarely mention it, but what is happening in America and worldwide are not some transient and unconnected events, but the infinitely sad story of the inexorable collapse of industrial civilization and of freedom due to overpopulation and to the malignant dictatorships that are the CCP (Chinese Communist Party) and Islam. Though these are the only important issues, they seldom are stated clearly in the endless debates and daily social convulsions, and few things in this article are ever discussed in any clear and intelligent way, in large part because the Diverse (i.e., those not of European ancestry) have a strangle hold on American and most Western media which make it impossible. Politics in democratic countries is dedicated almost entirely to providing the opportunity for every special interest group to get an ever-bigger share of the rapidly diminishing resources. The problem is that nearly all people are short-sighted, selfish, poorly educated, lacking experience and stupid and this creates an insoluble problem when there are 10 billion (by century's end), or when they constitute a majority of any electorate in a democratic system. It's one thing to make mistakes when there are time and resources to correct them, but quite another when it's impossible. The USA is the worst case as it seems to have vast resources and a resilient economy, and what I and most people grew up regarding as the wonderful traditions of democracy, diversity and equality, but I now see that these are invitations to exploitation by every special interest group and that giving privileges to everyone born, without imposing duties, has fatal consequences. Also, a system that operates this way cannot compete with ones that do not- Asia and above all China is eating America's lunch (and that of all non-Asian countries), and nothing is likely to stop it, but of course overpopulation dooms everyone (the minority who will survive after the great 22nd/23rd century die-off) to a hellish life. A world where everyone is free to replicate their genes and consume resources as they wish will soon have a hard landing. The fact is that democracy has become a license to steal -- from the government—i.e., from the shrinking minority who pay significant taxes, from the earth, from everyone everywhere, and from one's own descendants, and that diversity (multiculturalism, multipartisanism, etc.) in an overcrowded world leads to insoluble conflict and collapse. 9/11 was a direct result of the this.

The history in America is clear enough. In what can now be seen as the first major disaster stemming from the lunatic Christian idea of innate human rights, the politicians of the Northern states decided it was inappropriate for the South to have slaves. Slavery was certainly an outmoded and evil idea and was disappearing worldwide, and it would have been eliminated with economic and political pressures after emancipation via the 13th amendment. But then as now, the utopian delusions prevailed, and so they attacked the South, killing and crippling millions and creating poverty and dysgenic chaos (the death and debility of a large percentage of able-bodied Euro males) whose effects are still with us. The Africans replicated their genes at a higher rate, resulting in their coming to comprise an ever-increasing percentage of the country. Nobody realized it at the time and most still do not, but this was the beginning of the collapse of America and the defects in psychology which led the North to persecute the South were a continuation of the Christian fanaticisms which produced the murder and torture of millions during the middle ages, the Inquisition, the genocide of the new world Indians by the Europeans, the Crusades and the Jihads of the Muslims for the last 1200 years. ISIS, Al-Queda, the Crusaders and the Army of the North have a great deal in common.

Without asking the voters, a few thousand statesmen and congressmen and President Lincoln made ex-slaves citizens and gave them the right to vote via the 14th and 15th amendments. Gradually there came to be vast ghettos composed of ex slaves, where crime and poverty flourished, and where drugs (imported mostly by Hispanics) generated a vast criminal empire, whose users committed hundreds of millions of crimes every year. Then came the Democrats led by the Kennedys, who, raised in privilege and disconnected from the real world, and having like nearly all politicians no clue about biology, psychology, human ecology or history, decided in 1965 that it was only democratic and just that the country should change the immigration laws to decrease influx of Europeans in favor of 3rd world people (the Diverse). They passed the law and in 1965 president Lyndon Johnson signed it (see cover photo). There were misgivings from some quarters that this would destroy America, but they were assured that there would be "no significant demographic impact"! The American public never (to this day in 2019) had a chance to express their views (i.e., to vote), unless you count the Trump election as that chance, and congress and various presidents changed our democracy into a "Socialist Democracy", i.e., into a Neomarxist, third world supremacist fascist state. The Chinese are delighted as they do not have to fight the USA and other democracies for dominance, but only to wait for them to collapse.

A few decades ago, William Brennen, Chief Justice of the Supreme Court, suggested that a law passed a century before, to guarantee citizenship to former slaves (the first fatal legislative mistake, the second giving them the vote), should apply to anyone who happened to be born in America. Subsequently, other rulings of the court (not the people, who have never been asked) decided all those born in the USA, regardless of parental status (e.g., even if they were aliens from another solar system) had a right to US citizenship (anchor babies) and were subsequently permitted to make citizens of all their relatives — (the third and fourth fatal mistakes). Again, it never crossed the minds of congress or the courts that the constitution did not give any such rights, nor that the American public should be permitted to vote on this. In addition to the millions of 3rd world people here "legally" (i.e., with the permission of a few hundred in congress, but not the people) millions began entering illegally and all produced children at about 3 times the rate of existing Americans and generated ever increasing social problems. Most of the Diverse pay little or no taxes, and so they live partly or wholly on government handouts (i.e., taxes paid by the ever shrinking minority of Americans who pay any, as well as money borrowed from future generations to the tune of $2.5 billion a day, added to the $18 trillion in debt and the $90 trillion or more of unfunded future obligations—medicare, social security etc.), while the agricultural system, housing, streets and highways, sewers, water and electrical systems, parks, schools, hospitals, courts, public transportation, government, police, fire, emergency services and the huge defense spending needed to ensure the continued existence of our country and most others, were created, administered and largely paid for by Euros (i.e., those of European ancestry). The fact that the Diverse owe their well-being (relative to the Diverse still in the 3rd world) and their very existence (medicine, technology, agriculture, suppression of war and slavery) to Euros is never mentioned by anyone (see below).

Naturally, the Euros (and a minority of tax paying Diverse) are outraged to have to spend ever more of their working lives to support the legions of newly arrived Diverse, to be unsafe in their own homes and streets and to see their towns, schools, hospitals, parks etc. being taken over and destroyed. They try to protest, but the media are now controlled by the Diverse (with the help of deluded Euros who are dedicated to destroying their own descendants), and it is now almost impossible to state any opposition to the collapse of America and the world without being attacked as "racist", "white supremacist" or "a hater", and often losing one's job for exercising free speech. Words referring to the Diverse are almost banned, unless it's to praise them and assist their genuine racism (i.e., living at the expense of and exploiting and abusing in every way possible the Euro's, and their Diverse tax paying neighbors), so one cannot mention blacks, immigrants, Hispanics, Muslims etc. in the same discussion with the words rapist, terrorist, thief, murderer, child molester, convict, criminal, welfare etc., without being accused of "hatred" or "racism" or "white supremacy". They are of course oblivious to their own racism and third world supremacy. Keep in mind there is not and almost certainly will never be any evidence of a significant genetic difference between Euros and Diverse in psychology, or IQ, and that their tendency to excessive reproduction and other shortcomings is wholly due to culture.

Gradually, every kind of special interest group has succeeded in eliminating any negative reference to them in any easily identifiable way, so there has almost vanished from public discourse not only words referring to the Diverse, but to the short, tall, fat, thin, mentally ill, handicapped, genetically defective, disadvantaged, abnormal, schizophrenic, depressed, stupid, dishonest, crazy, lazy , cowardly, selfish, dull etc. until nothing but pleasant platitudes are heard and one is left puzzled as to who fills the jails, hospitals and mental wards to overflowing, litters the streets with garbage, destroys the parks, beaches and public lands, robs, riots, assaults, rapes and murders, and uses up all the tax money, plus an extra 2.5 billion dollars a day, added to the 18 trillion national debt (or over 90 trillion if you extend the real liabilities into the near future). Of course, it's not due all to the Diverse, but every passing day a larger percentage is as their numbers swell and those of the Euros decline.

It is now over fifty years after passing the new immigration act and about 16% of the population is Hispanic (up from less than 1% earlier), who have been reproducing at about 3X the rate of Euros , so that about half of children under 6 are now Hispanic, while some 13% of the country are blacks, rapidly being displaced and marginalized by Hispanics (though few blacks realize it, so they continue to support the politicians favoring further immigration and handouts and promising short term gains). Virtually nobody grasps the eventual collapse of America and the whole world, in spite of the fact that you can see it in front of your eyes everywhere. In America and worldwide, the Euros (and all the "rich" generally) are producing less than two kids per couple, so their populations are shrinking, and in America in 2014, for the first time since Euros came here in the 16th century, more of them died than were born, so their marginalization is certain. And, showing the "success" of the Neomarxist, third world supremacist immigration and welfare policies, the population of Hispanics in California passed 50%, so within a decade, the 6th largest economy in the world will be part of Mexico.

The Diverse will, in, this century, eliminate all American "racism" (i.e., any opposition or legal hindrance to takeover of all political power, and the appropriation of as much of their neighbor's money and property as they can manage,) except their own racism (e.g., graduated income tax which forces the Euro's to support them). Soon they will largely eliminate legal differences between citizens of Mexico and California and then Texas, who then will have full 'rights' (privileges) anywhere in the USA, so that citizenship will became increasingly

meaningless (and an ever-lower percentage of the Diverse will pay any significant taxes or serve in the military, and a far higher percentage will continue to receive welfare and to commit crimes, and to get free or heavily subsidized schooling, medical care etc.). One cannot mention in the media that the predominant racism in the USA is the extortion by the Diverse of anyone with money (mainly Euros but also any Diverse who have money), the elimination of free speech (except their own), the biasing of all laws to favor this extortion, and their rapid takeover of all political and financial
power, i.e., total discrimination against Euros and anyone belonging to the "upper classes", i.e., anyone who pays any significant taxes.

Gradually the poverty, drugs, gangs, environmental destruction and the corruption of police, army and government endemic in Mexico and most other 3rd world countries is spreading across America, so we will be able to cross over the increasingly porous border with Mexico without noticing we are in a different country –probably within a few decades, but certainly by the end of the century. The population continues to increase, and here as everywhere in the world, the increase is now 100% Diverse and, as we enter the next century (much sooner in some countries), resources will diminish and starvation, disease, crime and war will rage out of control. The rich and the corporations will mostly still be rich (as always, as things get worse they will take their money and leave), the poor will be poorer and more numerous, and life everywhere, with the possible exception of a few countries or parts of countries where population growth is prevented, will be unbearable and unsurvivable.

The cooperation among the Diverse to wrest control of society from Euros will crumble as society disintegrates and they will split into blacks, Hispanics, Muslims, Chinese, Filipinos, gays, seniors, disabled, and further where possible into endless subgroups. The rich will increasingly hire bodyguards, carry guns, drive bulletproof cars and use private police to protect them in their gated communities and offices, as is already commonplace in 3rd world countries. With much reduced quality of life and high crime, some will think of returning to their countries of origin, but there also overpopulation will exhaust resources and produce collapse even more severe than in the USA and Europe, and the racism in the 3rd world, temporarily suppressed by a relative abundance of resources and police and military presence, will become ever worse, so life will be hellish nearly everywhere. The population in the 22nd century will shrink as billions die of starvation, disease, drugs, suicide, and civil and international war. As third world nuclear countries collapse (Pakistan, India and maybe Iran by then, thanks to Obama) and are taken over by radicals, nuclear conflicts will eventually occur. Still, perhaps nobody will dare to suggest publicly that the prime cause of chaos was unrestricted motherhood.

Of course, much of this story has already played out in America, the U.K. and elsewhere, and the rest is inevitable, even without climate change and the ravenous appetites of China, which just make it happen faster. It's only a matter of how bad it will get where and when. Anyone who doubts this is out of touch with reality, but you can't fool mother nature, and their descendants will no longer debate it as they will be forced to live it.

The poor, and apparently, Obama, Krugman, Zuckerberg and most Democrats (Neomarxists), don't understand the most basic operating principle of civilization — there is no Free Lunch. You can only give to one by taking from another, now or in the future. No such thing as helping without hurting. Every dollar and every item has value because somewhere, someone destroyed the earth. And leftists have the delusion that they can solve all problems by stealing from the rich. To get some idea of the absurdity of this, all US taxpayers earning over a million dollars have a total after tax profit of about 800 billion, while the annual deficit is about 1.5 trillion, and even taking it all does nothing to pay off the existing 18 trillion debt or the approx. 90 trillion in near term unfunded liabilities (e.g., medicare and social security). Of course, you cannot increase their tax or corporate tax very much more or it will greatly depress the economy and produce a recession, job losses and the flight of capital, and they already pay the highest taxes, relative to what they earn as a % of the nation's income, of any industrialized country. And once again, the top 1% of earners pay about 50% of total personal federal income tax while the bottom 47% (mostly Diverse) pay nothing. So the fact is we only have a sort of democracy, as we have almost nothing to say about what the govt. does, and a sort of fascism, as the ever expanding govt. spies on our every move, controls ever more minutely our every action, and forces us at gunpoint to do whatever they decide, and a sort of communism as they steal whatever they want from whomever they want and use it to support anyone they like, here and all over the world, most of whom have no interest in democracy, justice, or equality, except as means to take advantage of our fatally flawed system to get as much money and services as they can in order to support replicating their genes and destroying the earth.

Speaking of Obama, Trump says that he is the worst president ever, and of course Obama, totally arrogant, dishonest and lacking any real grasp of the situation (or unwilling to be honest) just laughs, and babbles platitudes, but as I reflect a bit it's clearly true. Like Roosevelt, who gave us the first giant step into fascism and govt.

waste and oppression with an illegal and unconstitutional tax (social security), Obamacare let the govt. swallow 1/6 of the economy and created his own illegal tax (called 'penalties' of Obamacare, where FDR called them 'benefits' and 'contributions'). He tried to force the US to accept another 8 to 10 million illegals (nobody seems quite sure) which will 'birthright' into about 50 million by 2100. In the first 3 years of his office (2009 to 2012) the federal operating deficit increased about 44% from 10 to 15 trillion, the largest percent increase since WW2, while by mid 2015 it had increased to over 71% of fiscal operating budget -- over $18 trillion or about $57,000 for every person in the USA, including children. His deferral of the deportation of millions of illegals, all of whom now receive social security, tax credits, medicare etc., is estimated to have a lifetime cost to the govt. (i.e., to the minority of us who pay any significant taxes) of ca. $1.3 trillion. Of course, this does not include free school, use of judicial system, jails and police, free 'emergency' care (i.e., just going to emergency for any problem whatsoever), degradation of all public facilities etc. so it's likely at least twice as much. And we have seen 8 years of incompetent handling of the Iraq, Afghan and Syrian wars and the cancerous growth of the CCP and Islam. He probably gave the ability to make nuclear weapons to Iran, which is highly likely to lead to a nuclear war by 2100 or much sooner. He was clearly elected for classist, racist, third world supremacist reasons-- because he had visible African genes, while the Euros, having left Africa some 50,000 years earlier have invisible ones. He, and most of the people he appointed, had little competence or experience in running a country and they were picked, like himself, on the basis of Diverse genes and Neomarxist, third world supremacist sympathies. If he is not a traitor (giving aid and comfort to the enemy) then who is? It is clear as day that, like nearly everyone, he operates totally on automatic primitive psychology, with his coalitional sympathies (biases) favoring those who look and act more like him. He (like most Diverse) is in fact doing his best to destroy the country and system that made his exalted life possible. In an interview near the end of his term he said that the major reason for the backwardness of the third world was colonialism. As with all leftist third world supremacists, it has never crossed his mind that about 95% of all the third world people owe their existence and their relatively high standard of living to Euros and colonialism (i.e., medicine, agriculture, technology, science, trade, education, police and judicial system, communications, elimination of war and crime etc.), nor that the real enemies of the poor are other poor, who are just as repulsive as the rich, whom it is their greatest desire to emulate. I agree that, with the possible exception of Lincoln, he is the worst (i.e., most destructive to American quality of life and survival as a nation) for his lack of honesty, arrogance and assault on freedom and longterm survivability —a stunning achievement when his competition includes Nixon,

Johnson, the Bushes and the Clintons, and which makes even Reagan look good.

When considering bad presidents, we should start with Abraham Lincoln, who is revered as a saint, but he (with the help of congress) destroyed much of the country and the lives of millions of people fighting the totally unnecessary Civil War, and in many ways, the country will never recover as it led to the civil rights movement, the 1965 immigration act and the 1982 supreme court anchor baby ruling. Slavery would have come to an end soon without the war, as it did everywhere and of course it was Euros who provided the main impetus to bring it to an end here and everywhere. After the war the slaves could have been repatriated to Africa, or just given residence, instead of making them citizens (14th amendment) and then giving them the vote (15th amendment). He and his collaborators, like so many liberal upper class Euros then and now, was blinded by the utopian social delusions embodied in Christianity and democracy, which result from the inclusive fitness psychology of coalitional intuitions and reciprocal altruism, that was eugenic and adaptive in the EEA (Environment of Evolutionary Adaptation-i.e., from ca. 50,000 to several million years ago) but is fatally dysgenic and maladaptive in modern times.

Note the great irony of the quote from him that begins this book, which shows that even the brightest are victims of their own limits, and have no grasp of human biology, psychology or ecology. It never crossed his mind that the world would become horrifically overpopulated and that the Africans would grow to become a giant social problem, at home and for themselves and the world as Africa expands to over 4 billion. Likewise, in spite of the now clear disaster, it seems not to cross Obama's that the Diverse at home and abroad will destroy America and the world, though any bright ten year old can see it.

President Truman could have let McArthur use the atom bomb to end the Korean war, destroy communism and to avoid the continuing horror of China run by 25 sociopaths (the Politburo) or really just seven sociopaths (the Politburo Standing Committee) or perhaps actually just one sociopath (Xi Jinping). Johnson could have done likewise in Vietnam, Bush in Iraq and Obama in Afghanistan, Syria and Libya. China and probably many 3rd world countries would have used nuclear weapons if the situations were reversed. Once a radical Muslim country gets the bomb a preemptive strike by them or on them will likely ensue, and this is probable by 2100 and near certain by 2200. If Gaddafi had succeeded in his efforts to get the bomb it would very likely have happened. The US could have forced Japan, China and Korea, Iraq and Libya and all the countries of Europe (and the whole world for that matter) to pay for the costs of our military efforts in all the recent wars, and between wars, instead of taking on most of the cost and then helping them take over most of America's manufacturing. Of course, these decisions, critical to the country's survival, were made by a handful of politicians without consulting the voters. The Kennedy's were an important part of changing the immigration laws in the mid 60's, so they have to count as traitors and major enemies of America on a par with Obama, G.W Bush and the Clintons. We could have followed the universal pleas of US industry and refused to sign the GATT, which gave free access to all our patents years before they are granted, though of course the Chinese now hack and steal everything with impunity anyway. Eisenhower could have let the UK keep possession of the Suez canal, instead of blackmailing them into leaving Egypt, and on and on.

Some may be interested in a few statistics to give an idea of where we currently are on the road to hell. See the tables at the beginning. In the USA, the population of Hispanics will swell from about 55 million in 2016 (or as much as 80 million if you accept some estimates of 25 million illegals—it's a mark of how far the govt. has let things go that we don't really know) to perhaps 140 million midcentury and 200 million as we enter the 22nd century, at which time the US population will be soaring past 500 million, and the world population will be about 11 billion, 3 billion of that added from now to then in Africa and 1 billion in Asia (the official UN estimates at the moment). The Hispanics are reproducing so fast that Euros, now a 63% majority, will be a minority by midcentury and about 40% by 2100. Most of the increase in the USA from now on will be Hispanics, with the rest blacks, Asians and Muslims, and all the increase here and in the world will be 100% Diverse. About 500,000 people are naturalized yearly and since they are mostly from the 3rd world and produce children at about twice the rate of Euros, that will add perhaps 2 million midcentury and 5 million by 2100 for every year it continues.

To show how fast things got out of control after the "no demographic impact" TKO (technical knock out or Ted Kennedy Outrage, though we could equally call it the LBJ outrage, the Neomarxist outrage, the Liberal outrage etc.) immigration act of 1965, there are now more Hispanics in California than there are people in 46 other states. In 1970 just after the TKO, there were about 4 million Hispanics and now there are over 55 million "legals" (i.e., not made legal by the voters but by a handful of politicians and the Supremely Stupid court) and perhaps 80 million counting illegals. It never crosses the minds of the Democratic block-voting poor Diverse that the ones who will suffer by far the most from the "Diversification" of America are themselves. The U.S. has gone from 84 percent white, 11 percent black, 4 percent

Hispanic and 1 percent Asian in 1965, to 62 percent white, 11 percent black, 18 percent Hispanic and 6 percent Asian now, according to a recent Pew report. By 2055, no one group is expected to have a majority--a perfect scenario for chaos, but you can see countless idiots from academia (now a paradise for state funded Neomarxist third world supremacism) praising multipartisanism. The Asians are predicted to increase faster than any group, doubling their percentage in the next few decades, but at least they will have gone thru a minimal immigration procedure, except of course for anchor baby families (producing which is now a major industry as Asians fly here to give birth, though they are greatly surpassed by Hispanics who only have to walk across the border at night). Of course, the Asians are by and large a blessing for America as they are more productive and less trouble than any group, including Euros.

The US government (alone of major countries) pushes "diversity" but in countries all over the world and throughout history attempts to weld different races and cultures into one have been an utter disaster. Many groups have lived among or alongside others for thousands of years without notably assimilating. Chinese and Koreans and Japanese in Asia, Jews and gentiles in thousands of places, Turks, Kurds and Armenians etc., have lived together for millennia without assimilating and go for each other's throats at the slightest provocation. After over 300 years of racial mixing, the USA is still about 97% monoracial (i.e., white, Hispanic, black etc.) with only about 3% describing themselves as mixed race (and most of them were mixed when they came here). The Native Americans (to whom the whole New World really belongs if one is going to rectify past injustices against the Diverse, a fact which is never mentioned by the third world supremacists) are mostly still living isolated and (before the casinos) impoverished, as are the blacks who, 150 years after emancipation, largely still live in crime ridden, impoverished ghettos. And these have been the best of times, with lots of cheap land and natural resources, major welfare and affirmative action programs (largely unique to 'racist' America), a mostly healthy economy and a government which extorts over 30% of their money (i.e., 30% of their working lives, counting income tax, sales tax, real estate tax etc.), earned by the tax paying part of the middle and upper class, to give the poor massive handouts -- not only food stamps and other welfare, but police and emergency services, streets and parks, the government, the justice system, hospitals, national defense, schools, roads, bridges, power grid, etc., and the costs of environmental degradation, and the financial and emotional costs of crime and it's threat, etc., most of these never counted by anyone (and never mentioned by the Neomarxist third world supremacists) when considering the 'costs of welfare' or the huge downside to diversity.

In any case, the liberal, democratic delusion is that such largesse and social policies will weld our 'diverse' (i.e., fatally fragmented) society into one happy family. But government handouts need to continually increase (for social security, wars, health care, schools, welfare, infrastructure, etc.) while the relative tax base shrinks, and our debt and unfunded entitlements grow by trillions a year, so the economy is in the process of collapse. The average family has less real net earnings and savings now than two decades ago and could survive about 3 months without income, about 40% of retired Americans have less than $25,000 savings etc. And again, these are the best of times with lots of 'free' resources (i.e., stolen from others and from our descendants) worldwide and about 4 billion less people than there will be by the next century. As economies fail and starvation, disease, crime and war spread, people will split down racial and religious lines as always, and in the USA Hispanics and Blacks will still dominate the bottom. It rarely occurs to those who want to continue (and increase) the numbers of and the subsidization of the Diverse that the money for this is ultimately stolen from their own descendants, on whom falls the burden of over $90 trillion debt if one counts the current entitlements (or up to $220 trillion if liabilities continued without reduction of handouts and no tax increase), and a society and a world collapsing into anarchy.

As noted, one of the many evil side effects of diversity (e.g., massive increases in crime, environmental degradation, traffic gridlock, decreasing quality of schools, coming bankruptcy of local, state and federal governments, corruption of police and border officials, rising prices of everything, overloading of the medical system, etc.) is that our right to free speech has disappeared on any issue of possible political relevance and of course that means just about any issue. Even in private, if any negative comment on 'diversity' is recorded or witnessed by anyone credible, the racist, third world supremacist Diverse and their Euro servants will try to take away your job and damage your business or your person. This is certain when it involves public figures and racial or immigration issues, but nothing is off limits. Dozens of books in the last two decades address the issue including 'The New Thought Police: Inside the Left's Assault on Free Speech and Free Minds', 'End of Discussion: How the Left's Outrage Industry Shuts Down Debate, Manipulates Voters, and Makes America Less Free (and Fun)' and 'The Silencing: how the left is killing free speech', but nothing will dissuade the Democratic Socialists (i.e., closet communists) and the lunatic fringe liberals. As noted, I am writing this book because nobody in Academia, nor any public figure, dares to do it.

Another 'side effect' is the loss of much of our freedom and privacy as the government continues to expand its war on terror. There was never a compelling reason for admitting any serious number of Muslims (or any more Diverse for that matter). In any case, it seems a no-brainer to not admit and to expel single unmarried male Muslims aged 15 to 50, but even such obvious simple moves are beyond the capabilities of the retards who control congress and of course our beloved presidents, all of whom, with the members of congress, who voted for the immigration law changes starting in 1965, could be held personally responsible for 9/11, the Boston Marathon Bombing etc. Of course, Trump is trying to change this but it's too little, too late and barring his declaring martial law, running the country with the army, and deporting or quarantining 100 million of the least useful residents, America's date with destiny is certain.

A lovely example of how suppression of free speech leads to ever more insanity is the case of Major Hasan (courtesy Mark Steyn's "After America"). An army psychiatrist at Fort Hood who had SoA (Soldier of Allah) on his business card, he was frequently reprimanded when a student army intern for trying to convert patients to Islam, and many complaints were filed for his constant anti-American comments--one day he gave a Power Point lecture to a room full of army doctors justifying his radicalism. Free speech and common sense being no more available in the military than civilian life, he was then promoted to Major and sent to Fort Hood, where he commented to his superior officer on a recent murder of two soldiers in Little Rock: "this is what Muslims should do—stand up to the aggressors" and "people should strap bombs on themselves and go into Times Square", but the army did nothing for fear of being accused of bias. One day he walked out of his office with an assault rifle and murdered 13 soldiers. It turned out two different anti-terrorism task forces were aware that he had been in frequent email contact with top radical Islamist terrorists. The Army Chief of Staff General George Casey remarked: "What happened at Fort Hood was a tragedy, but I believe it would be an even greater tragedy if our diversity becomes a casualty here"!! Is it losing the 70 million on welfare or the 1.7 million in prison or the 3 million drug addicts that is more tragic?

The invasion of the Southwest by Hispanics gives the flavor of what is coming and Coulter in her book "Adios America" tells of trashed parks, schools that dropped from A to D grade, billions for 'free' (i.e., paid for by the upper middle and upper class and businesses) medical care and other services in Los Angeles alone etc. Anyone living there who remembers what Texas or California were like 30 years ago has no doubts about the catastrophic consequences of diversity as they see it every day. In California, which I know personally, the urban areas (and even most parks and beaches) that I used to enjoy are now crowded with Hispanics and often full of trash and spray painted with gang signs, while the highways are horrifically crowded and the cities and towns overrun with drugs and crime, so most of it is now uninhabitable and the world's 6th largest economy is headed for bankruptcy as it tries to move 20 million mostly lower class Hispanics into the upper middle class by using tax money from the Euros. One of the latest lunacies was to try to put all illegals on Obamacare. Some persons I know have had their annual medical coverage increase from under $1000 before Obamacare to about $4000 (2017 estimate) and the extra $3000 is what the Democrats are stealing from anyone they can to cover the costs of free or very low cost care for those who pay little or no taxes, and who already are bankrupting hospitals forced to give them free "emergency" care. Of course, the Republicans are trying to kill it, but like the whole government, it is already in a death spiral that only a huge increase in fees can fix.

One of the most flagrant violations of US law by the left-wing lunatics who support immigration is the creation of 'sanctuary cities'. The cities do not allow municipal funds or resources to be used to enforce federal immigration laws, usually by not allowing police or municipal employees to inquire about an individual's immigration status. This began with Los Angeles in 1979 (thus becoming the first large city donated to Mexico) and now includes at least 31 major American cities. Presumably, the President could order the army or the FBI to arrest the city officials who passed these regulations for obstruction of justice etc., but it's a murky legal area as (in another indication of the total ineptness of congress and the courts and the hopelessness of the democratic system as currently practiced) immigration violations are civil offenses and not federal or state felonies which they clearly should be. After I wrote this the courts (predictably) blocked Trump's attempt to cut off funds to sanctuary cities, forgetting that their purpose is to protect the citizens of America, and not those of other countries here illegally. And recently California declared itself a sanctuary state, i.e., it's now part of Mexico.

A competent government (maybe we could import one from Sweden, China or even Cuba?) could pass such legislation in a few weeks. Also, it could force compliance by cutting off most or all federal funds to any city or state that failed to comply with federal immigration laws, and at least one such bill has been introduced into congress recently, but the Democrats prevented its passage, and of course Obama or Clinton would have vetoed any attempt at giving American back to Americans. Trump of course has a different view, though he cannot save America via democratic means.

As long as the Democrats (soon to return to power and, rumor has it, to change their name to Neomarxist Third World Supremacist Party of Latin America, Asia, Africa and the Middle East) are in power, nothing will be done, and more cities and states will cease to be a part of America until Hispanics take over completely sometime in the second half of the century. Only a military coup can save America now and it's very unlikely the generals have the courage.

For this review, I read a few politically oriented books and articles in print and on the web of the kind that I have avoided for over 50 years, and in them and the comments on them saw repeated accusations of 'racist' against people who were only stating their desire to have the USA remain a prosperous and safe country. This claim is now almost always false in the normal meaning, but of course true in the new meaning—i.e., one opposed to letting Mexico and Africa annex America. So, I wrote a reply to this slander, since I have never seen a good one.

Actually, it's not 'racism' but self-defense –the Diverse in America are the racists, as on the average, your life here is largely an exploitation of other races, notably Europeans and Asians who actually pay taxes. For genuine racism look at how different groups native to your own country (or immigrants) are treated there. The vast majority of immigrants in the USA would not even be permitted to enter your countries, much less permitted citizenship, the privilege of voting, free or low cost housing, food, free or subsidized medical care, free school, affirmative action programs, the same privileges as natives etc. And in the USA, it is the Diverse who have taken away the tranquility, beauty, safety and free speech that existed here before a handful of stupid politicians and supreme court justices let you in. We never voted to let you enter or become citizens--it was forced on us by halfwits in our government, beginning with Lincoln and his partners in crime. If we had a chance to vote on it, few foreigners except medical, scientific and tech experts and some teachers would have been admitted and perhaps 75% of the Diverse would be deported. In many cases, you have an alien religion (some of which demand the murder of anyone you take a dislike to) and culture (honor killings of your daughters etc.), do not pay a fair share of taxes (typically none) and commit far more crimes per capita (e.g., 2.5x for Hispanics, 4.5x for blacks).

Furthermore, the middle class American pays about 30% of their income to the govt. This is about 66 days/year of their working life and maybe 20 days of that goes to support the poor, now mostly Diverse. And all the 'free' things such as welfare, food stamps, medical care and hospitals, schools, parks, streets, sanitation, police, firemen, power grid, postal system, roads and airports, national defense etc. exist largely because the 'racist' upper middle and upper class created, maintain and pay for them. Maybe another 4 working days goes to support the police, FBI, justice system, DHS, Border Patrol and other govt. agencies that have to deal with aliens. Add another 10 or so days to support the military, which is mostly needed to deal with the results of 3rd world overpopulation (the real major cause of the Korean War, the Vietnam War, Iraq, Afghanistan, Syria, Libya, Yemen and the major cause of most of the wars, social unrest and conflicts past, present and future), and this cost, added to welfare, medicare, social security and environmental degradation (an ever increasing percentage for immigrants and their descendants) is bankrupting the country, with the only possible solution being to decrease the benefits and increase the taxes, the burden of which will fall on everyone's descendants. You take advantage of the freedom of speech we created to tell malicious lies about us and prevent rational discussion! Most of you, if doing this in your country of origin, would wind up in prison or dead! Shameless liars! What is your problem? --poor education, no gratitude, malicious, stupid, no experience with civilized society? (pick 5). And anyone who doubts any of this just does not know how to use their brain or the net as it's all there. These comments are just the facts that anyone can see, along with simple extrapolations into the future.

Also, please let me ask the Diverse--do people in your country of origin work 30 days a year to support tens of millions of aliens who commit crimes at several times the rate of natives, overcrowd your schools, highways, cities and jails, trash your parks and beaches, spray paint graffiti on buildings and import and sell drugs to addicts who commit over a hundred million crimes a year (added to the 100 million or so they commit themselves)? And have you had a 9/11 and many bombings and murders at home? Do immigrants control the media so that you cannot even discuss these issues that are destroying your country and the world? Will your country be totally in their control in a few generations and be another impoverished, crime ridden, starving, corrupt 3rd world hellhole? Of course, for most of you it already is, and you came to America to escape it. But your descendants won't have to be homesick for the hellhole, as they will have re-created it here. The Diverse here (and their Euro servants) never tire of complaining in all the media every day about how they are not treated fairly and not given enough (i.e., the Euros and the relatively rich Diverse don't work hard enough to support them), and it never crosses their minds that if it were not for taxes paid mostly by Euros now and for over a century previous, there would be little or no police or fire or medical or school services or parks or public transport or streets or sewers in their communities, and of course there would not even be a country here, as it is mainly Euros who created, and support it and who serve in the military in all the wars. And it was primarily Euros and their descendants who created the net and the pc's that was used to create this and the electronic or print media you are reading this on, the tech that produces the food you eat and the medicine that keeps you alive. If not for the Euros technology and security, at least 90% of all the Diverse in the world would not exist. Everyone condemns colonialism, but it was the way that the Diverse were brought out of the dark ages into modern times via communications, medicine, agriculture, and enforcement of democratic government. Otherwise all their populations would have stayed very small, backwards, starving, disease ridden, impoverished, isolated and living in the dark ages (including slavery and its equivalents) to this day. To sum it up, the Euro's antipathy to Diversity ('racism') is due to a desire that their children have a country and a world worth living in. Again, this is for everyone's benefit, not just Euros or the rich.

Likewise, all my life I have been hearing third world people saying that their disproportionate problems with drugs, crime and welfare are due to racism, and certainly there is some truth to that, but I wonder why Asians, who must be subject to racism as well (insofar as it exists—and relative to most Diverse counties, it's quite minimal here), and most of whom came here much more recently, spoke little or no English, had no relatives here and few skills, have a fraction of the crime, drugs and welfare (all less than Euros and so way less than blacks or Hispanics) and average about $10,000 more income per family than Euros. Also, blacks never consider that they would not exist if their ancestors were not brought to the new world and they would never have been born or survived in Africa, that those who captured and sold them were usually African, that to this day Africans in Africa almost universally treat those of different tribes as subhuman (Idi Amin, Rwanda, Gaddafi etc. and far worse is soon to come as the population of Africa swells by 3 billion by 2100), and that if they want to see real racism and economic exploitation and police maltreatment, they should go live almost anywhere in Africa or the 3rd world. Returning to Africa or Mexico etc. has always been an option, but except for criminals escaping justice, nobody goes back. And it was the Euros who put an end to slavery worldwide and, insofar as possible, to serfdom, disease, starvation, crime and war all over the 3rd world. If it were not for colonialism and the inventions of Euros there would be maybe 1/10 as many Diverse alive and they would mostly still be living as they did 400 years ago. Likewise, it's never mentioned that if not for the Euro's, who were about 95% responsible for paying for and fighting and dying in WW2, the Germans and Japanese and/or the Communists would now control the world and only the Euros can prevent the CCP and/or the Muslims from doing so in the future. Also, it was mostly Euros who fought, are fighting and will be fighting the communists in Korea and Vietnam, and the Muslim fanatics in Iraq, Syria, Libya and Afghanistan and the many others soon to come.

Insofar as any revenge on the Euros is needed for their slavery (but slavery by other blacks in various forms has always existed), blacks have already had it abundantly. First, they have been largely supported and protected by the Euros for centuries. Second, the parasites they brought with them have infected and destroyed the lives of tens of millions of Euros. Malaria, schistosomes, filariasis, ascaris, yellow fever, smallpox etc., but above all hookworm, which was so common and so debilitating up to the early decades of this century that it was responsible for the widespread view of Southerners as stupid and lazy.

All this is crushingly obvious, but I bet there is not one grade school or college text in the world that mentions any of it, as it's clearly 'racist' to suggest that the Diverse owe anything to Euros or to point out that other Diverse in their countries of origin always have and always will treat them far worse than Euro do. And they are incapable of grasping the true horror that is coming or they would all be one in opposing any increase in the population by any group anywhere and any immigration into America. Well before 2100 the Hispanics will control America, and the rest of the world will be dominated by Chinese and the rest by Muslims, who will increase from about 1/5th of the world now to about 1/3rd by 2100 and outnumber Christians, and neither group is noted for embracing multiculturalism, women's rights, child rights, animal rights, gay rights, or any rights at all. So, the obvious fact is that overall the Euros have treated the Diverse much better than they have treated each other. And we now have the best of times, while by 2100 (give or take a generation or two) economic collapse and chaos will reign permanently except perhaps a few places that forcibly exclude Diverse. Again, keep in mind that in my view there is not, and almost certainly will never be, any evidence of a significant genetic difference between Euros and Diverse in psychology, or IQ, and that their tendency to excessive reproduction and other cultural limitations are accidents of history.

Likewise, it never crosses Diverse, leftist, third world supremacist, Neomarxist minds that every year maybe 500 billion dollars are spent in the USA by federal, state and city govts. on education, medicine, transportation (highways, streets, rail, bus and airline systems), police, fire and emergency care, numerous welfare programs, the government and judicial systems--the vast majority of it created, maintained and paid for by the Euros, assisted by the taxes of the small minority of well-off Diverse. Also, there is the FBI, NSA, CIA, and the armed forces of the USA (another 500 billion a year) and other Euro countries, without which there would be no USA and little or no peace, security or prosperity anywhere in the world, and they have also been created, run and staffed largely by the Euros, who constitute most of the dead and wounded in every war (less an issue for Hispanics who serve in the military at about half the rate of Euros) and in every police force from 1776 to now. Without medicine and public health measures, most of their ancestors (and the whole third world) would have suffered and often died of leprosy, malaria, worms, bacteria, flu, tuberculosis, smallpox, syphilis, HIV, hepatitis, yellow fever, encephalitis, and the tech for high cholesterol and blood pressure, heart, cancer, and liver surgery, transplants, MRI, XRAY, Ultrasound etc., etc., has almost all been invented, administered and overwhelmingly paid for by the Euro 'racists' and 'white supremacists'.

You think colonialism was bad? Just think what the 3rd world would be like without it, or what it would be like living under the Nazis, communists or Japanese (and will be like living under the Chinese or Muslims once the Diverse destroy America). This excuses nothing but just points out the facts of history. But fine, let's undo the 'injustice' and pass a Back to Africa (and Latin America and Asia etc.) law providing funds to repatriate everyone. They could sell their assets here and most could live like kings there, but of course there would be very few takers. And by the next century there will be 3 billion more Africans (the official estimate) and the whole continent will be a sewer, and 1 billion more Asians, and even India and China (who will add a hundred million or so each) will look like paradise in comparison to Africa, at least until the resources run out (oil, gas, coal, topsoil, fresh water, fish, minerals, forests).

If you look on the net you find the Diverse incessantly whining about their oppression, even when it occurred decades or centuries ago, but I don't see how anything that's done by others, even today, is my responsibility, and much less so in the past. If you want to hold every Euro responsible for what the vast majority now alive are completely innocent of, then we want to hold all Diverse responsible for all the crimes committed by any of them here or their relatives in their countries of origin over the last 400 years, and for their share of all the tens of trillions spent to build and defend the USA and to keep them safe, healthy and well fed. Yes, most blacks and Hispanics are poor due to historical factors beyond their control, just as Euros are often richer due to historical factors beyond theirs, but the important points are that we now alive did not cause this, and that here, as almost everywhere that the Diverse are a significant percentage, they commit most of the crime, collect most of the welfare, pay the least taxes and continue breeding excessively and dragging their countries and the world into the abyss.

Consider as well that the evils of colonialism are only prominent because they were recent. If we look carefully, we find that nearly every group in every country has an endless history of murder, rape, plunder and exploitation of their neighbors that continues today. It's not far off the mark to suggest that the best thing that could happen was to be conquered by the Euros.

Once again, keep in mind that there is not and almost certainly will never be any evidence of a significant genetic difference between Euros and Diverse and that their limitations are almost certainly due to culture. The problem is not the Diverse nor Euros, but that people are selfish, stupid, dishonest, lazy, crazy, and cowardly and will only behave decently, honestly, and fairly if forced to do so. Giving people rights instead of having privileges they must earn is a fatal mistake that will destroy any society and any world. In the tiny groups in which we evolved, where everyone was our relative, reciprocal altruism worked, but in a world soon swelling to 11 billion, this impulse to help others is suicidal. The world is totally preoccupied with terrorists, but their effects are actually trivial compared e.g., to traffic accidents, murders, drug addiction, disease, soil erosion etc., and every day the 7.7 billion do vastly more damage to the world just by living. The mothers of the third world increase the population by about 200,000 every day, and so do hugely more damage every hour than all the terrorists worldwide will do in the whole 21st century (until they get their hands on the bomb). Just the Diverse in the USA in one year will do far more damage to the USA and the world by destroying resources, eroding topsoil and creating CO_2 and other pollution than all terrorism worldwide in all of history. Is there even one politician or entertainer or business person who has a clue? And if they did would they say or do anything— certainly not—who wants to be attacked for 'racism'.

People everywhere are lazy, stupid and dishonest and democracy, justice and equality in a large Diverse welfare state are an open invitation to limitless exploitation of their neighbors and few will resist. In 1979 7% of Americans got means-tested govt. benefits while in 2009 it was over 30% and of course the increase is mostly the diverse. Food stamps rose from 17 million persons in 2000 to about 43 million now. In the first few years of Obama over 3 million enrolled to get 'disability' checks and over 20% of the adult population is now on 'disability' which according to the Census Bureau includes categories such as "had difficulty finding a job or remaining employed "and "had difficulty with schoolwork". There are now almost 60 million working age (16 to 65) adults who are not employed or about 40%

of the labor force. Illegal families get about $2.50 in direct benefits for every dollar they pay in taxes and about another $2.50 indirect benefits (and not counting their damage to the biosphere) so they are a huge and ever increasing drain in spite of frequent fake 'news stories' on the net about their great value.

Interest payments on our national debt are projected to rise to 85% of our total federal income by 2050. About half of our debt is owned by foreign govts., about a quarter by China, and if China continues to buy our debt at current rates, very soon our interest payments to them will cover their total annual military budget (ca. 80 billion vs U.S. of ca $600 billion) and (depending on interest rates) in a few years they would be able to triple or quadruple their military expenditures and it would all be paid for by US taxpayers. Actually, I have not seen it noted, but their lower costs mean that they are actually spending maybe 300 billion. And it is rarely mentioned why the US military budget is so enormous, and how it ties into the high lifestyle and huge govt. subsidies in Europe and worldwide for that matter. The USA is the world's free policeman, providing technology, money and troops for keeping the peace and fighting wars worldwide and is too stupid to ask the other countries to pay their share--until the recent comments by Trump. To a significant extent, the ability of the Europeans and countries worldwide to have a high standard of living is due to the American taxpayers (without of course being asked) paying for their defense for the last 75 years.

The CIS reports total immigration will reach about 51 million by 2023, about 85% of the total population increase (all the rest due to the Diverse already here) and will soon comprise about 15% of the total population—by far the largest percentage in any big country in recent history. It was reported that the Dept. of Homeland Security New Americans Taskforce was directed to process the citizenship applications of the 9 million green card holders ASAP to try to influence the 2016 election.

The federal govt. is a cancer which now takes about 40% of all income from the minority who pay significant taxes and federal govt. civilian employees are hugely overpaid, averaging ca. $81,000 salary and $42,000 benefits while private employees get about $51,000 salary and $11,000 benefits. About 25% of all the goods and services produced in the USA are consumed by the govt. and about 75% of total govt. income is given out as business and farm subsidies and welfare. If all federal taxes were increased by 30% and spending was not increased, the budget might balance in 25 years. Of course, the spending would increase immediately if more money was available, and also the economy would take a huge hit as there would be less incentive to earn or to stay in the USA and business investment and earnings would drop. It is estimated that private sector compliance with govt. regulations costs about 1.8 trillion a year or about 12% of our total GDP, and of course it is growing constantly, so we waste more on govt. paperwork every year than the GDP of most countries. The main push for evermore confiscation of our money (years of our working lives) by the govt. is the communism/socialism/fascism forced on us by the rapid increase of Diverse, but being the world's police force for free has cost us trillions, which also translates into years of our working lives as detailed elsewhere here.

The poor are almost always spoken of as though they were somehow superior to the rich and it is implicit that we ought to make sacrifices for them, but they are only the rich in waiting and when they get rich they are inevitably exactly as loathsome and exploitative. This is due to our innate psychology, which in the small groups in which we evolved made sense, as everyone was our relative, but in a world that is fast collapsing due to the expansion of the Diverse it makes no sense. The poor care no more about others than the rich.

Marvelous that even Obama and the Pope speak about the coming horrors of climate change, but of course not a word about the irresponsible parenthood that is its cause. The most you get from any govt. official, academic or TV documentary is a meek suggestion that climate change needs to be dealt with, but rarely a hint that overpopulation is the source of it and that most of it for the last century and all of it from now on is from the 3rd world. China now creates twice the C02 of the USA and this will rise as it is expected to about double the size of our GDP by 2030 or so, and USA Diverse create about 20% of USA pollution, which will rise to about 50% by the next century.

Ann Coulter in "Adios America" describes the outrageous story of what seems to be the only occasion on which Americans actually got to vote on the immigration issue—what some call "the great Prop 187 democracy ripoff".

In 1994 Californians, outraged to see ever more Hispanics crowding into the state and using up tax money, put on the ballot Proposition 187 which barred illegals from receiving state money. In spite of the expected opposition and outrageous lies from all the self-serving, boot licking Neomarxist third world supremacists, it passed overwhelmingly winning 2/3 of white, 56% of black, 57% of Asian and even 1/3 of Hispanic votes (yes, many middle and upper class Hispanics realize being taken over by Mexico will be a disaster). Note that all these people are 'racists' or 'white supremacists' (or in slightly more polite columns of the Carlos Slim Helu controlled NY Times etc. 'bigots' or 'nativists') according to the current use of this word by a large percentage of liberals, many Hispanics, the Sierra Club, the ACLU and even Nobel Prize winning economist Paul Krugman (who recently called Trump a 'racist' for daring to tell the truth while defending the USA from annexation by Mexico).

It even carried the hopeless Republican candidate for Governor, Pete Wilson to a landslide victory, with 1/3 of his voters stating his support for Prop 187 was their reason for voting for him. However, the "ACLU and other anti-American groups" (Coulter) brought suit and it was soon struck down by a Democratic appointed (i.e., 'honorary Mexican') District Court Judge for being unconstitutional (i.e., protecting Americans rather than aliens). As with the 1898 and 1982 Supreme Court decisions giving citizenship to anyone who is born here, it was another hallucinatory interpretation of our laws and a clear demonstration of the hopelessness of the court system, or any branch of the government (at least a Democrat dominated one) in protecting Americans from a third world takeover. It has been suggested that the ACLU change its name to the Alien Civil Liberties Union and that it, along with the many other organizations and individuals working to destroy the USA, be forced to register as agents of a foreign government or preferably, be classified as terrorists and all their employees and donors deported or quarantined.

In spite of this, neither the state nor federal govt. has done anything whatsoever to prevent the takeover, and Coulter notes that when G.W. Bush ran for president, he campaigned in America with the corrupt Mexican president Gortari (see comments on Carlos Slim below), had brother Jeb 'Illegal Immigration is an act of love' Bush speak in Spanish at the Republican National Convention, and after winning, gave weekly radio addresses in Spanish, added a Spanish page to the White House website, held a huge Cinco de Mayo party at the White House, and gave a speech to the blatantly racist National Council of La Raza, in which, among other outrages, he promised $100 million in federal money (i.e., our money) to speed immigration applications! Clearly with both the Republican and Democratic parties seeking annexation by Mexico, there is no hope for the democratic process in America unless it is drastically changed and clearly this will never happen by using the democratic process.

California is the 6th largest in economy in the world, ahead of France, Brazil, Italy,

South Korea, Australia, Spain, India, Russia, and Canada, and more than double that of Mexico, and in about 10 years, when their 10 million kids grow up and the total Hispanic population of Calif is about 22 million (counting only legals), they will own the state and it will have been annexed by Mexico.

In recent years, Calif. Governor Brown signed legislation granting drivers licenses to illegals, and paying for free medical care for their children (i.e., of course we the taxpayers pay). He agreed to let noncitizens monitor polls for elections, and they have been appointed to other government positions such as city councils without state govt. approval. He also forced all state officials to commit obstruction of justice by signing a law known as the Trust Act (i.e., trust they won't rob, rape, murder, sell drugs etc.), which specifies that unless immigrants have committed certain serious crimes, they cannot be detained (for delivery to the feds for deportation) past when they would otherwise become eligible for release. The batch of new "lets become part of Mexico" laws also included one that would allow immigrants without legal status to be admitted to the state bar and practice law in California. But he vetoed the bill allowing illegal aliens to serve on juries. So, the only thing that prevented the final step in turning over the Calif. Courts to Mexico was the arbitrary decision of one man! However, it won't be more than a few years before an Hispanic is Governor and then this and endless other atrocities will ensue, including presumably giving illegals the right to vote perhaps by passing another state law that violates or obstructs the federal one. In any case, there will soon by little distinction in California between being a citizen of the USA and a citizen of any other country who can sneak across the border. Note that as usual the Citizens of California were never permitted to vote on any of these issues, which were passed by the Democratic controlled state legislature. Why don't they just be honest and change the name to Neomarxist Party of Mexico? At least they should be forced to register as the agent of a foreign govt.

It is certain that California (and by the end of the century the USA) is lost to civilization (i.e., it will be like Mexico, which of course will be far worse by then since most of the world's resources will be gone and another 3 billion people will by demanding them) unless the govt. sends federal troops into California (and other states with sanctuary cities) to deport illegals and arrest all those (including numerous elected officials) who are violating federal law. Even this will only slow up the catastrophe unless a law is passed terminating anchor babies (i.e., those getting citizenship because they are born here), preferably retroactively to 1982 or better to 1898, and rescinding citizenship for them and all those who gained it from them—i.e. all their descendants and relatives. Also of course the 1965 immigration law must be declared unconstitutional and all those (and relatives and descendants) who immigrated since then have their status reviewed with the significant taxpayers remaining and the non or low payers repatriated. Hard to get precise statistics, as its 'racist' to even think about it, but in Stockton, California and Dallas, Texas about 70% of all births are to illegals and maybe 90% of the total counting all Hispanics, and of course the bills are almost all paid by Euros and 'rich' Diverse via forced taxation, which of course they never get to vote on.

To end birthright, a new law has to be passed and not an old one repealed, as there is no such law— this was an utterly arbitrary opinion of Justice Willie, "anchor baby" Brennan and only a handful of justices ever voted for this hallucinatory interpretation of the law. Those who want to see how the Supreme Court destroyed our country by eroding the boundary between being an American citizen and a person who was passing through (and the lack of basic common sense in the law and the hopelessness of the American legal system- and the contrary opinions of legal experts) can consult Levin's 'Men in Black' or see United States v. Wong Kim Ark, 169 U.S. 649 (1898) (yes it was a Chinese who began the assault on America over a century ago) where 6 lawyers (i.e., justices of the court) granted citizenship to the children of resident aliens and Plyler v. Doe, 457 U.S. 202 (1982) where 5 lawyers (with 4 disagreeing) granted citizenship to the children of illegal aliens and anyone giving birth while visiting. If just one of the 5 morons who voted for this had changed their mind, we would have maybe 10 million fewer on the welfare rolls now and perhaps 50 million fewer by 2100. Of course, none of the other 450 million or so adults alive between then and now have ever been permitted to vote on this or any of the basic issues leading inexorably to collapse. As we now see in the media every day, in a 'representative' democracy what is represented is not America's interests, but egomania, greed, stupidity and third world supremacism.

How many people did it take to hand America to Mexico? For the TKO Immigration disaster in 1965 there were 320 representatives and 76 senators, and for anchor babies the two Supreme Court decisions totaling 11 lawyers, most of these 'outstanding citizens' now dead, so out of the approx. 245 million adult Americans citizens alive now, about 120 very senior citizens actually voted for the handover. As clear a demonstration of the hopelessness of representative democracy (as practiced here) as one could want.

Clearly, if America is to remain a decent place to live for anyone, the 1965 act, and all subsequent ones, need to be repealed by a law that puts a moratorium on all immigration and naturalization, and preferably rescinds or at least reviews citizenship for everyone naturalized since 1965 (or preferably since the first absurd birthright ruling in 1898), along with all their relatives and descendants. All their cases could be reviewed and citizenship conferred on select individuals who scored high enough on a point scale, with welfare recipients, the chronically unemployed, felons, and their descendants ineligible, those with college or medical degrees, teachers, engineers, business owners etc., getting points towards eligibility, i.e., just basic common sense if America is to survive.

Following Ann Coulter ('Adios America'), we note that corporate tax in the USA is one the highest in the world of major countries at 39% and as the govt. continues to raise taxes to support the half of the country that is on some kind of welfare (if one includes social security, unemployment, food stamps, housing subsidies, welfare and veterans benefits), inevitably capital and jobs will leave, and entering the next century with vanishing resources, and since the entire annual population increase of 2.4 million is now Diverse, that means about 200 million more of them (for a total of around 350 million out of about 500 million) by 2100, a fragmented populace fighting for resources, and a drastically reduced standard of living with eventual collapse is inevitable, even without the predatory evils of the Seven Senile Sociopaths (i.e., the CCP)..

Regarding the tax situation, in 2013, those with gross incomes above $250,000 (nearly all of them Euros) paid nearly half (48.9%) of all individual income taxes, though they accounted for only 2.4% of all returns filed and their average tax rate was 25.6%. The bottom 50% of filers (those making under $34,000-maybe half Diverse and half Euros) paid an average of 1.2% federal income tax for total share of 2.4% while the next 35% of filers (those making $34k to $69k) averaged 21% tax rate for a total share of 10.5% of total federal income tax collected. So, it is obvious that contrary to the common view of the Democrats/third world supremacists/Neomarxists, the upper and upper middle class are giving the poor a largely free ride, and that we already have one foot in communism. However, we must not forget the $2.5 billion a day the US is going into debt and the total $80 trillion or more unfunded liabilities (e.g., social security and medicare), which will have to eventually be paid by some combo of increased taxes and decreased benefits to their descendants. Consider this: "When we combine the populations of non-payers and non-filers and look to see what overall percentage of each group is not paying taxes, we find that: 50.7 percent of African American households pay no income taxes, 35.5 percent of Asian American households do not, 37.6 percent of White American households do not, and 52 percent of (legal) Hispanics pay no income taxes." There are about 5X as many Euros (whites) as blacks and 4X as many

Euros as Hispanics in the USA, and there are about the same % of whites and blacks on welfare (39%) and about 50% of Hispanics, so percentage wise that means blacks are about 5X and Hispanics about 8X as likely to be on welfare as Euros.

Including property taxes, sales taxes etc. brings the average middle class ($34k to $69k income) tax up to about 30%, so 4 months/year or about 15 years labor in a 50 year lifetime goes to the government, a large percentage to support immigrants who are destroying America and the world, and another large percentage for the military, which is a free police force for the rest of the world.

Counting all support as enumerated above (i.e., not just food stamps etc., but the poor's fair share of all other expenses) the average middle-class family works roughly 5 weeks/year or 5 years of their working life to support the poor. Neither mass immigration, nor slavery, nor anchor babies, nor excessive breeding, nor unemployment, nor crimes and drugs are their fault, but the middle and upper class pay for the poor, and their kids will pay more (likely at least 10 years of their 50 year working life well before 2100) until the standard of living and quality of life is about the same as that of Diverse countries, and they will both drop continually every year until collapse, even if the Gang of Seven Sociopaths is destroyed.

Of course, every statistic has a counter statistic and the Neomarxist Third World Supremacists and the Fifty Cent Army of the CCP are busily spreading disinformation and trolling all social media, but as a rough guide we find a recent study that found that 37% of Hispanic immigrant households got the majority of their income from welfare while 17% of blacks did (whites were not reported but I would guess about 10%). Of the $ 3.5 trillion budget, about 595 billion is deficit and about 486 billion goes to welfare, so eliminating welfare would almost balance it and eliminating all the costs associated with persons and their descendants naturalized since 1965 would put the USA solidly in the black and would probably allow paying off the $18 trillion national debt before the end of the century, while implementing a Naturalized Citizens Repatriation Act would likely allow this closer to midcentury.

As I write this I see a 'news item' (i.e., one of the endless barrage of paid lies planted there every day by the Diverse and the Fifty Cent Army) on Yahoo that tells me that illegals are doing us a big favor as the majority are working and pay about $1000 each tax per year. But they don't tell us that they cost the country maybe $25,000 each in direct traceable costs and if you add their share of all the other costs (to maintain the govt. the police, the courts, the army, the streets etc., etc.) it's likely double that. As Coulter tells you on p47 of Adios America, a college educated person pays an average $29k taxes more per year than they get back in govt. services. Legal immigrants however get back an average $4344 more than they pay, while those without a high school degree get back about $37k more than they pay. She says that about 71% of illegal households get welfare.

About 20% of US families get 75% of their income from the govt (i.e., extorted from taxpayers and borrowed from banks at 2.5 billion/day) and another 20% get 40%. In the UK, which is about on a par with the USA on its Diverse/Neomarxist path to ruin, about 5 million persons or 10% of able adults live totally on welfare and have not worked a day since the Labour govt. took over in 1997, and another 30% receive partial support. Greece, famous for it's recent huge bailout, is a typical case of how the masses always drag a country into chaos if permitted. People normally retire on full govt. pensions in their 50's and as early as 45, and when retirement at 50 was permitted for a couple of hazardous jobs like bomb disposal, it soon was enlarged to cover over 500 occupations including hairdressers (hazardous chemicals like shampoo) and radio and TV announcers (bacteria on microphones)—no I am not joking.

People often praise European countries for their generous welfare, but in fact it is mainly possible because nearly all their defense since the 50's (to say nothing about the two world wars, the Korean and Vietnamese wars, Afghanistan, Iraq, Syria, Somalia, Serbia etc., etc.), i.e., about $10 trillion in direct costs and perhaps another $10 trillion indirect) has been paid for by the USA (and by American lives and injuries), i.e., by the 20% of US taxpayers who pay any significant tax, plus much of the $18 trillion debt. In fact, like all the world, they would not even be independent countries if not for the USA who defeated the Germans in two wars and the Japanese and kept the communists and now the Muslims under control for half a century. So not only is the U.S. bled dry by the poor and Diverse here, but we pay for them all over the world as well as helping the rich there get richer. Typical of all Europe, in France, where the Muslims have become a huge problem, even when not slaughtering people, most of them are on welfare, paid for in part by the USA. For about a decade the biggest voting bloc in the U.N is the Organization of Islamic Cooperation which controls e.g., the Human Rights Council, where they allow only the rights permitted by Islamic law, and so forget women's rights, children's rights, gay rights, freedom of religion, free speech etc. and in fact freedom of any kind. As the Muslims unrestrained breeding increases their percent of world population from 1/5 to 1/3 by 2100 or so and civilization collapses, this will get much worse.

Islam is defended with such ferocity because in the poor 3rd world countries it has been the only defense against selfishness, and it provides poor men with a guarantee of reproduction and survival. The same used to be the case for Christianity. It is also clear that as the 22nd century approaches and America collapses, China will replace it as the 'Great Satan' since it will be dominant worldwide, protecting its ever-growing investments and Chinese citizens, and eventually doing whatever it wants, as 'Diversification' results in control of America by Mexicans and Africans and it loses military superiority and the money and will to fight. And of course, the Chinese will not follow America's path and be 'diversified' into collapse, unless via some great misfortune they become democratic/Neomarxist (they are of course now only communist in name).

A bit off the mark but too nice to pass up is a lovely example of devolution (dysgenics) that is second only to overpopulation in bringing about the collapse of industrial civilization (though political correctness forbids discussion anywhere).
U.K. Pakistanis, who often import their cousins to marry and so are inbreeding with up to 5 children a family, sometimes with multiple wives, produce 30% of the rare diseases in the UK, though they are 2% of the population. Of course, most are on welfare and the defectives result in huge expenses for full time nursing care and special education (for those not deaf and blind). And the European High Court, like the US Supreme Court, has forgotten its real reason for existing and enraptured by Suicidal Utopian Delusions, has ruled the govt must pay full spousal benefits to all the wives and can't draw the line at two.

A good part of Coulter's book is spent on crime, and we should first note (Coulter does not seem to, though I expect she knows) that it is rarely considered that it is hugely underreported, especially among the poor and Diverse. Thus, the BJS says that about 3.4 million violent crimes per year go unreported and the figures for nonviolent ones (burglary, assault, petty theft, vandalism, drug dealing, etc.) must be in the hundreds of millions, disproportionately committed by (and suffered by) the Diverse. One finds that the percent of adult males incarcerated for whites is 0.7, for Hispanics 1.5 and for blacks 4.7. It appears impossible to find any precise national figures for the cost of incarceration but $35K/year seems a minimum, and perhaps $50K for the legal system, and perhaps another $50k in medical and psychological costs, rehab programs, loss of work by their victims etc. According to the BJS non-Hispanic blacks accounted for 39.4% of the prison and jail population in 2009, while non-Hispanic whites were 34.2%, and Hispanics (of any race) 20.6%. According to a 2009 report by the Pew Hispanic Center, in 2007 Latinos "accounted for 40% of all sentenced federal offenders--more than triple their share (13%) of the total U.S. adult population". Again, keep in mind there is not and almost certainly will never be any evidence of a significant genetic difference between Euros and Diverse in psychology, or IQ, and that their greater incidence of problems must be wholly due to their culture.

If one counted only illegals, the crime and imprisonment rate would likely be double that reported for legal Hispanics. As Coulter notes (p101-2) it's impossible to get the actual figures for immigrant crime since it's of course 'racist' to even suggest they should be collected (and as noted, all crime among Diverse is greatly underreported and many Hispanics are misclassified as whites), but it's definitely above that stated, so their actual rate could be near that of blacks. One set of data showed about 1/3 of the 2.2 million state and local prisoners are foreign born and maybe another 5% are American born Hispanics and another 30% black, leaving about 32% white. The foreign born were 70% more likely to have committed a violent crime and twice as likely a class A felony. As Coulter notes, virtually all immigrant groups have a higher crime rate than natives. As the invasion continues, bribery and extortion will see huge increases as they rise to the third world standard. Bribes (the mildest form of extortion) in cash or equivalent is the normal interaction between people in the third world and police, the military, customs and immigration officers, health and fire inspectors, teachers, school admissions officers, and even doctors, surgeons and nurses. I am not guessing here as I spent a decade of my life in the third world and experienced and heard countless stories about all of the above. As time passes, we can expect this to become routine here as well (first of course in California and the other Western states) and the nationwide norm thereafter. In addition to continued increases in crime of all kinds we will see the percentage of crimes solved drop to the extremely low levels of the third world. More resources are devoted to the solution of murders than any other crime and about 65% are solved in the USA, but in Mexico less than 2% are solved and as you get outside Mexico City the rate drops to near zero. Also note that the rate here used to be about 80%, but it has dropped in parallel with the increase in Diverse. Also 65% is the average but if you could get statistics, I am sure it would rise with the percent of Euro's in a city and drop as the percent of Diverse increases. In Detroit only 30% are solved. If you keep track of who robs, rapes and murders, it's obvious that black lives matter lots more to Euros than they do to other blacks.

Spanish may become the official and mandatory language and Roman Catholicism the official religion, and of course the Mexican cartels will be the dominant criminal organizations, at least for the Southwestern states by midcentury and likely the whole country by 2100.

Of course, as Coulter points out, it's very hard to get statistics on race and crime or increasingly on race and anything, as it's considered 'racism' even to ask and the govt. refuses to collect it. Finding the truth is made much more difficult since Hispanic special interest groups (i.e., third world supremacists), abetted by Euro liberals, who have lost or sold whatever common sense or decency they may have had, are hard at work spreading disinformation with hundreds of thousands of false or misleading items on the net and social media every week. She does not seem to mention the massive deception facilitated by Yahoo, Bing, Facebook and others, who present among their news items, paid disinformation which presents 'news' that is deliberately false or hugely misleading, such as the item mentioned above (repeated many times a day somewhere on the net) which says that illegals are a good thing as they are paying taxes.

In spite of being given a largely free ride, the Diverse take it all for granted (especially as it's 'racist', 'hate' and 'white supremacist' to point out their free ride, so you won't find it in the major media) and have no problem suing the police, hospitals, and every branch of government for any imagined infraction. The Euros should get a clue and sue them back! They and the US govt, now that Trump is president, could file millions of suits or criminal cases against people who riot in the streets, picket and protest disrupting traffic, smashing windows and causing business losses, psychological trauma, etc. Sue and/or arrest all the criminals and their families for the damages to property, police, loss of business income and work, etc. Also sue the police and every branch of government for failing to protect them every time a crime is committed, especially by illegal Diverse.

As I wrote this the parents of a young San Francisco woman murdered by an illegal alien criminal, who had been deported numerous times, and then shielded from deportation by the San Francisco police (obstruction of justice), is suing them and the feds (and they should sue the board of Supervisors and Governor Brown and the state legislature who voted for the sanctuary rules and Trust Act as well). Predictably he was found not guilty and in the sanctuary city of San Francisco (and now the sanctuary state of California) is able to live out his life of crime while being supported at public expense.

Hundreds of thousands are robbed, assaulted, raped or murdered by Diverse, and perhaps 100 million victimized in lesser ways every year, and the injured parties (most often Diverse) should sue every time. To facilitate this, the Euros could establish a fund and various organizations to eliminate illegals and crime against Euros. And of course, all the countries that foreign born criminals come from should be forced to pay the cost of policing and prosecuting them and of keeping them here—welfare, medical care, schooling, and their share of all the goods and services mentioned above, including national defense. Mexico should pay all the costs of policing the border and for all the crimes and for all the upkeep of illegals here since day one—i.e., back to say 1965. And they and Colombia etc. should pay for the cost of drug enforcement, addict treatment and jailing, and say a $20 million fine every time someone is raped, disabled or murdered by a drug addict or by an illegal or a naturalized citizen or descendant of a person originating in their country. If they won't we could expel everyone born there and cut off all trade and visas, or just confiscate their oil, mineral and food production. Like many of the ideas here it sounds bizarre because the cowardice and stupidity of 'our' leaders (i.e., not actually ours as we are never asked) has gotten us so used to being abused. We are the last country that should put up with abuse but the politicians and leftist morons have made us the easiest mark on the planet. Yes 9/11 is the most striking abuse, but in fact we suffer as many deaths and injuries from the Diverse every year (e.g., just from drugs and addicts or just from wars), and far more damage every day, if you extrapolate the consequences of their presence here into the future.

Much controversy was generated when Trump mentioned we were letting rapists into the country, but he was just stating the facts. Most crimes in Diverse communities are never reported, often because they are committed by the Hispanic gangs who control them. Coulter recounts a few (the publisher cut the book in half and she says she can easily produce 50 cases for every one cited) of the more outrageous immigrant rape crimes committed here, noting a study in which Latino women here reported childhood sexual abuse at about 80X the rate of other American women, and since it seems likely many did not want to talk about it, it could be higher. She notes that in much of Latin America raping teenagers is not considered a crime (e.g., the age of consent in Mexico is 12) and in any case, it is rare that anything is done about it, since it's often connected to gang members or their families and if you protest you die.

Coulter notes that illegals have made large areas of SouthWestern USA public lands and parks unsafe and some have been closed. Half of some 60 forest fires on federal or tribal land between 2006 and 2010 were started by illegals, many of them set deliberately to avoid capture. The cost of fighting these 30 alone might pay for a good start on a secure border fence.

I assume everyone knows about the massive marijuana growing operations conducted by the Mexican cartels in our national forests. In addition to the erosion and pollution, it is the norm for growers to kill numerous animals and threaten hikers. Most depressing of all is the sellout of the Sierra Club (who suddenly changed their tune after getting a $100 million contribution from billionaire David Gelbaum with the proviso that they support immigration—clearly confused as his right hand protects nature while the left destroys it), who are now devoted to mass immigration, denouncing anyone opposed as "white racists" even when they are Diverse. So, they are another group that should be made to register as an agent of a foreign government and their executives and major contributors made to join the other criminals quarantined on an island (the Aleutians would be perfect but even Cuba would do) where they can't do more harm. Considering the blatant trashing of California by Hispanics, and the clear as day end of nature in America as the immigrants about double the population during the next century or so, this is truly amazing from one viewpoint, but cowardice and stupidity are only to be expected.

One murder in the USA is said to total about $9 million lifetime costs and if they get death it is several million more. At about 15,000/year that would be about $150 billion/year just for homicides-most by Diverse. Mexico has about 5X the murder rate of the USA and Honduras about 20X and your descendants can certainly look forward to our rate moving in that direction. Coulter notes that Hispanics have committed about 23,000 murders here in the last few decades. As I write, this item appeared on the net. "In an undated file photo, Jose Manuel Martinez arrives at the Lawrence County Judicial Building in Moulton, Ala., before pleading guilty to shooting Jose Ruiz in Lawrence County, Ala., in March 2013. Martinez has admitted to killing dozens of people across the United States as an enforcer for drug cartels in Mexico." Not of course rare, just one of the few to make the headlines recently.

Figuring about 2.2 million prisoners (over 1% of the adult population) and a cost to put them in jail from the start of their criminal career of maybe $50,000 each or about $100 billion and the cost to keep them there of about $35,000 each or about $75 billion means a minimum of $150 billion a year, not including other governmental and social costs. I don't see any really clear estimates on the net for the total cost of crime in the USA, but in 2013 it was estimated that violent crime alone cost the UK (where guns are much less frequent and the Mexican and Colombian mafias don't operate significantly) ca. $150 billion or about $6000/household, or about 8% of GDP, but the USA has a much higher percentage of immigrants, guns and drugs, so including all the nonviolent crimes and figuring only 5% of the GDP, that would be about 900 billion per year. Figuring about 60% of crime due to the Diverse, or maybe 80% if you count that of Euros addicted to drugs imported by Diverse, we pay something like 700 billion a year to support Diverse crime.

Of course, all those guilty of felonies, regardless of national origin, history or status could have their citizenship rescinded and be deported or quarantined on an island, where their cost of upkeep could be from $0 to $1000/year rather than $35,000 and it could be made a one-way trip to avoid recidivism. Yes, its sci-fi now, but as the 22nd century approaches and civilization collapses, the tolerance of crime will diminish of necessity. For now, nothing will be done, and crime here will reach the levels in Mexico as the border continues to dissolve and environmental collapse and approaching bankruptcy dissolve the economy. Inside Mexico in 2014 alone, 100 U.S. citizens were known to have been murdered and more than 130 kidnapped and others just disappeared, and if you add other foreigners and Mexicans it runs into the thousands. Even a tiny lightly traveled country like Honduras manages some 10 murders and 2 kidnappings a year of US citizens. And of course, these are the best of times—it is getting steadily worse as unrestrained breeding and resource depletion bring collapse ever closer.

In another index of how far out of control Mexico is, the criminal cartels, believed to generate well over $21 billion each year from drugs, illegal mining, fishing and logging, theft, prostitution, extortion, kidnapping and embezzlement, are an increasing threat to Pemex, the Mexican oil monopoly. Between 2009 and 2016, thieves tapped the pipelines roughly every 1.4 kms along Pemex's approximately 14,000 km pipeline network, getting more than $1 billion in annual revenue from the gas which they sell on the black market. They are able to do this by terrorizing Pemex employees to obtain info on its operations, offering them the same as they do for everyone in Mexico—silver or lead, i.e., take the bribes or you and your family die.

Euros hear constantly about how bad they are not to want to give the Diverse even more. OK fine, lets agree to do it provided the third world country they are from lets in immigrants until they comprise about 30% of their population now and 60% by 2100, enforces legislation that gives all foreigners in their country, legally or not, citizenship for their babies, welfare, free food, free medical care, free schooling, immunity to deportation, free emergency care, drivers licenses, license to practice law, right to serve on juries, right to bring in all their relatives (who also get all these privileges), right to setup organizations that help them to lie on immigration forms, to evade deportation, to suppress free speech and to subvert the political process so that they can take over the country. Actually, let's make it easy and do it if even one of their countries implements even a few of these. Of course, it will never happen.

Naturally, those with every kind of mental or physical deficiency are dissatisfied with their level of welfare and are getting organized too. Those with autism, actually a spectrum of genetic deficiencies due to as many as 1000 genes, are now campaigning to be regarded as not deficient but 'neurodiverse' and 'neurotypicals' should regard them as peers or even their superiors. No problem for me if someone wants to have a 'friend' or spouse who cannot experience love or friendship and who feels the same when they die as they do when their goldfish does (except being more annoyed by the greater inconvenience). And those with more than mild cases will never hold a job and will be a burden to their relatives and society (i.e., the minority who pay taxes) all their lives, and have a strong tendency to pass the problem on to any offspring they have, so it will likely increase continually, the same as hundreds of other genetic problems with significant heritability. As diagnosis has improved, so has the incidence of autism, which now exceeds 1%, as does that for schizophrenia, schizotypal disorders, ADHD, drug addiction, alcoholism, alexithymia, low IQ, depression, bipolar disorder, etc., etc., so perhaps the combined incidence of disabling mental disorders exceeds 10% and those with physical problems who need partial or complete lifelong support is probably similar, and both are rising in number and percent, the inevitable results of 'civilization', 'democracy' and 'human rights'. Clearly, as the economy collapses, the costs of health care rise, and an ever-larger percentage are nonworking elderly and mentally or physically disabled, this lunatic system will collapse-i.e., the USA will eventually have about the same handouts for everyone as third world countries by the early 22nd century—none.

Coulter comments on Mexican citizen Carlos Slim Helu (the world's third richest person as I write this) in the context of the near universal lying about and evasion of immigration issues by the New York Times and other media. He gave a huge loan to the Times a few years ago, to save it from bankruptcy, and this likely accounts for its subsequent failure to cover immigration issues in a meaningful way. Slim is the world's premiere monopolist and his companies control 90% of the Mexican telephone market and many of its major industries (Mexican's refer to their country as Slimlandia). His wealth is the equivalent of roughly 5% of Mexico's GDP. To add perspective, since the USA has about 15 times Mexico's GDP, to be comparable, Bill Gates or Warren Buffet would have to be worth about a trillion dollars each or about 12X their worth as of 2019. California is the biggest money making US state for Slim, whose take of Mexican goods and services is about $140 million/day. To get the flavor of how things were when Slim managed to acquire the Mexican telephone company (and what can be expected here soon), Gortari (chosen by G.W. Bush to campaign with him) was president of the vicious Mexican political monopoly PRI, and in subsequent years Gortari's brother was found murdered, his relatives were apprehended by Swiss police when they tried to withdraw $84 million from his brother's bank account, and he fled Mexico for Ireland, where he remains. These are among the reasons Coulter calls Slim a robber baron and a baneful influence on Mexico and America. She notes that about $20 billion of Slim's yearly income from his telephone monopoly comes from Mexicans living here. He is Lebanese on both sides, so Mexico has experienced it's own foreign takeover.

The bleeding hearts insist Americans show ever more "humanity" and guarantee our own collapse to help the mob, but what humanity do the Diverse show? They breed like rabbits and consume without restraint, thus condemning everyone, including their own descendants, to Hell on Earth. There is nothing noble about the poor—they are just the rich in waiting. Showing the typical oblivion of the establishment, our Secretary of State Kerry praises China for 'lifting 200 million people out of poverty' but fails to note this placed a huge drain on the world resources, and is done by stealing from the future, including their own descendants, and that this is unsustainable. Ten or 11 billion (by 2100) all trying to stay out of poverty guarantees the collapse of the world. China's higher QOL, like our own, is only temporary, obtained at the cost of their own descendants and the worlds future.

How much Quality of Life (QOL- a general measure including wealth, crime rate, stress, traffic, drug problems, happiness etc.) might Americans gain by various measures? Banning anchor babies might up QOL 5% by mid-century and 10% by the end, relative to doing nothing. Making the ban retroactive to 1982, or preferably to 1898, and thus deporting most of those naturalized by being related to anchor babies, might raise QOL another 5% immediately. Banning immigration might raise it another 10% by end of century, while making the ban retroactive to 1965 and deporting most immigrants along with their descendants and naturalized relatives might give Americans (Diverse and Euros) another 20% more QOL immediately.

And there might be a Back to Africa or Slavery Restitution Act which sent all blacks, or at least those on welfare, unemployed or in prison, back to their homelands so we would never again have to listen to their inane complaints about being kidnapped (as noted, they never consider that if not for slavery they would not exist and if not for colonialism and Euro technology maybe 90% of the people in the third world would not exist), not to mention if not for Euro's they would now be living (or dying) under the Nazi's or the Japanese or the communists. Of course, one could do this on a case by case basis, keeping all the skilled (e.g., medical and hitech personnel). Instead of or prior to the slow deportation process, one could cancel the citizenship or at least the voting privileges of all the naturalized citizens and their descendants since 1965.

The 42 million African-Americans (about 74 million by 2100) who account for 4.5x as many prisoners per capita as Euros, get a largely free ride for all essential services and welfare, take over and render uninhabitable large areas of cities, increase the crowding and traffic by about 13% etc., so they may decrease the QOL of all Americans about 20% on average but to unliveable for those who are in poor neighborhoods. Hispanics amount to about 18% (or about 25% including illegals) and they account for a minimum of 2.5X as many prisoners as Euros and have all the other issues, thus causing a QOL drop of about 30% or again to unliveable in areas they dominate, which soon will include the whole southwestern USA. So overall, it's a fair guess that deporting most Diverse would about double the QOL (or say from just bearable to wonderful) right now for the average person, but of course much more increase for the poorer and less for the richer. If one compares likely QOL in 2119 (i.e., a century from now), if all the possible anti-diversity measures were adopted, relative to what it will be if little or nothing is done, I expect QOL would be about 3X higher or again from intolerable to fantastic.

After documenting the incompetence of the INS and the govt., and the countless treasonous and blatantly anti-white racist (in the original meaningful sense of racist) organizations (e.g., the National Council of La Raza) helping to swamp us with immigrants (partial list on p247 of Adios America) Coulter says "The only thing that stands between America and oblivion is a total immigration moratorium" and "The billion dollar immigration industry has turned every single aspect of immigration law into an engine of fraud. The family reunifications are frauds, the "farmworkers" are frauds, the high-tech visas are frauds and the asylum and refugee cases are monumental frauds." Her book is heavily documented (and most data were left out due to size constraints) and of course nearly all the data can be found on the net.

As Coulter notes, a 2015 poll shows that more Americans had a favorable opinion of North Korea (11%) than wanted to increase immigration (7%,) but most Democrats, the Clintons, the Bush's, Obama, casino mogul Sheldon Adelson, Hedge

Fund billionaire David Gelbaum, Carlos Slim, Nobel Prize winning economist Paul Krugman and megabillionaire Facebook founder Mark Zuckerberg don't want Americans to ever vote on it. She also mentions that then Florida Governor Jeb Bush (with a Mexican wife) pushed for a bill to give drivers licenses to illegal aliens (copying California) just 3 years after 13 of the 9/11 terrorists had used Florida drivers licenses to board the planes. Yes, the same Jeb Bush who recently called Illegal immigration "an act of love" (of course he means love for Mexico and hatred for the USA, or at least its Euros).

The inexorable collapse of the USA (and other first world countries in Europe are just a step or two behind, as they have let in Diverse who are producing children at about 3 times Euro rates) shows the fatal flaws in representative democracy. If they are to survive and not turn into third world hellholes, they must establish a meritocracy. Change the voting age to 35 minimum and 65 maximum, with minimum IQ 110, proof of mental stability, lack of drug or alcohol dependence, no felony convictions, and a minimum score on the SAT test that would get one into a good college. But the sorry state of what passes for civilization is shown by a recent Gallup poll which found that about 50% of Americans believed the Devil influences daily events, and that UFO's are real, while 36% believe in telepathy and about 25% in ghosts. A yes on any of these would seem to be a good reason for lifetime exclusion from voting and preferably loss of citizenship as should a 'yes' or 'possibly' or 'probably' answer to "Do you think O.J. Simpson is innocent".

Perhaps it will lessen the pain slightly to realize that it is not only the American government that is moronic and treasonous, as versions of its suicide are happening in other democracies. In Britain, the National Children's Bureau has urged daycare teachers to report any 'racist' utterance of children as young as three. About 40% of Britons receive some form of welfare. London has more violent crime than Istanbul or New York and is said to have almost 1/3 of the world's CCTV cameras, which record the average citizen about 300 times a day. Of course, as usual, there are no trustworthy statistics for China, where some of the most successful electronics companies are in the CCTV business and where facial recognition software can often identify any random person in minutes. The UK has the highest rate in Europe of STD's, unwed mothers, drug addiction and abortion. One fifth of all children have no working adult in their house, almost a million people have been on sick leave for over a decade, the courts forced the govt. to give a disabled man money to fly to Amsterdam to have sex with a prostitute because to deny it would be a "violation of his human rights". The number of indictable offenses per 1000 rose from about 10 in the 1950's to about 110 in the 1990's in parallel with the increase in

Diverse. Thanks to Mark Steyn's "After America", which is required reading for all bright, civilized Americans who want their country to survive, though barring a military coup, there is not a chance.

Coulter points out the absurdity of politicians fawning on the Hispanic voters (Hispandering). If presidential candidate Mitt Romney had won 71% of the Hispanic vote instead of 27% he still would have lost, but if he had won only 4% more of the white vote he would have won. In fact, 72% of voters are non-Hispanic white, so even if someone got ALL the nonwhite votes, a presidential candidate could still win by a landslide, as we saw in the Trump election. The problem is a sizeable percent of white voters are morons and lunatics who are unable to act in their own self-interest. The absurdity of letting average citizens vote was shown when many were seriously considering Ben Carson for president in 2016--a Seventh Day Adventist bible thumping creationist Detroit ghetto homeboy of such obvious immaturity and stupidity that no sane country would permit him to occupy any public office whatsoever (of course one could say the same of most people and most politicians). He has however, the huge advantage that his defects give him much in common with the average American. It appears to me his limitations include autism-the reason for his famous "flat affect". Do not be fooled by his occasional simulations of laughter--autistics learn to mimic emotions at an early age and some even have successful careers as comedians. Famous comedian Dan Aykroyd had this to say about his Asperger's -- "One of my symptoms included my obsession with ghosts and law enforcement -- I carry around a police badge with me, for example. I became obsessed by Hans Holzer, the greatest ghost hunter ever. That's when the idea of my film Ghostbusters was born."

"Gentle Ben" Carson wants to outlaw abortion, even in cases of rape and incest, thinks we should ditch Medicare, and adheres to many weird conspiracy theories, such as the pyramids not being built by the pharaohs as tombs, but by the biblical Joseph for the storage of grain! He proposes to turn the Department of Education into a fascist overseer of proper morals, with students reporting professors who displayed political bias (i.e., anyone whatsoever) to the government so universities' funding could be cut. "I personally believe that this theory that Darwin came up with was something that was encouraged by the Adversary." The Adversary is a nickname for the devil; it's the actual translation of the word "Satan." He also dismissed the Big Bang, calling it a "fairy tale." Like all creationists, that means that he rejects most of modern science--i.e., everything that lets us make sense of biology, geology, physics and the universe and puts them on all fours with people who lived 100,000 years ago--i.e., Neanderthals. Of course, to the sane, intelligent and educated, "fairy tales" are about heaven, hell, angels and devils, but these are at exactly the right level for the average low class American, Diverse or Euro. Hard to believe we could do worse than the Clinton's, Nixon, Reagan, Obama and G.W. Bush, but it will happen, and your descendants will see an endless line of politicians who's only real qualifications are greed, dishonesty, stupidity, sociopathy, dark skin or a Spanish surname. In any case, it's unavoidable in a mobocracy that morons, lunatics and the merely clueless will take over and run the show until it collapses, which is inevitable unless democracy as currently practiced changes radically and Diversity decreases.

Now that we have a reasonably sane, intelligent, patriotic person as president (though seeing this thru the massive disinformation and libel produced by the Neomarxist Third World Supremacists can be difficult) and enough Republicans in congress (the Democrats having sold out their country long ago) we could theoretically deport the illegals, but unless we terminate immigration and retroactively deport most of those naturalized since 1965, it will only slow the disaster and not stop it. However nearly everything Trump tries to do is blocked by the Neomarxist judges and the democrats who long ago ceased to represent America's interests.

Hillary Clinton was preferable to Obama, who was trained as a constitutional lawyer, so he knew our systems fatal weaknesses, and how much further he could go in creating a communist state enforced by fascism, like his much-admired model Cuba. I can easily forgive Hillary for Benghazi and her emails and Bill for Monica, but not for their utterly cynical pardoning of clients of Hillary's brother Hugh, tax cheat Marc Rich and four Hasids convicted in 1999 of bilking the federal government of more than $30 million in federal housing subsidies, small business loans and student grants, in order to curry favor with N.Y. Jews. This is very well known and in fact just about everything I say here is easily findable on the net.

Even though our mobocracy is a slow-motion nightmare, if we had a direct democracy (as we easily could in the computer age) and people were actually polled on important issues, perhaps most of our major problems would be disposed of quickly. Suppose tomorrow there was a vote of every registered voter with an email address or smartphone on questions something like this:

Should all illegal aliens be deported within one year? Should welfare be cut in half within 1year? Should all convicted felons born in another country or one of whose parents were, have their citizenship canceled and be deported within 90 days? Should all immigration be terminated except temporary work visas for those with special skills? Should all child molesters, rapists, murderers, and drug addicts have their citizenship canceled and deported, or if a native citizen, quarantined on an island?

So much the better if voting was restricted to those whose parents and/or all four grandparents are native born, who are non- felons, who have paid more than 5% of their income in taxes the last 3 years and passed mental health, current events and IQ tests. Again, the biggest benefactors would be the Diverse who remained here, but of course the majority will resist any change that requires intelligence or education to grasp.

I am not against a Diverse society, but to save America for your children (recall I have no descendants nor close relatives), it should be capped at say 20% and that would mean about 40% of the Diverse here now would be repatriated. Actually I would not object to keeping the % Diverse we have now (about 37%) provided half the ones here were replaced by carefully screened Asians or by people from anywhere provided they are carefully screened (i.e., no criminals, mental or physical defectives, no religious nuts, no drug addicts, well educated with a proven useful profession), and that they agree to have no more than two children, with immediate deportation if they produce a third, commit a major felony, or remain on welfare for more than one year. And no relatives are permitted entry. In fact, it would be a huge step forward to replace all the Euro criminals, drug addicts, mental cases, welfare users, and chronically unemployed etc. with suitable Diverse. Of course, it's impossible now, but as civilization collapses and the Seven Sociopaths of the CCP take over, many amazing things will happen, all of them extremely unpleasant for billions of people, with the Diverse having the most suffering and dying. Coulter jokingly suggests inviting Israel to occupy the border with Mexico, as they have shown how to guard one. However, I would suggest really doing it— either giving them the Southern portion of each border state or perhaps just occupying the border section of Mexico (which we could do in a few days). Israel should be delighted to have a second country, since their position in Israel will become untenable as the USA, France etc. lose the ability to be the world's policemen, and nuclear capable third world countries collapse. However, we should require the Israelis to leave the strict orthodox at home where the Muslims will soon get them, as we already have enough rabbit breeding religious lunatics.

Speaking of the collapse of nuclear capable third world countries, it should be obvious that as this happens, probably before the end of this century, but certainly in the next, with H Bombs in possession of fanatics, it is just a matter of time before they begin vaporizing American and European cities. The only definitive defense will be preemptive "nucleation" of any such country that collapses, or where Muslim radicals take over. It must be obvious to Israel that they will have no other choice but a preemptive strike on Pakistan, Iran and maybe others. Another lovely gift from the Diverse.

In a late 2015 poll by You.Gov, 29 percent of respondents said they can imagine a situation in which they would support the military taking control of the federal government – that translates into over 70 million American adults. And these again are the best of times. At this time in the next century, give or take a few decades, (much sooner in many third world countries), with industrial civilization collapsing, starvation, crime, disease and war worldwide, military coups will be happening everywhere. It's almost certainly the only cure for America's problems, but of course nobody will get to vote on it.

In sum, this is the American chapter of the sad story of the inexorable destruction of the world by unrestrained motherhood. Fifty-four years ago, 396 US politicians voted to embrace the destruction of America by the third world, via the "no significant demographic impact" immigration act. Without the changes they and the Supreme Idiots Court made (along with failure to enforce our immigration laws), we would have about 80 million fewer people now and at least 150 million fewer in 2100, along with tens of trillions of dollars in savings. We would have a chance to deal with the immense problems America and the world face. But, burdened with a fatally fragmented (i.e., Diverse) population about twice the size we might have had, half of which will not contribute to the solution, but rather constitute the problem, it is impossible. What we see is that democracy as practiced here and now guarantees a fatally inept government. Peace and prosperity worldwide will vanish and starvation, disease, crime, military coups, terrorism and warlords will become routine, probably in this century, certainly during the next.

To me it's clear that nothing will restrain motherhood and that there is no hope for America or the world regardless of what happens in technology, green living or politics anywhere. Everything tranquil, pure, wild, sane, safe and decent is doomed. There is no problem understanding the stupidity, laziness, dishonesty, self-deception, cowardice, arrogance, greed and insanity of hairless monkeys, but it ought to seem a bit odd that so many reasonably sane and more or less educated people could welcome into their country (or at least permit the entry and tolerate the presence of) large numbers of immigrants who proceed to take over and destroy it. Monkey psychology (shared by all humans) is only capable of seriously considering oneself and immediate relatives for a short time into the future (reciprocal altruism or inclusive fitness), maybe decades at most, so there is no internal restraint. Democracy is the ideal breeding ground for catastrophe.

Most people are neither smart nor well educated, but one can see collapse happening in front of us, and above all in the big urban areas and in the Southwest, especially California and Texas. Sheer laziness, ignorance and a lack of understanding of ecology and the nature of population growth is part of it, but I think that the innate reciprocal altruism we share with all animals must have a big role. When we evolved in Africa we lived in small groups, probably seldom more than a few hundred and often less than 20, and so all those around us were our close relatives, and our behavior was selected to treat them reasonably well as they shared our genes (inclusive fitness) and would reciprocate good deeds (reciprocal altruism). We stopped evolving and began devolving, replacing evolution by natural selection with devolution (genetic degeneration) by unnatural selection about 100,000 years ago, when culture evolved to the point where language, fire and tools gave us a huge advantage over other animals, and there was no longer major selective force for changing behavior or increasing or maintaining health and intelligence. So, to this day we still have the tendency, when we do not feel in immediate physical danger, to act in a more or less friendly manner to those around us. The temporary peace, brought about by advanced communications and weaponry and the merciless rape of the planets resources, has expanded this 'one big family' delusion. Though the more intelligent and reflective persons (which of course includes many Diverse) can see the danger to their descendants, those who are poorly educated, dull witted, or emotionally unstable, sociopathic, autistic, or mentally ill (i.e., the vast majority) won't see it or won't act on it. But how about Adelson, Zuckerberg, Gelbaum, Biden, Clinton, Obama, Krugman and a very long list of the rich and famous? They have at least some education and intelligence, so how can they want to destroy their country and their own children's future? Actually, they are no more well educated, perceptive and future oriented than the average college graduate (i.e., not very), and also, they and their relatives live in gated communities and often have bodyguards, so they will not be seriously concerned about or even aware of trashed neighborhoods, beaches and parks, drive by shootings, home invasions, rapes and murders, nor about paying taxes or making ends meet. They are just not thinking about the fate of their great grandchildren, nor anyone's, or if it does cross their mind, like the vast majority, they don't have clue a about human ecology, nor dysgenics, and can't see the inexorable path to collapse. Insofar as they do, they will not risk personal discomforts by saying or doing anything about it (selfishness and cowardice).

A reader suggested I was talking about 'ethnic cleansing' of Diverse by Euros, but what's happening worldwide is exactly the reverse. I had not actually thought of the destruction of America and industrial civilization by Diverse as genocide, but since the number of Euros of all types (and many groups of Diverse such as Japanese and Koreans) will steadily decline, and their countries be taken over by Diverse, it does have that aspect, though it's the Euros failure to produce enough children that is responsible for their declining numbers. A few zealots (but not so few in the future as Muslims will increase from about 1/5 of the world to about 1/3 by 2100, stimulating the conditions which breed fanaticism) like Al Qaeda and ISIS want to eliminate all Euro's (and Jews and Sunni's and Feminists and Christians etc., etc.) and the Arabs will certainly demolish Israel by and by, but otherwise there is little motivation to get rid of those who are giving you a free lunch (though of course few Diverse will grasp how big the lunch really is until it stops and civilization collapses). However, as time passes and the competition for space and resources gets ever more desperate, genocide of all Euro groups may become an explicit goal, though mostly it will be far overshadowed by attacks of various Diverse groups on others, which has always been the case and always will. In any event, all Euro and many Diverse groups are certainly doomed--we are talking roughly 2100 and beyond, when the USA (then a part of Mexico) and Europe will no longer have the money or the will to suppress anarchy everywhere, as they will be unable to control it at home.

Shocking as it is for me to come to these realizations (I never really thought about these issues in a serious way until recently), I don't see any hope for America or the other 'democracies' (America has one foot in Fascism and the other in Communism already) without a drastic change in the way "democracy" works, or in its complete abandonment. Of course, it's going to be pretty much the same elsewhere and both Euros and Diverse ought to pray the Chinese adopt democracy soon (so they collapse too) or they are doomed from outside and inside. That democracy is a fatally flawed system is not news to anyone with a grasp of history or human nature. Our second president John Adams had this to say in 1814:

"I do not say that democracy has been more pernicious on the whole, and in the long run, than monarchy or aristocracy. Democracy has never been and never can be so durable as aristocracy or monarchy; but while it lasts, it is more bloody than either. … Remember, democracy never lasts long. It soon wastes, exhausts, and murders itself. There never was a democracy yet that did not commit suicide. It is in vain to say that democracy is less vain, less proud, less selfish, less ambitious, or less avaricious than aristocracy or monarchy. It is not true, in fact, and nowhere appears in history. Those passions are the same in all men, under all forms of simple government, and when unchecked, produce the same effects of fraud, violence, and cruelty. When clear prospects are opened before vanity, pride, avarice, or ambition, for their easy gratification, it is hard for the most considerate philosophers and the most conscientious moralists to resist the temptation. Individuals have conquered themselves. Nations and large bodies of men, never." John Adams, The Letters of John and Abigail Adams

The most basic facts, almost never mentioned, are that there are not enough resources in America or the world to lift a significant percentage of the poor out of poverty and keep them there. The attempt to do this is bankrupting America and destroying the world. The earth's capacity to produce food decreases daily, as does our genetic quality. And now, as always, by far the greatest enemy of the poor is other poor and not the rich. Without dramatic and immediate changes, there is no hope for preventing the collapse of America, or any country that follows a democratic system.

So, it is clear that Ann Coulter is right and unless some truly miraculous changes happen very soon, it's goodbye America and hello Third World Hellhole. The only consolations are that we older folk can take comfort in knowing it will not be finalized during our lifetime, that those like myself who are childless will have no descendants to suffer the consequences, and, since the descendants of those who let this happen (i.e., nearly everyone) will be as loathsome as their ancestors, they will richly deserve hell on earth.

How the Seven Sociopaths Who Rule China are Winning World War Three and Three Ways to Stop Them

Michael Starks

Abstract

The first thing we must keep in mind is that when saying that China says this or China does that, we are not speaking of the Chinese people, but of the Sociopaths who control the CCP -- Chinese Communist Party, i.e., the Seven Senile Sociopathic Serial Killers (SSSSK) of the Standing Committee of the CCP or the 25 members of the Politburo etc..

The CCP's plans for WW3 and total domination are laid out quite clearly in Chinese govt publications and speeches and this is Xi Jinping's "China Dream". It is a dream only for the tiny minority (perhaps a few dozen to a few hundred) who rule China and a nightmare for everyone else (including 1.4 billion Chinese). The 10 billion dollars yearly enables them or their puppets to own or control newspapers, magazines, TV and radio channels and place fake news in most major media everywhere every day. In addition, they have an army (maybe millions of people) who troll all the media placing more propaganda and drowning out legitimate commentary (the 50 cent army).

In addition to stripping the 3rd world of resources, a major thrust of the multi-trillion dollar Belt and Road Initiative is building military bases worldwide. They are forcing the free world into a massive high-tech arms race that makes the cold war with the Soviet Union look like a picnic.

Though the SSSSK, and the rest of the world's military, are spending huge sums on advanced hardware, it is highly likely that WW3 (or the smaller engagements leading up to it) will be software dominated. It is not out of the question that the SSSSK, with probably more hackers (coders) working for them then all the rest of the world combined, will win future wars with minimal physical conflict, just by paralyzing their enemies via the net. No satellites, no phones, no communications, no financial transactions, no power grid, no internet, no advanced weapons, no vehicles, trains, ships or planes.

There are only two main paths to removing the CCP, freeing 1.4 billion Chinese prisoners, and ending the lunatic march to WW3. The peaceful one is to launch an all-out trade war to devastate the Chinese economy until the military gets fed up and boots out the CCP.

An alternative to shutting down China's economy is a limited war, such as a targeted strike by say 50 thermobaric drones on the 20th Congress of the CCP, when all the top members are in one place, but that won't take place until 2022 so one could hit the annual plenary meeting. The Chinese would be informed, as the attack happened, that they must lay down their arms and prepare to hold a democratic election or be nuked into the stone age. The other alternative is an all-out nuclear attack. Military confrontation is unavoidable given the CCP's present course. It will likely happen over the islands in the South China Sea or Taiwan within a few decades, but as they establish military bases worldwide it could happen anywhere (see Crouching Tiger etc.). Future conflicts will have hardkill and softkill aspects with the stated objectives of the CCP to emphasize cyberwar by hacking and paralyzing control systems of all military and industrial communications, equipment, power plants, satellites, internet, banks, and any device or vehicle connected to the net. The SS are slowly fielding a worldwide array of manned and autonomous surface and underwater subs or drones capable of launching conventional or nuclear weapons that may lie dormant awaiting a signal from China or even looking for the signature of US ships or planes. While destroying our satellites, thus eliminating communication between the USA and our forces worldwide, they will use theirs, in conjunction with drones to target and destroy our currently superior naval forces. Of course, all of this is increasingly done automatically by AI.

By far the biggest ally of the CCP is the Democratic party of the USA.

The choice is to stop the CCP now or watch as they extend the Chinese prison over the whole world.

Of course, universal surveillance and digitizing of our lives is inevitable everywhere. Anyone who does not think so is profoundly out of touch.

Of course, it is the optimists who expect the Chinese sociopaths to rule the world while the pessimists (who view themselves as realists) expect AI sociopathy (or AS as I call it – i.e., Artificial Stupidity or Artificial Sociopathy) to take over, perhaps by 2030.

Those interested in further details on the lunatic path of modern society may consult my other works such as Suicide by Democracy-an Obituary for America and the World 4th Edition 2019 and Suicidal Utopian Delusions in the 21st Century: Philosophy, Human Nature and the Collapse of Civilization 5th ed (2019)

The first thing we must keep in mind is that when saying that China says this or China does that, we are not speaking of the Chinese people, but of the Sociopaths who control of CCP (Chinese Communist Party, i.e., the Seven Senile Sociopathic Serial Killers (SSSSK) of the Standing Committee of the CCP or the 25 members of the Politburo. I recently watched some typical leftist fake news programs (pretty much the only kind one can find in the media, i.e., nearly everything now –i.e., Yahoo, CNN, The New York Times, etc.) on YouTube, one by VICE which mentioned that 1000 economists (and 15 Nobel Prize winners) sent a letter to Trump telling him that the trade war was a mistake, and another which interviewed an academic economist who said that Trump's move was a provocation for starting

World War 3. They are right about the disruption of global trade, but have no grasp of the big picture, which is that the Seven Sociopaths have total world domination, with the elimination of freedom everywhere, as their goal, and that there are only two ways to stop them—a total trade embargo that devastates the Chinese economy and leads their military to force out the CCP and hold elections, or WW3, which can be limited (conventional arms with maybe a few nukes) or total (all the nukes at once). Clear as day, but all these "brilliant" academics can't see it. If the Sociopaths are not removed now, in as little as 15 years it will be too late and your descendants slowly but inexorably will be subject to the same fate as Chinese—total surveillance with kidnapping, torture and murder of any dissenters.

Of course, the CCP started WW3 long ago (you could see their invasions of Tibet or Korea as the beginning) and is pursuing it in every possible way, except for bullets and bombs, and they will come soon. The CCP fought the USA in Korea, invaded and massacred Tibet, and fought border skirmishes with Russia and India. It conducts massive hacking operations against all industrial and military databases worldwide and has stolen the classified data on virtually all current US and European military and space systems, analyzed their weaknesses and fielded improved versions within a few years. Tens of thousands, and maybe hundreds of thousands, of CCP employees have been hacking into military, industrial, financial and social media databases worldwide since the early days of the net and there are hundreds of known recent hacks in the USA alone. As the major institutions and military have hardened their firewalls, the SSSSK have moved to minor institutions and to defense subcontractors and to our allies, which are easier targets. While it ignores the crushing poverty of hundreds of millions and the marginal existence of most of its people, it has built up a massive military and space presence, which grows larger every year, and whose only reason for existence is waging war to eliminate freedom everywhere. In addition to stripping the 3rd world of resources, a major thrust of the multi-trillion dollar Belt and Road Initiative is building military bases worldwide. They are forcing the free world into a massive high-tech arms race that makes the cold war with the Soviet Union look like a picnic. The Russians are not stupid, and in spite of pretending friendship with the Sociopaths, they surely grasp that the CCP is going to eat them alive, that their only hope is to ally themselves with the West, and Trump is right on the money in befriending Putin. Of course, the Neomarxist Third World Supremacist Fascists (i.e., the Democratic Party) will likely take total control of the USA in 2020 and nothing could be more to the liking of the CCP. Snowden (another clueless twenty something) helped the SSSSK more than any other single individual, with the possible exception of all the American presidents since WW2, who have pursued the suicidal policy of appeasement. The USA has no choice but to monitor all communications and to compile a dossier on everyone, as it's essential not only to control criminals and terrorists, but to counter the SSSSK, who are rapidly doing the same thing, with the intent of removing freedom completely.

Though the SSSSK, and the rest of the world's military, are spending huge sums on advanced hardware, it is highly likely that WW3 (or the smaller engagements leading up to it) will be software dominated. It is not out of the question that the SSSSK, with probably more hackers (coders) working for them then all the rest of the world combined, will win future wars with minimal physical conflict, just by paralyzing their enemies via the net. No satellites, no phones, no communications, no financial transactions, no power grid, no internet, no advanced weapons, no vehicles, trains, ships or planes.

Some may question that the CCP (and of course the top tiers of the police, army and 610 Office) are really mentally aberrant, so here are some of the common characteristics of sociopaths (formerly called psychopaths) that you can find on the net. Of course, some of these are shared by many autistics and alexithymics, and sociopaths differ from "normal" people only in degree.

Superficial Charm, Manipulative and Cunning, Grandiose Sense of Self, Lack of Remorse, Shame or Guilt, Shallow Emotions, Incapacity for Love, Callousness/Lack of Empathy, Poor Behavioral Controls/Impulsive Nature, Believe they are all-powerful, all-knowing, entitled to every wish, no sense of personal boundaries, no concern for their impact on others. Problems in making and keeping friends. Aberrant behaviors such as cruelty to people or animals, Stealing, Promiscuity, Criminal or Entrepreneurial Versatility, Change their image as needed, Do not perceive that anything is wrong with them, Authoritarian, Secretive, Paranoid, Seek out situations where their tyrannical behavior will be tolerated, condoned, or admired (e.g., CCP, Police, Military, Predatory Capitalism), Conventional appearance, Goal of enslavement of their victims, Seek to exercise despotic control over every aspect of other's lives, Have an emotional need to justify their actions and therefore need their victim's affirmation (respect, gratitude), Ultimate goal is the creation of a willing victim. Incapable of real human attachment to another, Unable to feel remorse or guilt, Extreme narcissism and grandiosity, Their goal is to rule the world. Pathological Liars.

This last is one of the most striking characteristics of the CCP. Virtually everything they say in opposition to others is an obvious lie, or distortion, mostly so absurd that any well-educated ten year old will laugh at them. Yet they persist in saturating all the media every day (an estimated $10 billion annual budget just for foreign propaganda) with preposterous statements. The fact that they are so out of touch with reality that they think they will be taken seriously clearly shows what any rational person will regard as mental illness (sociopathy).

There are only two main paths to removing the CCP, freeing 1.4 billion Chinese prisoners, and ending the lunatic march to WW3. The peaceful one is to launch an all-out trade war to devastate the Chinese economy until the military gets fed up and boots out the CCP. The USA needs, by any means necessary, to join all its allies in reducing the trade with China to near zero—no imports of any product from China or any entity with more that 10% Chinese ownership anywhere in the world, including any product with any component of such origin. No export of anything whatsoever to China or any entity that reexports to China or that has more than 10 % Chinese ownership, with severe and immediate consequences for any violators. Yes, it would temporarily cost millions of jobs and a major worldwide recession, and yes I know that a large part of their exports are from joint ventures with American companies, but the alternative is that every country will become the dog of the Seven Sociopaths (and like all edible animal they keep dogs in small cages while they fatten them for the kill) and/or experience the horrors of WW3. Other possible steps are to send home all Chinese students and workers in science and tech, freeze all assets of any entity more than 10% Chinese owned, forbid foreign travel to any Chinese citizen, prohibit any Chinese or any entity more than 10% owned by Chinese from buying any company, land, product or technology from the USA or any of its allies. All these measures would be phased in as appropriate.

We should keep in mind that the Chinese monster is largely due to the suicidal utopian delusions, cowardice and stupidity of our politicians. Truman refused to let McArthur nuke them in Korea, President Carter gave them the right to send students to the USA (there are currently about 300,000), use our intellectual property without paying royalties, gave them most favored nation trading status, and by decree canceled our recognition of Taiwan and our mutual defense agreement (i.e., with no vote by anyone – he should be an honorary CCP member, along with the Bushes, the Obamas, the Clintons, Edward Snowden, etc.). These were the first in a long series of conciliatory gestures to the world's most vicious dictatorship which made it possible for them to prosper, and set the stage for their coming invasion of Taiwan, the South Sea Islands and other countries as they wish. These measures along with our failure to invade in the 40's to prevent their takeover of China, our failure to nuke their army and hence the CCP out of existence during the Korean War, our failure to prevent their massacre of Tibet, our failure to do anything when they exploded their first nuclear weapons, our failure to take them out in 1966 when they launched their first nuclear capable ICBM, our (or rather Bush's) failure to do anything about the Tiananmen massacre, our failure to shut down the Confucius Institutes present in many universities worldwide, which are fronts for the CCP, our failure to ban the purchase of companies , property, mining rights etc. worldwide, which is another way to acquire high-tech and other vital assets, our failure to do anything over the last 20 years about their continual industrial and military espionage and hacking into our databases stealing nearly all our advanced weaponry, our failure to stop their allies North Korea and Pakistan from developing nukes and ICBM's and receiving equipment from China (e.g., their mobile missile launchers, which they claim were for hauling logs and it was pure coincidence they exactly fit the Korean missiles), our failure to stop them from violating our embargo on Iran's oil (they buy much of it, registering their ships in Iran), and its nuclear program (equipment and technicians go back and forth to N. Korea via China), our failure to stop them from providing military tech and weapons worldwide (e.g., North Korea, Iran, Pakistan, the cartels in Mexico, and over 30 other countries), our failure to stop the flow of dangerous drugs and their precursors directly or indirectly (e.g., nearly all Fentanyl and Carfentanyl sent worldwide, and meth precursors for the Mexican cartels come from China), and our failure to do anything about their building "ports" (i.e., military bases) all over the world, which is ongoing.

An alternative to shutting down China's economy is a limited war, such as a targeted strike by say 50 thermobaric drones on the 20th Congress of the CCP, when all the top members are in one place, but that won't take place until 2022 so one could hit the annual plenary meeting. The Chinese would be informed, as the attack happened, that they must lay down their arms and prepare to hold a democratic election or be nuked into the stone age. The other alternative is an all-out nuclear attack. Military confrontation is unavoidable given the CCP's present course. It will likely happen over the islands in the South China Sea or Taiwan within a few decades, but as they establish military bases worldwide it could happen anywhere (see Crouching Tiger etc.). Future conflicts will have hardkill and softkill aspects with the stated objectives of the CCP to emphasize cyberwar by hacking and paralyzing control systems of all military and industrial communications, equipment, power plants, satellites, internet, banks, and any device or vehicle connected to the net. The SS are slowly fielding a worldwide array of manned and autonomous surface and underwater subs or drones capable of launching conventional or nuclear weapons that may lie dormant awaiting a signal from China or even looking for the signature of US ships or planes. While destroying our satellites, thus eliminating communication between the USA and our forces worldwide, they will use theirs, in conjunction with drones to target and destroy our currently superior naval forces. Perhaps worst of all is the rapid development of robots and drones of all sizes and capabilities which will inevitably be employed by criminals and terrorists to act from anywhere in the world, and massive swarms of which will be used by or instead of soldiers to fight ever more numerous and vicious wars. Of course, all of this is increasingly done automatically by AI.

All this is totally obvious to anyone who spends a little time on the net. Two of the best sources to start with are the book Crouching Tiger (and the five YouTube videos with the same name), and the long series of short satirical pieces on the China Uncensored channel on YouTube or their new one www.chinauncensored.tv. The CCP's plans for WW3 and total domination are laid out quite clearly in Chinese govt publications and speeches and this is Xi Jinping's "China Dream". It is a dream only for the tiny minority (perhaps a few dozen to a few hundred) who rule China and a nightmare for everyone else (including 1.4 billion Chinese). The 10 billion dollars yearly enables them or their puppets to own or control newspapers, magazines, TV and radio channels and place fake news in most major media everywhere every day. In addition, they have an army (maybe millions of people) who troll all the media placing more propaganda and drowning out legitimate commentary (the 50 cent army).

The rule of the SSSSK (or 25 SSSK if you focus on the Politburo rather than it's standing committee) is a surrealistic tragicomedy like Snow White and the Seven Dwarves, but without Snow White, endearing personalities, or a happy ending. They are the wardens of the world's biggest prison, but they are by far the worst criminals, committing by proxy every year millions of assaults, rapes, robberies, bribes, kidnappings, tortures, and murders, most of them presumably by their own secret police of the 610 Office created on June 10, 1999 by Jiang Zemin to persecute the qigong meditators of Falun Gong, and anyone else deemed a threat, now including anyone making any critical comment and including all religious and political groups not under their direct rule. By far the biggest ally of the Seven

Dwarves is the Democratic party of the USA, which, at a time when America needs more than ever to be strong and united, is doing everything possible to divide America into warring factions with ever more of its resources going to sustain the burgeoning legions of the lower classes and driving it into bankruptcy, though of course they have no insight into this whatsoever. The CCP is by far the most evil group in world history, robbing, raping, kidnapping, imprisoning, torturing, starving to death and murdering more people that all the other dictators in history (an estimated 100 million dead), and in a few years will have a total surveillance state recording every action of everyone in China, which is already expanding worldwide as they include data from hacking and from all who pass thru territories under their control, buy tickets on Chinese airlines etc.

Though the SSSSK treat us as an enemy, in fact, the USA is the Chinese people's greatest friend and the CCP their greatest enemy. From another perspective, other Chinese are the greatest enemies of Chinese, as they demolish all the world's resources.

Of course, some say that China will collapse of its own accord, and it's possible, but the price of being wrong is the end of freedom and WW3 or a long series of conflicts which the Seven Sociopaths will almost certainly win. One must keep in mind that they have controls on their population and weapons that Stalin, Hitler, Gaddafi and Idi Amin never dreamed of. CCTV cameras (currently maybe 300 million and increasing rapidly) on highspeed networks with AI image analysis, tracking software on every phone which people are required to use, and GPS trackers on all vehicles, all transactions payable only by phone already dominant there and universal and mandatory soon, total automatic monitoring of all communications by AI and an estimated 2 million online human censors. In addition to millions of police and army cadres, there may be as many as 10 million plainclothes secret police of 610 Office created by Jiang Zemin, with black prisons (i.e., unofficial and unmarked), instant updating of the digital dossier on all 1.4 billion Chinese and soon on everyone on earth who uses the net or phones. It's often called the Social Credit System and it enables the Sociopaths to shut down the communications, purchasing ability, travel, bank accounts etc. of anyone. This is not fantasy but already largely implemented for the Muslims of Xinjiang and spreading rapidly—see YouTube, China Uncensored etc. Of course, universal surveillance and digitizing of our lives is inevitable everywhere. Anyone who does not think so is profoundly out of touch.

The choice is to stop the CCP now or watch as they extend the Chinese prison over the whole world.

The biggest ally of the CCP is the Democratic Party of the USA.

Of course, it is the optimists who expect the Chinese sociopaths to rule the world while the pessimists (who view themselves as realists) expect AI sociopathy (or AS as I call it – i.e., Artificial Stupidity or Artificial Sociopathy) to take over. It is the opinion of many thoughtful persons- Musk, Gates, Hawking etc., including top AI researchers (see the many TED talks on YouTube) that AI will reach explosive self-growth (increasing its power thousands or millions of times in days, minutes or microseconds) at some time in the next few decades – 2030 is sometimes mentioned, escaping through the net and infecting all sufficiently powerful computers. AS will be unstoppable, especially since it appears that it will be running on quantum computers which will increase its speed more thousands or millions of times). If you are optimistic, it will keep humans and other animals around as pets and the world will become a zoo with a eugenic captive breeding program, if a pessimist, it will eliminate humans or even all organic life as an annoying competition for resources. The science fiction of today is likely to be the reality of tomorrow.

Made in the USA
Lexington, KY
17 October 2019